Contents

Introduction to Educational Research

Chapter 1. Introduction to Educational Research

This chapter will address the following learning objectives:
• Define educational research according to the American Educational Research Association (AERA).   • Describe the interdisciplinary nature of educational research and its role in advancing knowledge and practice in education.   • Explain the purpose and significance of educational research in shaping the future of education and empowering learners.   • Discuss the value of educational research in improving teaching practices, enhancing student learning outcomes, informing policy and decision-making, addressing equity and social justice issues, fostering innovation, and building a knowledge base in education.   • Analyze examples of educational research projects across different areas.   • Differentiate between educational research designs.   • Outline the stages of the research process in educational research.   • Examine the impact of digital technology on educational research.   • Evaluate the ethical considerations in conducting educational research, particularly in the digital age.   • Explain the overarching goal of educational research and its importance in providing evidence-based insights to inform educational practice and policy.

Educational research is a dynamic and interdisciplinary field that encompasses a wide range of inquiries aimed at advancing knowledge and practice in education. By fostering collaboration between researchers, educators, policymakers, and other stakeholders, educational research plays a critical role in shaping the future of education and empowering learners to reach their full potential.

Educational research is a systematic inquiry conducted to understand, evaluate, and improve various aspects of education. It encompasses a broad range of topics, including teaching methods, curriculum design, learning outcomes, educational policies, and the social and psychological factors influencing education. Educational research employs rigorous methods to gather and analyze data, aiming to generate evidence-based insights that inform educational practice, policymaking, and theory development. Below are some examples of educational research projects:

1. **Impact of Technology on Learning Outcomes**: A study examining the effectiveness of using interactive educational software in mathematics classrooms compared to traditional instructional methods. Researchers could measure students' mathematical achievement, engagement, and attitudes towards learning using pre- and post-assessments, surveys, and classroom observations.

Introduction to Educational Research

2. **Teacher Professional Development**: A research project evaluating the effectiveness of a professional development program designed to enhance teachers' cultural competency in diverse classrooms. Researchers could use pre- and post-surveys, classroom observations, and interviews to assess changes in teachers' knowledge, attitudes, and instructional practices.

3. **Early Childhood Education Intervention**: A longitudinal study investigating the long-term effects of a preschool intervention program on children's academic achievement, social-emotional development, and school readiness. Researchers could follow participants from preschool through elementary school, collecting data on standardized test scores, behavior ratings, and academic performance.

4. **Parental Involvement and Student Achievement**: A correlational study exploring the relationship between parental involvement in education and students' academic achievement. Researchers could survey parents and students to gather data on parental involvement practices, such as homework help, communication with teachers, and participation in school events, and then analyze the data to identify any associations with student outcomes.

5. **Inclusive Education Practices**: A qualitative research project examining the experiences of students with disabilities in inclusive classrooms. Researchers could conduct interviews and focus groups with students, teachers, and parents to explore perceptions of inclusion, barriers to participation, and strategies for promoting inclusivity in schools.

6. **Teacher Burnout and Job Satisfaction**: A mixed-methods study investigating factors contributing to teacher burnout and job satisfaction. Researchers could administer surveys to teachers to assess levels of burnout, job satisfaction, and perceived stress, as well as conduct follow-up interviews to explore underlying causes and potential interventions.

One widely accepted definition of educational research comes from the American Educational Research Association (AERA). According to AERA, educational research is defined as "the field of inquiry concerned with the study and practice of teaching and learning processes, both formal and informal, from pre-kindergarten through postsecondary education and lifelong learning contexts" (American Educational Research Association, 2021). This definition highlights the interdisciplinary nature of educational research and its focus on understanding the complexities of teaching and learning across diverse educational settings and contexts.

One of the key goals of educational research is to inform and improve educational practice. By conducting rigorous studies and analyzing data, researchers can identify effective teaching strategies, assess the impact of educational interventions, and develop evidence-based recommendations for educators, policymakers, and other stakeholders (Creswell, 2014).

Educational research is characterized by its commitment to objectivity, validity, and reliability. Researchers use a variety of research methods, including quantitative, qualitative, and mixed methods approaches, to collect and analyze data. They adhere to ethical guidelines to ensure the rights and well-being of research participants are protected.

In essence, educational research serves as a vital tool for advancing our understanding of education and driving positive change in educational systems worldwide and plays a vital role in advancing our understanding of how people learn and how education can be improved to meet the needs of diverse learners. It contributes to the development of innovative educational practices, informs policy decisions, and helps create more equitable and effective educational systems.

The Value of Educational Research

Educational research serves as the cornerstone for understanding and improving the complex dynamics of teaching and learning. It delves into the multifaceted aspects of education, exploring effective teaching practices, student learning outcomes, equity in education, policy development, and innovation. In this introduction, we will discuss the invaluable contributions of educational research in shaping the present and future of education.

At its core, educational research is driven by a commitment to enhancing the quality and effectiveness of educational practices. By systematically investigating various facets of education, researchers uncover insights that inform teaching methodologies, curriculum design, and assessment strategies. These insights not only benefit educators in refining their approaches but also contribute to fostering optimal learning environments for students of all backgrounds and abilities.

Moreover, educational research plays a pivotal role in addressing societal challenges related to equity and social justice in education. Through rigorous inquiry, researchers identify disparities in educational access and outcomes, shedding light on the root causes and advocating for policies and practices that promote inclusivity and fairness. By amplifying marginalized voices and championing equitable education opportunities, educational research serves as a catalyst for positive social change.

Furthermore, educational research informs policy development and decision-making at various levels of the education system. Policymakers rely on evidence-based findings to craft effective educational policies, allocate resources efficiently, and adapt to the evolving needs of diverse student populations. By bridging the gap between research and practice, educational research ensures that policy interventions are grounded in empirical evidence, thus maximizing their impact on educational outcomes.

In addition to its practical implications, educational research fosters a culture of innovation and continuous improvement within the education sector. By exploring emerging trends, experimenting with novel approaches, and evaluating their efficacy, researchers inspire educators to embrace change and adapt to the evolving landscape of education. This spirit of innovation not only drives improvements in teaching and learning but also fuels advancements in educational technology, pedagogy, and curriculum development.

In summary, research in education is valuable for several reasons:

1. **Improving Teaching Practices**: Educational research helps identify effective teaching methods and strategies, allowing educators to refine their practices to better support student learning. For example, studies on different instructional approaches, classroom management techniques, and assessment methods provide insights into what works best in different contexts (Hattie, 2009).

2. **Enhancing Student Learning Outcomes**: By identifying factors that influence student achievement, educational research helps educators tailor instruction to meet the diverse needs of learners. This includes understanding the impact of factors such as class size, curriculum design, and technology integration on student outcomes (OECD, 2019).

3. **Informing Policy and Decision-Making**: Educational research provides evidence to inform policy decisions at the institutional, local, and national levels. Policymakers rely on research findings to develop effective educational policies and allocate resources efficiently (Levin, 2013).

4. **Addressing Equity and Social Justice**: Research in education helps identify disparities in educational access, opportunities, and outcomes. By examining factors such as socioeconomic status, race, gender, and disability, researchers can advocate for policies and practices that promote equity and social justice in education (Ladson-Billings, 2006).

5. **Fostering Innovation and Continuous Improvement**: Educational research drives innovation by exploring new teaching methods, technologies, and approaches to education. It encourages educators to experiment with new ideas and adapt their practices based on empirical evidence (Fullan, 2016).

6. **Building a Knowledge Base**: Through systematic inquiry and dissemination of findings, educational research contributes to the accumulation of knowledge in the field. This knowledge base serves as a foundation for future research and professional development initiatives (Creswell, 2014).

Overall, research in education plays a crucial role in advancing the quality and effectiveness of teaching and learning practices, promoting equity and social justice, and informing policy decisions to improve educational systems. Educational research serves as a linchpin for advancing the quality, equity, and effectiveness of education. By generating empirical evidence, informing policy decisions, and fostering innovation, educational research empowers educators, policymakers, and stakeholders to navigate the complexities of education and work collaboratively towards a brighter future for learners worldwide.

Types of Educational Research

Educational research encompasses a diverse array of methods and approaches designed to investigate various aspects of teaching, learning, and educational systems. Below are some common types of educational research:

1. **Quantitative Research**: This type of research involves the collection and analysis of numerical data to understand educational phenomena. Quantitative studies often use statistical techniques to examine relationships, patterns, and trends. Examples include experimental studies, correlational research, and surveys. Quantitative research provides insights into the effectiveness of interventions, the impact of variables on student outcomes, and trends in educational practices (Creswell, 2014).

2. **Qualitative Research**: Qualitative research focuses on exploring complex phenomena in-depth, often through the collection and analysis of non-numerical data such as interviews, observations, and textual analysis. Qualitative studies seek to understand the experiences, perspectives, and contexts that shape educational processes. Examples include ethnographic research, case studies, and phenomenological inquiry. Qualitative research provides rich, nuanced insights into the lived experiences of students and educators, as well as the socio-cultural dynamics of educational settings (Merriam, 2009).

3. **Mixed-Methods Research**: Mixed-methods research combines quantitative and qualitative approaches within a single study to provide a comprehensive understanding of educational phenomena. Researchers collect and analyze both numerical and non-numerical data, allowing them to triangulate findings, explore complex relationships, and gain multiple perspectives on a phenomenon. Mixed-methods research is particularly useful for addressing multifaceted research

questions and gaining a holistic understanding of educational issues (Creswell & Plano Clark, 2018).

4. **Action Research**: Action research is a participatory approach in which educators engage in systematic inquiry to address practical problems or improve teaching and learning in their own classrooms or schools. Action research typically involves cycles of planning, action, observation, and reflection, with the aim of informing and transforming educational practices. This collaborative and iterative process empowers educators to take ownership of their professional development and enact meaningful change in their educational contexts (Stringer, 2013).

5. **Experimental Research**: Experimental research involves the manipulation of one or more variables to observe the effects on student outcomes. Researchers randomly assign participants to experimental and control groups and compare their performance to assess the impact of interventions or treatments. Experimental studies provide rigorous evidence of causal relationships and are often used to evaluate the effectiveness of educational interventions, programs, or instructional methods (Trochim & Donnelly, 2008).

6. **Quasi-Experimental Research**: Quasi-experimental research shares similarities with experimental research but lacks random assignment of participants to experimental and control groups. This type of research allows researchers to study the effects of interventions or treatments in real-world settings where random assignment may not be feasible or ethical. Quasi-experimental designs include pretest-posttest designs, nonequivalent control group designs, and interrupted time series designs. While they provide valuable insights into cause-and-effect relationships, quasi-experimental studies may be susceptible to selection bias and threats to internal validity (Campbell & Stanley, 1963).

7. **Causal-Comparative Research**: Causal-comparative research, also known as ex post facto research, investigates the relationship between independent and dependent variables without direct manipulation by the researcher. Unlike experimental research, causal-comparative studies do not establish causality but instead seek to identify associations or differences between variables. Researchers often compare groups that already differ on the independent variable of interest, such as comparing students from different socioeconomic backgrounds on academic achievement. Causal-comparative studies are valuable for exploring patterns and relationships in naturally occurring data but are limited in their ability to infer causality (Gay, Mills, & Airasian, 2011).

8. **Correlational Research**: Correlational research examines the relationship between two or more variables without intervening or manipulating them. Researchers use correlational designs to assess the degree and direction of association between variables, often through statistical techniques such as Pearson's correlation coefficient. Correlational studies can provide insights into patterns of behavior or characteristics within a population, but they do not imply causality. While correlational research is less invasive and more ecologically valid than experimental designs, it does not, in most cases, establish cause-and-effect relationships (Creswell, 2014).

9. **Survey Research**: Survey research involves collecting data from a sample of individuals through questionnaires or interviews to gather information about attitudes, beliefs, behaviors, or characteristics. Surveys are a popular method in educational research for assessing opinions, experiences, and perceptions of students, teachers, parents, or other stakeholders. Researchers use various types of survey instruments, including Likert scales, multiple-choice questions, and open-ended responses, to gather quantitative and qualitative data. Survey research allows for large-

scale data collection and generalization to broader populations but requires careful attention to sampling, questionnaire design, and data analysis techniques to ensure validity and reliability (Dillman, Smyth, & Christian, 2014).

Each type of research design has its strengths and limitations, and researchers must carefully select the most appropriate approach based on their research questions, hypotheses, and practical constraints.

Educational Research in the Digital Age

Educational research in the digital age is characterized by the integration of technology into various aspects of the research process, from data collection and analysis to dissemination of findings. The digital age impacted the field of educational research in the following ways:

1. **Data Collection**: Digital technologies have revolutionized data collection methods in educational research. Researchers can now gather data through online surveys, digital assessments, learning management systems, and educational apps. These digital tools not only streamline the data collection process but also allow for real-time data capture and analysis, providing researchers with richer and more timely insights into educational phenomena (Bartlett-Bragg & Smith, 2005).

2. **Data Analysis**: The availability of sophisticated data analysis software has facilitated more complex and nuanced analyses in educational research. Researchers can employ techniques such as data mining, machine learning, and social network analysis to uncover patterns, trends, and relationships within educational datasets. Advanced statistical software packages enable researchers to conduct multivariate analyses and predictive modeling, enhancing the depth and accuracy of research findings (Spector, 2006).

3. **Virtual Learning Environments**: The proliferation of virtual learning environments, such as online courses, virtual classrooms, and educational simulations, has opened new avenues for educational research. Researchers can investigate the efficacy of online learning platforms, the impact of virtual reality on learning outcomes, and the effectiveness of gamified learning experiences. Virtual learning environments also offer opportunities for longitudinal studies and international collaborations, transcending geographical boundaries and traditional constraints of educational research (Dalgarno & Lee, 2010).

4. **Digital Scholarship and Open Access**: The digital age has democratized access to educational research through open-access journals, digital repositories, and online preprint archives. Researchers can disseminate their findings more widely and rapidly, reaching a global audience of scholars, practitioners, policymakers, and the public. Digital scholarship platforms also facilitate collaboration, citation tracking, and interdisciplinary exchange, fostering a more dynamic and inclusive research ecosystem (Veletsianos & Kimmons, 2012).

5. **Ethical Considerations**: The digital age has introduced new ethical considerations and challenges in educational research. Researchers must navigate issues such as data privacy, informed consent, digital literacy, and algorithmic bias. Ethical guidelines and institutional review boards play a crucial role in safeguarding the rights and well-being of research participants in the digital realm, ensuring that educational research adheres to the highest standards of integrity and transparency (Bromley, 2016).

In summary, educational research in the digital age is characterized by the integration of technology into all stages of the research process, from data collection and analysis to dissemination and ethical considerations. By harnessing the power of digital technologies, researchers can conduct more innovative, rigorous, and impactful studies that advance our understanding of teaching, learning, and educational practice.

The Process of Educational Research

The research process in educational research typically follows a systematic and iterative approach, involving several key stages from conceptualization to dissemination of findings. Below is an overview of the research process:

- **Identifying the Research Problem**: The research process begins with identifying a research problem or question that addresses a gap in the existing literature or seeks to explore a new area of inquiry. Researchers conduct a thorough review of relevant literature to understand the context, theoretical frameworks, and prior research findings related to the chosen topic.

- **Formulating Research Objectives and Hypotheses**: Based on the identified research problem, researchers formulate clear and specific research objectives or research questions. In quantitative research, researchers may also develop hypotheses that predict the relationship between variables under investigation.

- **Selecting Research Design and Method**: Researchers choose an appropriate research design and method based on the nature of the research problem, research objectives, and available resources. Common research designs in educational research include experimental, quasi-experimental, correlational, descriptive, and qualitative designs. Researchers also select data collection methods, such as surveys, interviews, observations, experiments, and document analysis, based on the research design and research questions.

- **Data Collection**: Researchers collect data according to the selected research design and data collection methods. This may involve administering surveys, conducting interviews, observing participants in natural settings, conducting experiments, or analyzing existing datasets. Researchers must ensure that data collection procedures adhere to ethical guidelines and obtain informed consent from participants when necessary.

- **Data Analysis**: Once data collection is complete, researchers analyze the collected data using appropriate statistical or qualitative analysis techniques. Quantitative data analysis may involve descriptive statistics, inferential statistics, regression analysis, or factor analysis, depending on the research design and hypotheses. Qualitative data analysis may involve thematic analysis, content analysis, or grounded theory, aiming to identify patterns, themes, and meanings within the data.

- **Interpreting Findings**: Researchers interpret the findings of the data analysis in relation to the research objectives or research questions. They examine the implications of the findings, discuss their significance in the context of existing literature, and identify potential limitations or areas for further research.

- **Drawing Conclusions**: Based on the interpretation of findings, researchers draw conclusions that address the research problem and objectives. Conclusions should be supported by empirical evidence and provide insights into the phenomenon under investigation.

- **Communicating Results**: Researchers communicate their research findings through scholarly publications, conference presentations, reports, or other dissemination channels. They adhere to the conventions of academic writing and citation practices, ensuring that their research is accessible and contributes to the broader scholarly community.

- **Reflecting and Iterating**: The research process is often iterative, with researchers reflecting on their methods, findings, and conclusions to refine their approach or explore new avenues of inquiry. Researchers may also respond to feedback from peers, reviewers, or stakeholders to strengthen the quality and relevance of their research.

Overall, the research process in educational research involves a systematic and rigorous approach to investigating educational phenomena, generating new knowledge, and contributing to the advancement of the field.

Summary

The introduction to educational research provides a comprehensive overview of the field, highlighting its interdisciplinary nature, its role in advancing knowledge and practice in education, and its importance in shaping the future of education. It outlines the key characteristics of educational research, including its systematic inquiry, focus on understanding, evaluating, and improving various aspects of education, and its rigorous methodologies. The chapter also provides examples of educational research projects across different areas, such as the impact of technology on learning outcomes, teacher professional development, and parental involvement in student achievement. Additionally, it presents a widely accepted definition of educational research from the American Educational Research Association (AERA) and emphasizes its goal of informing and improving educational practice. The chapter concludes by discussing the value of educational research in addressing societal challenges, informing policymaking, fostering innovation, and promoting equity and social justice in education. Finally, it introduces different types of educational research, including quantitative, qualitative, mixed-methods, action research, experimental, quasi-experimental, causal-comparative, correlational, and survey research, each with its own strengths and limitations. Overall, the introduction provides a comprehensive foundation for understanding the scope, purpose, and significance of educational research.

Suggestions for Students

Key Questions

Use the following questions and prompts to check your understanding, discuss, and reflect upon the content of this chapter:

1. What is the primary focus of educational research?

2. Describe the interdisciplinary nature of educational research.

3. Why is educational research considered important in shaping the future of education?

4. What examples of topics fall within the scope of educational research?

5. What distinguishes educational research from other types of research?

6. How does educational research contribute to improving teaching and learning practices?

7. What is the role of evidence-based recommendations in educational research?

8. What is the role of ethical considerations in educational research?

9. What are three common types of educational research methods?

10. How does educational research inform policymaking in education?

11. Why is it important for educational research to address equity and social justice issues?

12. What are the key characteristics of quantitative research in educational research?

13. What are the key characteristics of qualitative research in educational research?

14. How does the digital age impact educational research?

15. What are some examples of educational research projects?

Suggestions for Instructors

Suggested Learning Activities

The following learning activities are designed to engage students in active learning, critical thinking, and application of key concepts from this chapter. They can be adapted or modified to suit different instructional formats, class sizes, and learning objectives.

Research Project Presentation: Divide students into small groups and assign each group one of the examples of educational research projects mentioned in the text (e.g., impact of technology on learning outcomes, teacher professional development). Have each group conduct further research on their assigned topic, prepare a presentation summarizing their findings, and present it to the class. Encourage classmates to ask questions and engage in discussions about research projects.

Case Study Analysis: Provide students with a case study involving an educational research dilemma or ethical issue (e.g., conflicting interests of stakeholders, data privacy concerns in digital research). In small groups, students analyze the case study, identify the key ethical considerations, and propose solutions or actions based on ethical principles discussed in the text.

Research Design Workshop: Organize a workshop where students explore different types of research designs mentioned in the text (e.g., quantitative, qualitative, mixed methods). Divide students into groups and assign each group a specific research design. Have groups brainstorm research questions and hypotheses, select appropriate data collection methods, and outline a research plan for investigating an educational phenomenon of their choice.

Digital Research Tools Exploration: Introduce students to various digital tools and technologies commonly used in educational research (e.g., online survey platforms, statistical software, virtual learning environments). Allow students to explore these tools hands-on, conduct mock data collection or analysis activities, and reflect on the advantages and limitations of using digital technology in educational research.

Debate on Educational Policy Issues: Select a current educational policy issue or debate relevant to the topics discussed in the text (e.g., standardized testing, inclusion practices). Divide the class into two groups representing different perspectives on the issue (e.g., educators vs. policymakers). Have students research their assigned perspective, prepare arguments supported by evidence from educational research, and engage in a structured debate.

Critical Analysis of Research Articles: Provide students with a selection of research articles from educational journals representing different research designs and methodologies. In pairs or small groups, have students critically analyze the articles, focusing on the research questions, methods, findings, and implications. Facilitate discussions where students compare the strengths and limitations of each study.

Ethical Dilemma Role-Playing: Create scenarios depicting ethical dilemmas commonly encountered in educational research (e.g., conflicting interests of researchers and participants, plagiarism concerns). Assign roles to students and have them role-play the scenarios, considering perspectives of researchers, participants, institutional review boards, and other stakeholders. Encourage students to negotiate solutions and reflect on the ethical implications of their decisions.

Research Proposal Development: Guide students through the process of developing a research proposal for an educational research study. Provide templates or frameworks for structuring the proposal and encourage students to incorporate elements such as research questions, objectives, methodology, ethical considerations, and potential impact of the study. Provide feedback and opportunities for revision to strengthen students' proposal-writing skills.

Guest Speaker Presentation: Invite a guest speaker with expertise in educational research or a related field to present to the class. The speaker could share insights from their own research projects, discuss current trends or challenges in educational research, and provide practical advice for students interested in pursuing research careers or further studies in education.

Reflective Journaling: Assign students to maintain a reflective journal throughout the course, where they document their thoughts, questions, and insights related to the topics covered in the text. Encourage students to reflect on their learning experiences, connections between theory and practice, and personal growth as emerging researchers or educators. Provide prompts or discussion topics to guide students' reflections and facilitate class discussions based on their journal entries.

References

American Educational Research Association. (2021). About AERA. Retrieved from https://www.aera.net/About-AERA

Bartlett-Bragg, A., & Smith, C. (2005). Constructing an educational psychology of digital knowledge construction. In W. Sims, D. Gibson, C. Haynes, & J. Price (Eds.), Proceedings of the 12th Annual Conference of the Australian Society for Computers in Learning in Tertiary Education (ASCILITE), (pp. 73-82).

Introduction to Educational Research

Bromley, M. (2016). Ethical considerations in educational research in the digital age. British Journal of Educational Technology, 47(6), 1052-1062.

Campbell, D. T., & Stanley, J. C. (1963). Experimental and quasi-experimental designs for research. Houghton Mifflin.

Creswell, J. W. (2014). Educational Research: Planning, Conducting, and Evaluating Quantitative and Qualitative Research (4th ed.). Pearson.

Creswell, J. W., & Plano Clark, V. L. (2018). Designing and conducting mixed methods research. Sage Publications.

Dalgarno, B., & Lee, M. J. W. (2010). What are the learning affordances of 3-D virtual environments? British Journal of Educational Technology, 41(1), 10-32.

Dillman, D. A., Smyth, J. D., & Christian, L. M. (2014). Internet, phone, mail, and mixed-mode surveys: The tailored design method. John Wiley & Sons.

Fullan, M. (2016). The new meaning of educational change (5th ed.). Teachers College Press.

Gall, M. D., Gall, J. P., & Borg, W. R. (2007). Educational research: An introduction. Pearson.

Gay, L. R., Mills, G. E., & Airasian, P. (2011). Educational research: Competencies for analysis and applications. Pearson.

Hattie, J. (2009). Visible Learning: A synthesis of over 800 meta-analyses relating to achievement. Routledge.

Ladson-Billings, G. (2006). From the achievement gap to the education debt: Understanding achievement in U.S. schools. Educational Researcher, 35(7), 3-12.

Leedy, P. D., & Ormrod, J. E. (2014). Practical research: Planning and design. Pearson.

Levin, B. (2013). To know is not enough: Research knowledge and its use. Review of Educational Research, 83(3), 388-394.

Merriam, S. B. (2009). Qualitative research: A guide to design and implementation. Jossey-Bass.

OECD. (2019). Teaching for the Future: Effective Classroom Practices to Transform Education. OECD Publishing.

Spector, J. M. (2006). Toward a philosophy of instructional technology. Educational Technology, 46(3), 5-15.

Stringer, E. T. (2013). Action research (4th ed.). Sage Publications.

Trochim, W. M., & Donnelly, J. P. (2008). The research methods knowledge base (3rd ed.). Atomic Dog Publishing.

Veletsianos, G., & Kimmons, R. (2012). Assumptions and challenges of open scholarship. The International Review of Research in Open and Distributed Learning, 13(4), 166-189.

Chapter 2. Research Problems and Research Questions

This chapter will address the following learning objectives:
• Explain the importance of identifying a research problem in educational research.
• State key considerations for selecting relevant and significant research problems in education.
• Analyze examples of research problems across various areas of education.
• Explain the significance of clarity and specificity in formulating research questions.
• Assess the importance of feasibility in the development of research questions.
• Discuss the importance of relevance and significance in shaping research questions.
• Explain the concept of openness to inquiry and its role in developing research questions.
• Discuss the ethical considerations involved in the development of research questions.
• Synthesize the importance of research questions in guiding educational research endeavors.

Research Problems

Identifying a research problem is a crucial first step in any educational research endeavor. It lays the foundation for the entire research process, guiding researchers in defining the scope of their study, formulating research questions, and determining the direction of their inquiry. In the field of education, research problems are diverse and multifaceted, reflecting the complex dynamics of teaching, learning, and educational systems.

The identification of a research problem involves recognizing a gap or issue in the existing literature or educational practice that warrants further investigation. The process of identifying a research problem involves careful consideration of various factors, including the current state of knowledge, gaps in the existing literature, practical challenges or issues faced by educators, and the broader societal context. Researchers must critically analyze these factors to pinpoint a research problem that is both relevant and significant, addressing key questions or concerns within the field of education.

This introduction will explore the importance of identifying a research problem, discuss key considerations in selecting a research topic, and provide guidance on how to formulate clear and focused research questions.

The following table provides several examples of research problems across various areas of education:

Introduction to Educational Research

Research Topic	Research Problem
Student Engagement	Despite efforts to enhance student engagement in classrooms, some students still exhibit low levels of participation and interest in learning activities.
Digital Literacy Education	With the increasing reliance on digital technologies in education, there is a growing need for effective digital literacy education to ensure that students develop essential skills for navigating the digital landscape.
Teacher Professional Development	Many teachers face challenges in keeping pace with the rapidly evolving demands of the education landscape and implementing evidence-based instructional practices in their classrooms.
Inclusive Education	Despite efforts to promote inclusive education, students with disabilities continue to face barriers to full participation and meaningful engagement in inclusive classroom settings.
Assessment and Feedback	Traditional methods of assessment may not adequately capture students' diverse strengths, skills, and knowledge, and provide timely and constructive feedback for improvement.
Parental Involvement	Despite the recognized importance of parental involvement in supporting students' academic success, some parents face barriers to active engagement in their children's education.
Educational Equity	Disparities persist in educational access, opportunities, and outcomes, particularly along lines of race, socioeconomic status, and geographic location, leading to inequities in educational attainment and achievement.

These examples illustrate the diverse range of educational research problems that researchers may explore to address pressing issues, inform evidence-based practices, and contribute to positive change in education. Each research problem presents unique challenges and opportunities for inquiry, requiring careful consideration of relevant theories, methods, and ethical considerations in the research process.

The following section will explore the importance of identifying a research problem in educational research, discuss key considerations for selecting a research problem, and provide practical guidance for researchers embarking on this critical phase of the research process.

Importance of Identifying a Research Problem

Identifying a research problem is the critical first step in the research process, setting the stage for subsequent stages of inquiry, data collection, analysis, and interpretation. By selecting a clear, relevant, and significant research problem, researchers can make meaningful contributions to the field of education, address pressing challenges, and advance knowledge and practice in teaching and learning.

Through careful consideration of the existing literature, practical relevance, theoretical framework, feasibility, and ethical considerations, researchers can effectively identify research problems that are both academically rigorous and socially impactful. By engaging with stakeholders, piloting research questions, and documenting the rationale for their choices, researchers can ensure that their research is well-informed, transparent, and responsive to the needs of the educational community.

Educational research aims to advance knowledge and practice in the field of education by addressing pressing issues, exploring new ideas, and generating evidence-based insights. At the heart of every research endeavor lies a research problem—a question or issue that requires investigation to deepen understanding, inform decision-making, or drive positive change. Identifying a clear and well-defined research problem is essential for multiple reasons:

Focus and Direction. A well-defined research problem provides focus and direction for the entire research process. It helps researchers clarify their research objectives, delineate the scope of their study, and identify specific research questions or hypotheses to address.

Relevance and Significance. The research problem should address a relevant and significant issue within the field of education. By tackling pressing challenges or exploring emerging trends, researchers can contribute new knowledge, insights, and solutions to enhance educational practice and policy.

Contribution to Knowledge. A carefully formulated research problem contributes to the advancement of knowledge in the field of education. It builds upon existing research findings, fills gaps in the literature, and generates new theoretical or practical insights that can inform future research, practice, and decision-making.

Stakeholder Engagement. Engaging stakeholders, such as educators, policymakers, students, and community members, is essential in educational research. A well-defined research problem can facilitate stakeholder involvement by clearly articulating the relevance and potential impact of the research, fostering collaboration and partnership throughout the research process.

Considerations for Selecting a Research Problem

Selecting a research problem requires thoughtful consideration of various factors:

Literature Review. Conducting a comprehensive literature review is critical to identify gaps, trends, and debates within the existing body of research. Researchers should examine relevant scholarly articles, books, reports, and other sources to assess the current state of knowledge and identify areas where further research is needed.

Scope and Specificity: Researchers should define the scope and specificity of their research topic to ensure that it is neither too broad nor too narrow, allowing for a focused and manageable research study.

Practical Relevance. Researchers should consider the practical relevance of the research problem to educational practice, policy, or community needs. By addressing real-world challenges or opportunities, research findings are more likely to have meaningful impacts and implications for stakeholders.

Theoretical Framework. The selection of a research problem should be guided by a clear theoretical framework or conceptual framework. Researchers should consider theoretical perspectives, models, or frameworks that provide a lens for understanding the phenomena under investigation and guiding the research design and analysis.

Feasibility and Resources. Researchers must assess the feasibility of addressing the research problem within the constraints of time, resources, and expertise available. Considerations such as access to data, research participants, research facilities, and funding sources should be considered when selecting a research problem.

Ethical Considerations. Ethical considerations are paramount in educational research. Researchers must ensure that their research problem is ethically sound and aligns with ethical guidelines and principles, including the protection of human subjects, confidentiality, informed consent, and integrity in research conduct.

Personal Interest and Expertise: Researchers should choose a topic that aligns with their personal interests, expertise, and passion for contributing to the field of education.

Stakeholder Perspectives: Engaging with stakeholders, such as educators, students, parents, or policymakers, can provide valuable insights into pressing issues or areas of interest that warrant further investigation.

Practical Guidance for Researchers

To effectively identify a research problem in educational research, researchers can follow these practical steps:

1. **Define the Scope**: Clearly define the scope of the research, including the educational context, population of interest, and key variables or concepts to be studied. Consider the level of analysis (e.g., classroom, school, district, national) and the temporal scope (e.g., cross-sectional, longitudinal) of the research.

2. **Brainstorm Research Questions**: Brainstorm potential research questions or hypotheses that align with the research problem and objectives. Consider the specific aims of the study, the gaps identified in the literature, and the theoretical or conceptual framework guiding the research.

3. **Consult with Stakeholders**: Engage with stakeholders, such as educators, administrators, policymakers, students, and community members, to gather input and perspectives on potential research problems. Consultation with stakeholders can help ensure that the research is relevant, meaningful, and responsive to the needs of the target audience.

4. **Pilot Testing**: Pilot test potential research questions or hypotheses to assess their clarity, feasibility, and relevance. Seek feedback from colleagues, mentors, or peers in the field of education to refine and iterate on the research problem before finalizing it for the study.

5. **Document Rationale**: Document the rationale and justification for selecting the research problem, including a synthesis of the literature, the practical significance of the research, and the theoretical or conceptual framework guiding the study. Clearly articulate why the research problem is worth investigating and how it contributes to the broader field of education.

In summary, identifying a research problem is a foundational step in educational research, requiring careful thought, deliberation, and collaboration. By approaching this process systematically and thoughtfully, researchers can embark on research endeavors that contribute to the improvement of educational practice, policy, and outcomes for learners worldwide.

Research Questions

Once a research problem has been selected, the next step is to formulate clear and focused research questions. Research questions serve as the guiding framework for the research study, guiding the selection of research methods, data collection procedures, and data analysis techniques.

Introduction to Educational Research

The following table provides examples of research questions for the research problems discussed in the first section of this chapter:

Research Topic	Research Problem	Research Question
Student Engagement	Problem: Despite efforts to enhance student engagement in classrooms, some students still exhibit low levels of participation and interest in learning activities.	What factors contribute to student disengagement in the classroom? What strategies can educators implement to promote greater student engagement?
Digital Literacy Education	With the increasing reliance on digital technologies in education, there is a growing need for effective digital literacy education to ensure that students develop essential skills for navigating the digital landscape.	How can digital literacy education be integrated into the curriculum to equip students with the necessary skills to critically evaluate online information, communicate effectively in digital environments, and protect their digital privacy and security?
Teacher Professional Development	Many teachers face challenges in keeping pace with the rapidly evolving demands of the education landscape and implementing evidence-based instructional practices in their classrooms.	What types of professional development programs are most effective in supporting teachers' ongoing learning and professional growth? How can schools and districts ensure sustained implementation of effective teaching strategies?
Inclusive Education	Despite efforts to promote inclusive education, students with disabilities continue to face barriers to full participation and meaningful engagement in inclusive classroom settings.	What are the key challenges and opportunities associated with implementing inclusive education practices? How can schools foster a more inclusive learning environment that meets the diverse needs of all students?
Assessment and Feedback	Traditional methods of assessment may not adequately capture students' diverse strengths, skills, and knowledge, and provide timely and constructive feedback for improvement.	What alternative assessment methods and feedback strategies can educators employ to better assess students' learning progress, promote metacognitive skills development, and enhance overall learning outcomes?
Parental Involvement	Despite the recognized importance of parental involvement in supporting students' academic success, some parents face barriers to active engagement in their children's education.	What are the most effective strategies for promoting parental involvement in education, particularly among underrepresented or marginalized communities? How can schools and communities collaborate to strengthen home-school partnerships?
Educational Equity	Disparities persist in educational access, opportunities, and outcomes, particularly along lines of race, socioeconomic status, and geographic location, leading to	What systemic barriers contribute to educational inequities? What policies, practices, and interventions can be implemented to promote greater equity and access to

Research Topic	Research Problem	Research Question
	inequities in educational attainment and achievement.	high-quality education for all students?

When formulating research questions, researchers should consider the following principles:

1. **Clarity and Specificity**: Research questions should be clear, specific, and focused, articulating the key variables or concepts under investigation and the intended outcomes of the study.

2. **Feasibility**: Research questions should be feasible to answer within the constraints of the research study, considering factors such as available resources, time frame, and access to participants or data.

3. **Relevance and Significance**: Research questions should address a significant gap or issue in the existing literature or educational practice, demonstrating relevance and potential impact on the field of education.

4. **Openness to Inquiry**: Research questions should be open-ended and exploratory, allowing for multiple perspectives, interpretations, and avenues of investigation.

5. **Ethics**: Research questions should be ethical to ensure that the research process respects the rights, dignity, and well-being of all individuals involved, including participants, researchers, and other stakeholders. Ethical research questions uphold principles of integrity, fairness, and respect for human rights, promoting trust and accountability in the research process.

Clear and Specific Research Questions

Clarity and specificity are fundamental aspects of developing research questions in any field, including educational research. Clear and specific research questions provide a focused framework for inquiry, guiding researchers in their investigation and ensuring that the study's objectives are well-defined and achievable. Clarity and specificity are crucial for the following reasons:

Guiding the Research Process: Clear and specific research questions serve as a roadmap for the entire research process. They help researchers stay focused on the key objectives of their study, guiding decisions regarding research design, data collection methods, and data analysis techniques.

Facilitating Communication: Clear research questions make it easier for researchers to communicate their study's purpose and objectives to others, including colleagues, stakeholders, and research participants. This clarity fosters understanding and collaboration, ensuring that everyone involved in the research is on the same page.

Enhancing Validity and Reliability: Specific research questions enable researchers to design studies that are more valid and reliable. By clearly defining the variables and concepts under investigation, researchers can ensure that their measurements are consistent and that their findings accurately reflect the phenomenon of interest.

Minimizing Bias and Ambiguity: Clear and specific research questions help minimize bias and ambiguity in the research process. They make it easier for researchers to formulate hypotheses, select appropriate research methods, and interpret their findings objectively, reducing the risk of misinterpretation or misrepresentation.

Introduction to Educational Research

Facilitating Replication and Extension: Clear research questions pave the way for future research by providing a solid foundation for replication and extension studies. Other researchers can build upon existing research by replicating the study's methods or extending the investigation to new contexts or populations.

Examples of Clear and Unclear Research Questions:
Clear Research Question: "What is the impact of parental involvement on students' academic achievement in elementary schools?" ***Explanation:*** In the clear research question, the variables (parental involvement and academic achievement) are clearly defined, and the context (elementary schools) is specified. This question provides a clear focus for the study and suggests a specific direction for inquiry. ***Unclear Research Question:*** "How do parents affect their children's performance in school?" ***Explanation:*** In contrast, the unclear research question lacks specificity and clarity. The term "parents" is vague and could refer to various aspects of parental influence, while "performance in school" is a broad and ambiguous concept that could encompass academic achievement, behavior, or other factors. Without clear definitions and context, it's challenging to determine the scope and objectives of the study.

Clear and specific research questions are essential for guiding the research process, facilitating communication, enhancing validity and reliability, minimizing bias and ambiguity, and facilitating replication and extension of research findings. By ensuring that research questions are clear and specific, researchers can conduct studies that are focused, rigorous, and meaningful.

Feasible Research Questions

Feasibility is a critical consideration in the development of research questions as it determines the practicality and achievability of conducting the research study. Feasibility refers to the extent to which a research question can be answered within the constraints of available resources, time, and access to data or participants. Feasibility is important for the following reasons:

Resource Allocation. Feasible research questions ensure that resources, such as time, funding, and personnel, are allocated efficiently. Researchers must consider the feasibility of their research questions to ensure that they can conduct the study within the available resources without overextending themselves.

Time Constraints. Research projects are often conducted within a limited timeframe, making it essential to choose research questions that can be answered within the allotted time. Feasible research questions are realistic in terms of the time required for data collection, analysis, and reporting.

Access to Participants and Data. Feasibility also relates to the availability of participants and data required for the study. Researchers must consider whether they can access the necessary population or dataset to answer their research questions effectively.

Ethical Considerations. Feasible research questions take into account ethical considerations, such as participant privacy, informed consent, and potential harm. Researchers must ensure that their study can be conducted ethically and in accordance with relevant guidelines and regulations.

Practical Considerations. Feasible research questions consider practical factors, such as the researcher's expertise, the research setting, and the complexity of data collection and analysis methods. Researchers must choose research questions that align with their skills and resources.

Examples of Feasible and Unfeasible Research Questions

Feasible Research Question: "Does the implementation of a mindfulness-based intervention improve students' self-regulation skills in a high school setting?"

Explanation: This research question is feasible because it specifies a clear intervention (mindfulness-based intervention) and outcome measure (students' self-regulation skills) that can be assessed within a high school setting. The research design could involve implementing the intervention in select classrooms and measuring changes in self-regulation skills through pre- and post-intervention assessments.

Unfeasible Research Question: "How does global climate change impact student performance in mathematics across different continents?"

Explanation: This research question is unfeasible due to several reasons. Firstly, measuring the impact of global climate change on student performance in mathematics would require extensive data collection across various continents, which is logistically challenging and resource-intensive. Additionally, attributing changes in student performance solely to climate change would be methodologically complex, as numerous other factors influence academic achievement.

Feasible research questions are essential for ensuring that research studies are practical, manageable, and can be executed within the constraints of available resources, time, and ethical considerations. By focusing on specific populations, contexts, and variables, researchers can design studies that yield meaningful insights and contribute to the advancement of knowledge in their respective fields.

Relevant and Significant Research Questions

Formulating research questions that are both relevant and significant is essential in guiding meaningful inquiry and ensuring the impact of research findings. Below are some reasons why relevance and significance are crucial:

Addressing Real-World Issues. Relevant research questions address pressing issues or gaps in knowledge within the field of study. By focusing on topics that are relevant to the current needs and challenges faced by practitioners, policymakers, and stakeholders, researchers can ensure that their findings have practical implications and can contribute to addressing real-world problems.

Informing Decision-Making. Research questions that are significant have the potential to inform decision-making processes at various levels, from individual practice to institutional policy. By generating evidence-based insights into important educational issues, researchers can empower stakeholders to make informed decisions that lead to positive changes in educational practice, programs, and policies.

Introduction to Educational Research

Contributing to Literature. Relevant and significant research questions contribute to the advancement of knowledge within the field by building upon existing research, challenging assumptions, and generating new insights. By addressing gaps or controversies in literature, researchers can expand the theoretical and empirical understanding of educational phenomena and contribute to the development of the field.

Engaging Stakeholders. Research questions that are relevant and significant are more likely to engage stakeholders and garner support for the research endeavor. By demonstrating the importance and potential impact of their research, researchers can foster collaboration, partnership, and participation from practitioners, policymakers, and other stakeholders, enhancing the relevance and applicability of their findings.

Examples of Relevant and Irrelevant Research Questions

Relevant Research Question: "What are the most effective strategies for promoting inclusive education in diverse classrooms, and how do they impact student learning outcomes?"

Explanation: This research question is relevant because it addresses the pressing issue of promoting inclusive education in diverse classrooms, which is a priority for educators, policymakers, and advocates for educational equity. It is also significant because it has the potential to inform the development of inclusive practices and policies that improve student learning outcomes and promote social inclusion.

Irrelevant Research Question: "What is the favorite color of students in middle school?"

Explanation: This research question lacks relevance and significance because it does not address any pressing educational issues or contribute to advancing knowledge within the field. While it may be of interest to some individuals, it does not have practical implications for educational practice, policy, or theory.

By formulating research questions that are both relevant and significant, researchers can ensure that their studies address important issues, inform decision-making processes, contribute to the literature, and engage stakeholders effectively. This helps to maximize the impact and relevance of research findings, ultimately leading to positive changes in educational practice and policy.

Opened Research Questions

Openness to inquiry is essential in the development of research questions as it encourages exploration, discovery, and the pursuit of new knowledge. Openness to inquiry is crucial for the following reasons:

Encouraging Exploration. Open research questions allow for exploration of diverse perspectives, alternative explanations, and unexpected findings. By remaining open to different possibilities and interpretations, researchers can uncover new insights and generate innovative solutions to complex problems.

Fostering Creativity and Innovation. Open research questions stimulate creativity and innovation by encouraging researchers to think critically, question assumptions, and explore unconventional ideas. By embracing uncertainty and ambiguity, researchers can push the boundaries of knowledge and make groundbreaking discoveries.

Promoting Rigor and Objectivity. Open research questions promote rigor and objectivity by encouraging researchers to approach their inquiry with an open mind and consider multiple viewpoints. By critically evaluating evidence, challenging biases, and engaging in reflexivity, researchers can ensure the validity and reliability of their findings.

Facilitating Collaboration and Interdisciplinary Exchange. Open research questions facilitate collaboration and interdisciplinary exchange by inviting input from diverse stakeholders, disciplines, and perspectives. By fostering dialogue and collaboration, researchers can leverage collective expertise and resources to address complex problems and generate comprehensive solutions.

Examples of Open and Closed Research Questions

Open Research Question: "How does technology influence the learning experiences of students in diverse educational settings?"

Explanation: This open research question invites exploration of the multifaceted ways in which technology impacts student learning experiences across different educational contexts. It allows for consideration of various factors, such as pedagogical approaches, student characteristics, and socio-cultural dynamics, and encourages researchers to adopt a holistic perspective in their inquiry.

Closed Research Question: "Does technology improve student learning outcomes?"

Explanation: This closed research question presupposes a binary answer (yes or no) and limits the scope of inquiry to a specific technology and outcome measure. It does not allow for exploration of alternative perspectives, contextual factors, or unintended consequences associated with technology use in education.

By embracing openness to inquiry in the development of research questions, researchers can foster exploration, creativity, rigor, and collaboration, ultimately leading to more nuanced understanding and innovative solutions to complex problems in education and beyond.

Ethical Research Questions

Ethics play a crucial role in the development of research questions as they guide researchers in conducting studies that uphold the rights, dignity, and well-being of research participants. Below are some ethical principles that must be considered in the development of research questions:

Respecting Participant Rights. Ethical research questions prioritize the rights and welfare of research participants, ensuring that their autonomy, privacy, and confidentiality are respected throughout the research process. By considering the potential risks and benefits of participation, researchers can design studies that prioritize participant well-being and minimize harm.

Ensuring Informed Consent. Ethical research questions promote informed consent by providing participants with clear and comprehensive information about the study purpose, procedures, risks, and benefits. By obtaining voluntary and informed consent from participants, researchers ensure that individuals have the opportunity to make autonomous decisions about their involvement in the research.

Avoiding Harm and Exploitation. Ethical research questions aim to minimize the risk of harm and exploitation to research participants, particularly vulnerable populations such as children, minorities, and individuals with limited decision-making capacity. By considering the potential impact of research on participants' physical, psychological, social, and cultural well-being, researchers can mitigate risks and protect against exploitation.

Maintaining Integrity and Trust. Ethical research questions uphold the principles of integrity, honesty, and transparency in research conduct. By adhering to ethical guidelines and professional standards, researchers build trust and credibility with participants, colleagues, and the broader community, enhancing the integrity and reliability of their research findings.

Examples of Ethical and Unethical Research Questions

Ethical Research Question: "How do parental involvement practices influence student academic achievement in elementary schools, and what strategies can educators implement to promote meaningful parental engagement?"

Explanation: This ethical research question respects the rights and dignity of both students and parents by focusing on a topic of educational significance and proposing to explore ways to enhance parental involvement in a constructive manner. It prioritizes participant well-being and autonomy by seeking to generate insights that benefit both students and parents without causing harm or exploitation.

Unethical Research Question: "What are the psychological effects of bullying on middle school students, and how can researchers manipulate social dynamics to exacerbate these effects?"

Explanation: This unethical research question raises serious ethical concerns as it involves intentionally inflicting harm on research participants (middle school students) by subjecting them to bullying experiences. It prioritizes research interests over participant welfare and violates ethical principles of beneficence, non-maleficence, and respect for persons. Such research questions are unethical and should be avoided.

By considering ethical principles in the development of research questions, researchers can conduct studies that prioritize participant welfare, uphold integrity and trust, and contribute to the advancement of knowledge in a responsible and ethical manner.

In conclusion, identifying a research problem is a critical first step in educational research, laying the groundwork for meaningful inquiry and discovery. By selecting a research topic that is relevant, feasible, and aligned with stakeholder needs, and formulating clear and focused research questions, researchers can embark on a journey of inquiry that contributes to the advancement of knowledge and practice in the field of education.

Summary

The text discusses the foundational aspects of educational research, focusing on the identification of research problems and the formulation of research questions. It highlights the significance of identifying relevant and significant research problems, emphasizing their role in guiding the research process and addressing pressing issues in education. The text provides examples of research problems across various educational domains, illustrating the diversity of topics that researchers may explore.

Furthermore, it discusses the importance of clarity, specificity, feasibility, relevance, significance, openness to inquiry, and ethics in the development of research questions. Clear and specific research questions provide a focused framework for inquiry, while feasible questions ensure practicality within the constraints of available resources and ethical considerations. Relevant and significant research questions address real-world issues, inform decision-making, and contribute to the advancement of knowledge in the field. Open research questions encourage exploration, creativity, and collaboration, fostering innovative solutions to complex problems. Lastly, ethical research questions prioritize the rights, dignity, and well-being of research participants, ensuring integrity and trust in the research process.

Throughout the text, examples of clear and unclear, feasible and unfeasible, relevant and irrelevant, and ethical and unethical research questions are provided to illustrate key concepts. By considering these principles and examples, researchers can effectively identify research problems and formulate research questions that drive meaningful inquiry and contribute to positive changes in education.

Suggestions for Students

Key Questions

Use the following questions and prompts to check your understanding, discuss, and reflect upon the content of this chapter:

1. What is the importance of identifying a research problem in educational research?

2. How can researchers identify relevant and significant research problems?

3. Provide examples of research problems in various areas of education.

4. What are the key considerations for selecting a research problem?

5. Discuss the significance of clarity and specificity in the development of research questions. Provide examples of clear and unclear research questions.

6. Why is feasibility important in the development of research questions? Give examples of feasible and unfeasible research questions.

7. Explain the importance of relevance and significance in formulating research questions. Provide examples of relevant and significant research questions, as well as non-relevant/non-significant ones.

8. Discuss the concept of openness to inquiry in developing research questions. Include examples of open and closed research questions.

9. Why is it essential for research questions to be ethical? Provide examples of ethical and unethical research questions.

10. How can researchers ensure that their research questions align with ethical principles?

Suggestions for Instructors

Suggested learning activities

The following activities provide opportunities for students to engage with the content of this chapter, apply theoretical concepts to real-world scenarios, and develop essential research skills in educational research.

Case Studies. Provide students with case studies related to educational research problems and ask them to identify the research problem, formulate research questions, and discuss the importance of each step in the research process.

Group Discussions. Divide students into small groups and assign each group a research problem from the text. Ask them to brainstorm potential research questions and discuss the relevance, significance, and feasibility of each question. Encourage groups to present their findings to the class and facilitate a discussion.

Research Proposal Development. Have students work individually or in pairs to develop a research proposal based on one of the research problems provided in the text. They should outline the research problem, research questions, literature review, methodology, and ethical considerations. Provide feedback on their proposals to help them refine their ideas.

Ethical Dilemma Scenarios. Present students with ethical dilemma scenarios related to educational research questions. Ask them to analyze each scenario and discuss the ethical implications of the research questions involved. Encourage students to propose solutions to address ethical concerns while still conducting valuable research.

Research Question Analysis. Provide students with a set of research questions and ask them to evaluate each question based on clarity, specificity, feasibility, relevance, significance, and ethical considerations. This activity will help students understand the criteria for developing effective research questions.

Guest Speaker Presentation. Invite a guest speaker who is actively engaged in educational research to discuss their experience in identifying research problems and formulating research questions. Encourage students to ask questions and engage in a dialogue with the speaker to gain insights into the research process.

References

American Educational Research Association, American Psychological Association, & National Council on Measurement in Education. (2014). Standards for educational and psychological testing. American Educational Research Association.

Creswell, J. W. (2014). Research design: Qualitative, quantitative, and mixed methods approaches. Sage publications.

Leedy, P. D., & Ormrod, J. E. (2014). Practical research: Planning and design. Pearson.

Merriam, S. B. (2009). Qualitative research: A guide to design and implementation. John Wiley & Sons.

Stake, R. E. (1995). The art of case study research. Sage.

Yin, R. K. (2017). Case study research and applications: Design and methods. Sage publications.

Chapter 3. Reviewing the Literature

This chapter will address the following learning objectives:
• Define literature reviews in educational research.
• Explain the significance of literature reviews in educational research.
• Discuss the impact of the digital age on literature reviews.
• Identify the key objectives of literature reviews in educational research.
• Compare and contrast various methods and approaches for conducting literature reviews in educational research.
• Identify different writing styles and conventions used in literature reviews.
• Utilize the diverse range of sources available for literature reviews in educational research.
• Evaluate the challenges associated with conducting literature reviews.
• Apply practical guidelines for conducting literature reviews effectively.
• Summarize strategies to avoid plagiarism in conducting literature reviews.
• Utilize plagiarism detection tools to ensure academic integrity in literature reviews.

In the realm of educational research, reviewing existing literature serves as the cornerstone for the advancement of knowledge and the formulation of informed conclusions. It is through this process that researchers engage in a comprehensive examination of previous studies, theoretical frameworks, and empirical evidence relevant to their area of inquiry. By delving into the existing body of literature, researchers not only identify gaps and inconsistencies but also build upon the foundations laid by their predecessors.

A literature review in educational research is a critical analysis and synthesis of existing scholarly literature on a specific topic or research question within the field of education. It involves identifying, evaluating, and synthesizing relevant research studies, theoretical frameworks, and empirical findings to provide a comprehensive understanding of the topic under investigation. Literature reviews serve to contextualize research within the broader academic discourse, identify gaps in existing knowledge, and inform the development of research hypotheses or questions. Gall et al. (2003) defined literature reviews as follows:

"A literature review in educational research is a systematic, comprehensive, and critical analysis of scholarly literature related to a specific topic or research question within the field of education. It involves identifying, evaluating, and synthesizing relevant studies, theories, and findings to provide a comprehensive understanding of the topic and inform future research directions."

Reviewing the literature in educational research is a multifaceted endeavor that requires critical analysis, synthesis, and interpretation of diverse sources. It involves navigating through a vast array of scholarly articles, books, reports, and other academic publications to extract valuable insights and identify key themes and trends. Moreover, it necessitates a discerning eye to evaluate the quality and credibility of the sources, considering factors such as methodology, validity, and relevance to the research question at hand.

Through this process, researchers gain a deeper understanding of the current state of knowledge in their field, identify potential avenues for further exploration, and refine the focus of their own research inquiries. Furthermore, by situating their work within the broader context of existing scholarship, researchers contribute to the ongoing dialogue and collective advancement of educational theory and practice.

In this chapter, we will explore the significance of literature review in educational research, its key objectives, methods, challenges, as well as provide practical guidelines for conducting a thorough and effective review of the literature.

The Importance of Literature Reviews

In the dynamic landscape of educational research, the process of reviewing literature stands as an indispensable pillar, guiding scholars through a labyrinth of ideas, studies, and theories. This critical examination of existing scholarship serves as both a compass and a roadmap, illuminating the path toward deeper understanding and meaningful contributions to the field. The importance of reviewing the literature in educational research cannot be overstated, as it underpins the foundation upon which new knowledge is constructed and insights are gleaned.

At its core, the literature review is a journey of exploration and discovery, allowing researchers to navigate the vast expanse of scholarly work that precedes their own. It is a journey marked by inquiry, analysis, and synthesis, as researchers engage with a diverse array of sources to uncover patterns, trends, and gaps in knowledge. Through this process, they gain valuable insights into the historical context, theoretical frameworks, and empirical evidence that shape the landscape of educational inquiry.

Moreover, reviewing the literature serves as a catalyst for critical thinking and scholarly dialogue. By interrogating existing theories, methodologies, and findings, researchers are prompted to question assumptions, challenge established paradigms, and push the boundaries of knowledge. This spirit of inquiry not only enriches individual research endeavors but also contributes to the broader intellectual discourse within the field of education.

Furthermore, the literature review plays a pivotal role in shaping the trajectory of research inquiry. It provides researchers with a solid foundation upon which to build their own studies, guiding the formulation of research questions, hypotheses, and methodologies. By synthesizing existing knowledge and identifying gaps in the literature, researchers are empowered to design studies that address pressing issues, expand theoretical frameworks, and generate new insights.

The examples below illustrate the breadth and depth of literature reviews in educational research, which serve to synthesize existing knowledge, identify key trends and patterns, and inform future research directions and educational practices.

Introduction to Educational Research

Examples Literature Review Topics in Educational Research:
Literature Review on Student Engagement in Online Learning: This review synthesizes existing research on factors influencing student engagement in online learning environments. It examines the role of instructional design, technology integration, instructor presence, and learner characteristics in promoting meaningful engagement and learning outcomes. The review highlights the importance of fostering interaction, collaboration, and self-regulated learning strategies to enhance student engagement in online courses.
Literature Review on the Impact of Socioeconomic Status on Academic Achievement: This review explores the relationship between socioeconomic status (SES) and academic achievement among students. Drawing on a range of empirical studies, the review examines the influence of family background, parental involvement, school resources, and community factors on academic outcomes. It identifies disparities in educational attainment based on SES and discusses implications for educational policy and practice.
Literature Review on the Effectiveness of Inquiry-Based Learning in Science Education: This review evaluates the effectiveness of inquiry-based learning (IBL) approaches in promoting student understanding and engagement in science education. Drawing on theoretical frameworks and empirical studies, the review examines the impact of IBL on student motivation, conceptual understanding, and scientific inquiry skills. It identifies best practices for implementing IBL strategies and discusses challenges and opportunities for incorporating IBL into science curriculum.
Literature Review on Culturally Responsive Teaching Practices: This review synthesizes research on culturally responsive teaching (CRT) practices aimed at addressing the diverse needs of students from culturally and linguistically diverse backgrounds. It explores strategies for creating inclusive and culturally affirming learning environments, such as incorporating students' cultural assets into the curriculum, promoting critical consciousness, and fostering positive teacher-student relationships. The review discusses the importance of culturally responsive pedagogy in promoting academic success and equity in education.
Literature Review on the Impact of Early Childhood Education Programs: This review examines the evidence on the long-term impact of early childhood education (ECE) programs on children's cognitive, social-emotional, and academic development. Drawing on longitudinal studies and meta-analyses, the review assesses the effectiveness of different types of ECE interventions, such as pre-kindergarten programs, Head Start, and early intervention services. It discusses the potential benefits of high-quality ECE programs in narrowing achievement gaps and promoting lifelong learning outcomes.

In addition to informing the direction of research, the literature review also enhances the rigor and validity of scholarly work. By critically evaluating the quality, relevance, and credibility of existing sources, researchers ensure that their own studies are grounded in a solid evidence base. This rigorous approach not only strengthens the validity of research findings but also fosters transparency and accountability within the scholarly community. The literature review holds paramount importance in educational research for several compelling reasons:

Contextualizing Research. Educational research does not exist in isolation. Instead, it builds upon existing knowledge and theories. A thorough literature review provides the necessary context by outlining the historical development, current state, and key debates within the field. This contextualization helps researchers understand where their work fits within the larger landscape of educational scholarship.

Identifying Gaps and Research Questions. By reviewing the literature, researchers can identify gaps, inconsistencies, and unresolved questions in previous studies. This process helps in formulating clear research questions and objectives that address the existing gaps in knowledge. Identifying these gaps is crucial for advancing the field and contributing to meaningful scholarly discourse.

Building Theoretical Frameworks. Educational research often relies on theoretical frameworks to guide inquiry and interpretation. Literature review enables researchers to explore and evaluate different theoretical perspectives relevant to their topic. By synthesizing existing theories, researchers can develop robust conceptual frameworks that provide a foundation for their study and help make sense of their findings.

Informing Methodological Choices. The literature review informs researchers about the methods used in previous studies, including their strengths, limitations, and applicability to different research contexts. This knowledge guides researchers in selecting appropriate research methods, data collection techniques, and analytical approaches for their own study. Additionally, it helps in avoiding pitfalls and challenges encountered by previous researchers.

Validating Findings and Interpretations. By grounding their work in existing literature, researchers can validate their findings and interpretations. Referencing prior studies that support their arguments lends credibility to their research and enhances its impact. Moreover, engaging with contrasting viewpoints and conflicting evidence allows researchers to critically evaluate their own findings and consider alternative explanations.

Contributing to Knowledge Development. Through the literature review, researchers not only consume existing knowledge but also contribute to its expansion. By synthesizing and synthesizing existing research, researchers can identify emerging trends, new perspectives, and areas for further exploration. This process fosters intellectual dialogue and collective advancement within the field of education.

In essence, the literature review serves as the foundation upon which educational research is built. It provides researchers with the necessary tools to situate their work within the broader scholarly discourse, develop robust research questions and methodologies, and contribute meaningfully to the advancement of knowledge in the field of education.

In summary, the importance of reviewing the literature in educational research lies in its ability to inform, inspire, and enrich the pursuit of knowledge. By engaging with existing scholarship, researchers gain valuable insights, identify research questions, and contribute to the advancement of theory and practice in education. In the pages that follow, we will explore the various dimensions of the literature review process, offering practical guidance and insights for scholars embarking on their own research journeys.

Literature Reviews in the Digital Age

The digital age has had a profound impact on the accessibility, dissemination, and synthesis of sources for conducting literature reviews in educational research. Digital technologies have facilitated the rapid dissemination of scholarly work, enabling researchers to access a vast array of sources from anywhere in the world. Online databases, digital repositories, and academic search engines have democratized access to knowledge, empowering researchers of all backgrounds to engage in scholarly inquiry and contribute to the advancement of educational research.

Furthermore, the digital age has facilitated new methods and approaches for conducting literature reviews, such as systematic reviews, meta-analyses, and text mining. These computational techniques leverage digital tools and algorithms to systematically search, analyze, and synthesize large volumes of literature, enabling researchers to identify patterns, trends, and insights that may not be apparent through traditional methods. The digital age has thus opened new possibilities for conducting rigorous, evidence-based literature reviews that inform policy, practice, and theory in educational research.

In summary, the digital age has transformed the landscape of educational research, offering researchers unprecedented access to sources and tools for conducting literature reviews. Understanding the types of sources available and their impact in the digital age is essential for researchers to navigate this dynamic terrain and harness its full potential for advancing knowledge and scholarship in the field of education.

Literature Review Objectives

In educational research, literature reviews serve multifaceted objectives, each contributing to the advancement of knowledge, theory, and practice within the field. Let's delve into the primary objectives:

1. **Identifying Existing Knowledge**: One of the fundamental objectives of a literature review is to identify and synthesize existing knowledge and scholarship related to the research topic. By thoroughly examining previous studies, theoretical frameworks, and empirical evidence, researchers gain a comprehensive understanding of the current state of knowledge within their area of inquiry. This foundational knowledge serves as a springboard for further exploration and informs the direction of the research.

2. **Identifying Gaps and Inconsistencies**: Literature reviews enable researchers to identify gaps, inconsistencies, and unresolved questions in the existing literature. By critically analyzing previous studies, researchers can pinpoint areas where further research is needed to address unanswered questions or reconcile conflicting findings. This process of gap identification is essential for advancing knowledge and guiding the formulation of research questions and hypotheses.

3. **Building Theoretical Frameworks**: Educational research often relies on theoretical frameworks to guide inquiry and interpretation. Literature reviews play a crucial role in building and refining theoretical frameworks by synthesizing existing theories and perspectives relevant to the research topic. By integrating diverse theoretical perspectives, researchers can develop robust conceptual frameworks that provide a theoretical lens through which to interpret their findings.

4. **Informing Methodological Choices**: Literature reviews inform researchers about the methodologies used in previous studies, including their strengths, limitations, and applicability to different research contexts. By examining the methodological approaches employed by previous researchers, researchers can make informed decisions about the research design, data collection methods, and analytical techniques best suited to their own study. This ensures methodological rigor and enhances the validity and reliability of research findings.

5. **Validating Findings and Interpretations**: By grounding their work in existing literature, researchers can validate their findings and interpretations. Referencing prior studies that support their arguments lends credibility to their research and enhances its impact. Moreover, engaging with contrasting viewpoints and conflicting evidence allows researchers to critically evaluate their own findings and consider alternative explanations, thereby strengthening the validity and robustness of their conclusions.

6. **Contributing to Knowledge Development**: Literature reviews not only consume existing knowledge but also contribute to its expansion. By synthesizing and synthesizing existing research, researchers can identify emerging trends, new perspectives, and areas for further exploration. This process fosters intellectual dialogue and collective advancement within the field of education, ultimately contributing to the growth and development of knowledge, theory, and practice.

In summary, literature reviews in educational research serve a multitude of objectives, ranging from identifying existing knowledge and gaps in the literature to informing theoretical frameworks, methodological choices, and interpretations of research findings. By fulfilling these objectives, literature reviews play a pivotal role in advancing knowledge, theory, and practice within the field of education.

Literature Review Methods

Reviewing the literature in educational research involves several methods and approaches, each tailored to the specific research question, objectives, and context. Here are some commonly used methods:

Systematic Literature Review. Systematic literature reviews involve a structured and comprehensive search of relevant literature using predefined criteria and rigorous methodological procedures. These reviews aim to minimize bias and ensure transparency by following a systematic approach to study selection, data extraction, and synthesis. Systematic reviews often employ techniques such as meta-analysis to quantitatively synthesize the findings of multiple studies on a particular topic. This method is particularly useful for synthesizing large bodies of literature and providing evidence-based recommendations for practice and policy in education (Kitchenham, 2004).

Narrative Literature Review. Narrative literature reviews involve a qualitative synthesis of the existing literature on a particular topic. Unlike systematic reviews, narrative reviews do not follow a predefined protocol and may include a broader range of sources and perspectives. Researchers conducting narrative reviews typically focus on synthesizing key themes, trends, and debates within the literature to provide a comprehensive overview of the topic. While narrative reviews may lack the rigor of systematic reviews, they offer flexibility and allow researchers to explore complex and multifaceted issues in education (Green et al., 2006).

Scoping Review. Scoping reviews aim to map the existing literature on a broad topic or research area, identifying key concepts, sources, and gaps in knowledge. Unlike systematic reviews, scoping reviews may include a wider range of study designs and sources, making them suitable for exploring diverse and emerging topics in education. Scoping reviews typically involve a systematic search of literature followed by a narrative synthesis of findings, providing researchers with a comprehensive understanding of the breadth and depth of research on a particular topic (Arksey & O'Malley, 2005).

Meta-ethnography. Meta-ethnography is a qualitative synthesis method commonly used in educational research to integrate findings from multiple qualitative studies on a particular topic.

Meta-ethnography involves a systematic process of translating, synthesizing, and reinterpreting findings across studies to generate new insights or theoretical understandings. This method allows researchers to explore the underlying meanings, themes, and patterns within qualitative data and develop higher-order interpretations or theories (Noblit & Hare, 1988).

Content Analysis. Content analysis involves a systematic analysis of textual data to identify patterns, themes, and relationships within a body of literature. In educational research, content analysis may be used to examine the representation of key concepts, theories, or methodologies across multiple studies. Researchers conducting content analysis typically develop coding schemes or frameworks to categorize and analyze textual data, allowing them to identify recurring themes, trends, or gaps in the literature (Krippendorff, 2018).

Descriptive (Mapping) Literature Review. Descriptive literature reviews, also known as mapping reviews, aim to provide a comprehensive overview of the existing literature on a particular topic or research area. These reviews typically involve mapping the key concepts, themes, theories, and empirical evidence present in the literature without necessarily aiming for a synthesis or critique. Descriptive reviews help researchers identify the scope, breadth, and depth of research on a given topic, facilitating a broad understanding of the field. They are particularly useful for exploring emerging topics or complex interdisciplinary areas where the extent of existing literature may be unclear (Grant & Booth, 2009).

Aggregative Literature Review. Aggregative literature reviews involve synthesizing and summarizing the findings of multiple studies to draw overarching conclusions or identify common patterns and trends. Unlike systematic reviews, which often focus on quantitative data and employ meta-analysis, aggregative reviews may include both quantitative and qualitative studies and use narrative synthesis techniques. These reviews aim to provide a comprehensive synthesis of the existing evidence on a particular topic, offering insights into the cumulative findings of multiple studies. Aggregative reviews are useful for synthesizing diverse sources of evidence and generating new interpretations or theoretical insights (Hannes & Macaitis, 2012).

Realist Literature Review. Realist literature reviews, rooted in realist philosophy, aim to explore how and why social interventions or programs work in particular contexts. These reviews focus on identifying and unpacking the underlying mechanisms, contexts, and outcomes of interventions, rather than simply synthesizing study findings. Realist reviews typically involve developing and refining program theories or hypotheses based on the existing literature and empirical evidence. They aim to provide insights into the causal mechanisms that explain how interventions produce outcomes in different contexts, offering valuable lessons for policy and practice (Pawson et al., 2004).

Critical Literature Review. Critical literature reviews involve a critical analysis and evaluation of the existing literature on a particular topic, with a focus on identifying assumptions, biases, and limitations in the literature. These reviews aim to interrogate the underlying assumptions, ideologies, and power dynamics that shape research and knowledge production in a given field. Critical reviews may employ a variety of theoretical frameworks, such as feminist theory, critical race theory, or postcolonial theory, to unpack the social, cultural, and political dimensions of the literature. They aim to challenge dominant discourses, highlight marginalized perspectives, and promote reflexivity and critical engagement among researchers (Denzin & Lincoln, 2018).

These methods represent some of the many approaches to reviewing the literature in educational research. These types of literature reviews offer different approaches to synthesizing and interpreting the existing literature in educational research, each with its own strengths and limitations. Researchers should carefully consider the objectives, scope, and methodology of their review when selecting the most appropriate approach.

Writing Styles and Conventions

Writing styles. In the development of literature reviews in educational research, writing styles can vary depending on factors such as the research question, objectives, audience, and disciplinary conventions. Here are some common writing styles used in literature reviews, along with references for further exploration:

Narrative Style. Narrative writing style involves presenting the literature review in a coherent and engaging narrative format. This style often follows a chronological or thematic organization, with the author synthesizing and summarizing the literature in their own words. Narrative literature reviews aim to provide a comprehensive overview of the existing literature, highlighting key themes, debates, and findings (Green et al., 2006).

Descriptive Style. Descriptive writing style focuses on providing a detailed description of the literature, without necessarily offering a critical analysis or synthesis. Descriptive literature reviews often involve summarizing individual studies or sources, presenting their main findings, methods, and conclusions. This style is useful for mapping the scope and breadth of research on a particular topic (Grant & Booth, 2009).

Analytical Style. Analytical writing style involves critically analyzing and synthesizing the literature to identify patterns, trends, and relationships. This style requires the author to engage with the literature in a deep and reflective manner, evaluating the strengths, weaknesses, and contributions of each source. Analytical literature reviews aim to generate new insights, interpretations, or theoretical frameworks based on the existing literature (Booth et al., 2016).

Argumentative Style. Argumentative writing style involves presenting a clear and persuasive argument or thesis based on the literature. This style requires the author to critically evaluate the evidence, construct logical arguments, and support their claims with relevant examples and citations. Argumentative literature reviews aim to advance a particular perspective, theory, or interpretation of the literature (Randolph, 2009).

Systematic Style. Systematic writing style follows a structured and systematic approach to reviewing the literature, often adhering to predefined criteria and methods. This style is common in systematic literature reviews, which involve a rigorous and transparent process of study selection, data extraction, and synthesis. Systematic literature reviews aim to minimize bias and ensure the reliability and validity of the findings (Tranfield et al., 2003).

Integrative Style. Integrative writing style involves integrating diverse sources, perspectives, and methodologies to provide a comprehensive synthesis of the literature. This style emphasizes the interconnectedness of ideas and findings across different studies, disciplines, or theoretical frameworks. Integrative literature reviews aim to generate new insights or theoretical understandings by synthesizing and reconciling conflicting perspectives (Torraco, 2005).

These writing styles can be adapted and combined to suit the specific requirements and objectives of the literature review in educational research. Researchers should carefully consider the intended audience, purpose, and context of their literature review when selecting the most appropriate writing style.

Writing Conventions. In the development of literature reviews in educational research, adhering to specific writing conventions is essential for ensuring clarity, coherence, and scholarly rigor. Here are some key writing conventions commonly observed in literature reviews, along with references for further exploration:

Clear Organization. Literature reviews should be well-organized and structured to guide readers through the review process. Typically, literature reviews begin with an introduction that outlines the scope, objectives, and significance of the review. This is followed by a discussion of the methods used to search and select the literature, a synthesis of the findings organized thematically or chronologically, and a conclusion that summarizes key insights and implications (Booth et al., 2016).

Critical Analysis. Literature reviews should involve a critical analysis and evaluation of the literature, rather than merely summarizing or describing existing studies. Authors should assess the strengths, weaknesses, and limitations of each source, as well as the overall quality and credibility of the literature. Critical analysis helps to identify gaps, contradictions, and areas for further research (Randolph, 2009).

Appropriate Language and Tone. Authors should use clear, concise, and scholarly language in their literature reviews, avoiding jargon or overly technical terminology that may obscure meaning. The tone of the review should be objective and impartial, focusing on presenting evidence and arguments rather than personal opinions or biases. Formal academic language and third-person perspective are typically employed (Hart, 1998).

Integration of Sources. Literature reviews should integrate diverse sources, perspectives, and methodologies to provide a comprehensive synthesis of the literature. Authors should strive to connect ideas, findings, and theories from different studies, disciplines, or theoretical frameworks, highlighting their interconnections and implications. Integration fosters a nuanced understanding of the topic and promotes interdisciplinary dialogue (Torraco, 2005).

Effective Use of Citations. Proper citation and referencing are crucial in literature reviews to acknowledge the contributions of previous research and avoid plagiarism. Authors should accurately cite each source consulted in the review, following the citation style specified by their discipline or publication venue (APA, MLA, Chicago, etc.). Citations should be used strategically to support arguments, provide evidence, and direct readers to relevant literature (Purdue OWL, n.d.).

Synthesis and Interpretation. Literature reviews should go beyond summarizing individual studies to provide synthesis and interpretation of the findings. Authors should analyze common themes, patterns, and trends across the literature, drawing connections and offering insights into the broader implications for theory, practice, and future research. Synthesis involves making sense of the collective evidence and generating new knowledge (Booth et al., 2016).

By adhering to these writing conventions, authors can develop literature reviews that are informative, credible, and impactful in advancing knowledge and scholarship in educational research.

Sources for Conducting Literature Reviews

In the realm of educational research, conducting a thorough literature review is an essential step towards building a strong foundation for scholarly inquiry. The process involves engaging with a diverse range of sources that offer insights, perspectives, and empirical evidence relevant to the research topic. Understanding the types of sources available for conducting literature reviews is crucial for researchers to navigate the vast landscape of educational scholarship effectively.

In the ever-evolving landscape of educational research, technology has revolutionized the way scholars engage with and access sources for conducting literature reviews. The proliferation of digital technologies has not only expanded the breadth and depth of available sources but has also transformed the methods and approaches used in reviewing the literature. In this digital era, researchers have access to a vast array of online repositories, databases, and scholarly platforms that offer unprecedented opportunities for exploration, discovery, and synthesis of knowledge. Understanding the types of sources available for conducting a literature review in educational research and their impact in the digital age is essential for navigating this dynamic terrain and harnessing its full potential.

In this section, we will explore various sources commonly utilized in educational research literature reviews and highlight their significance in shaping the discourse, theory, and practice in the field.

Peer-Reviewed Journal Articles: Peer-reviewed journals remain a cornerstone source for conducting literature reviews in educational research. Access to online databases such as JSTOR, PubMed, and Google Scholar has made it easier for researchers to identify and access a wide range of peer-reviewed articles spanning various subfields of education. These articles provide in-depth analyses of theoretical frameworks, research methodologies, empirical findings, and critical discussions relevant to educational research.

Books and Monographs: Books written by leading scholars in the field of education continue to be valuable sources for literature reviews. Electronic books (e-books) and online libraries such as Google Books and Project Gutenberg offer researchers instant access to a vast collection of educational literature. Monographs and edited volumes provide comprehensive insights into specific topics, theories, and research methodologies, facilitating deeper exploration and synthesis of knowledge.

Research Reports and Policy Documents: Research reports and policy documents published by government agencies, research institutes, and educational organizations are invaluable sources for literature reviews in educational research. These documents are often available online through institutional websites, digital repositories, and open-access platforms. They offer insights into current trends, challenges, and priorities in education, as well as data, analyses, and policy recommendations relevant to educational research.

Conference Proceedings: Academic conferences and symposia provide platforms for researchers to present and discuss their work, making conference proceedings a valuable source for literature reviews in educational research. Conference proceedings are often archived and accessible online through conference websites, digital libraries, and academic databases. They offer insights into cutting-edge research, emerging trends, and debates within the field of education, providing researchers with valuable leads for further exploration.

Dissertations and Theses: Graduate-level dissertations and theses represent original research conducted by students under the guidance of faculty mentors, making them valuable sources for literature reviews in educational research. Electronic theses and dissertations (ETDs) are increasingly available online through institutional repositories and digital libraries. They offer insights into specific research topics, methodologies, findings, and theoretical perspectives within educational research.

Digital Repositories and Open Educational Resources (OER): The digital age has witnessed the emergence of digital repositories and open educational resources (OER) that provide access to a wide range of educational materials, including teaching materials, textbooks, multimedia resources, and research publications. Platforms such as OpenStax, MERLOT, and OER Commons offer researchers access to a wealth of educational content that can inform literature reviews and support scholarly inquiry in educational research.

Grey Literature: Grey literature refers to unpublished or non-commercially published material, such as working papers, white papers, and technical reports. While not subjected to the same peer review process as scholarly articles, grey literature may sometimes provide valuable insights, particularly on practical issues and program evaluations within education.

When conducting a literature review, it's important to use a combination of these sources to ensure a comprehensive understanding of the topic. Additionally, critically evaluating the quality, relevance, and credibility of each source is essential for maintaining the rigor and validity of the literature review.

In summary, the sources available for conducting literature reviews in educational research encompass a wide range of scholarly materials, including peer-reviewed journal articles, books, research reports, conference proceedings, and dissertations. By engaging with these sources, researchers gain valuable insights, perspectives, and evidence relevant to their research topics, enriching the discourse, theory, and practice in the field of education.

Challenges in Conducting Literature Reviews

Conducting literature reviews in educational research can be a complex and challenging process, fraught with various obstacles and pitfalls. Some of the key challenges include:

Information Overload. The sheer volume of literature available in educational research can be overwhelming, making it difficult for researchers to identify relevant sources and synthesize key findings. With the exponential growth of scholarly publications and online databases, researchers may struggle to keep pace with new research and emerging trends (Allen, 2016).

Access to Resources. Accessing relevant resources, particularly subscription-based journals and databases, can be a barrier for researchers, especially those working in resource-constrained settings or institutions with limited access to scholarly publications. Limited access to resources may restrict researchers' ability to conduct comprehensive literature reviews and access the latest research findings (Elbaz-Luwisch, 2018).

Quality Control. Ensuring the quality and credibility of sources is a critical challenge in conducting literature reviews. With the proliferation of predatory journals and low-quality publications, researchers must exercise caution when selecting sources and critically evaluate the validity, reliability, and relevance of each study (Shamseer et al., 2017).

Heterogeneity of Sources. Educational research encompasses a wide range of disciplines, methods, and theoretical perspectives, leading to heterogeneity in the sources available for review. Synthesizing diverse sources with varying methodological approaches and epistemological orientations can be challenging, requiring researchers to employ appropriate methods and techniques for integration (Boote & Beile, 2005).

Time Constraints. Conducting a thorough literature review requires significant time and effort, from searching and screening relevant sources to synthesizing and analyzing findings. Researchers may face time constraints, particularly when balancing multiple responsibilities such as teaching, administrative duties, and other research projects (Fink, 2014).

Bias and Subjectivity. Researchers' own biases, perspectives, and disciplinary backgrounds can influence the selection and interpretation of literature, potentially leading to bias in the review process. Ensuring objectivity and rigor in the review requires researchers to be transparent about their methodological approach, criteria for inclusion/exclusion, and potential sources of bias (Hart, 1998).

Language and Cultural Barriers. Language and cultural barriers can pose challenges for researchers conducting literature reviews, particularly when accessing sources published in languages other than their own or exploring research conducted in diverse cultural contexts. Overcoming these barriers may require collaboration with colleagues or experts fluent in relevant languages and familiar with cultural nuances (Boslaugh & Watters, 2009).

Addressing these challenges requires researchers to adopt systematic and rigorous approaches to literature reviews, including clear criteria for inclusion/exclusion, transparent reporting of methods, and critical appraisal of sources. Collaboration with colleagues, librarians, and experts in the field can also help researchers navigate the complexities of conducting literature reviews in educational research.

Practical Guidelines for Conducting Literature Reviews

Conducting a literature review in educational research requires careful planning, systematic methods, and rigorous attention to detail. Here are some practical guidelines to help researchers navigate the process effectively:

1. **Define the Scope and Objectives**. Clearly define the scope and objectives of your literature review. Identify the specific research question(s) or topic(s) you wish to explore, as well as the key concepts, themes, and variables of interest. This will help guide your search strategy and ensure that your review remains focused and relevant (Boote & Beile, 2005).

2. **Develop a Search Strategy**. Develop a systematic search strategy to identify relevant sources for your literature review. Start by selecting appropriate keywords, phrases, and subject headings related to your topic, and use them to search relevant databases, journals, and repositories. Consider consulting with a librarian or information specialist to refine your search strategy and identify additional sources (Booth et al., 2016).

3. **Select Relevant Sources**. Screen the search results to identify relevant sources for inclusion in your literature review. Assess each source based on predefined inclusion/exclusion criteria, such as publication date, study design, methodology, and relevance to your research question(s). Be systematic and transparent in your selection process to ensure the integrity and reliability of your review (Grant & Booth, 2009).

4. **Critically Appraise the Literature**. Critically appraise the quality and credibility of the sources included in your literature review. Evaluate each source based on criteria such as the validity of the research design, the reliability of the findings, the relevance to your research question(s), and the authority of the author(s). Consider using established appraisal tools or guidelines to assist you in this process (Higgins & Green, 2011).

5. **Synthesize and Analyze Findings**. Synthesize and analyze the findings of the selected sources to identify key themes, patterns, and trends in the literature. Organize the literature thematically or chronologically to facilitate a coherent and structured presentation of your review. Compare and contrast the findings of different studies, highlighting areas of consensus, controversy, and ambiguity (Creswell, 2014).

6. **Identify Gaps and Future Directions**. Identify gaps, limitations, and unanswered questions in the existing literature. Reflect on the implications of these gaps for theory, practice, and future research in education. Consider proposing recommendations for addressing these gaps and advancing knowledge in the field (Booth et al., 2016).

7. **Provide Clear and Concise Reporting**. Provide clear and concise reporting of your literature review, adhering to established guidelines and conventions in educational research. Structure your review logically, including an introduction, methodology, findings, discussion, and conclusion. Use clear and precise language to convey your ideas and findings effectively (Hart, 1998).

8. **Engage in Reflective Practice**. Engage in reflective practice throughout the literature review process, continuously questioning assumptions, biases, and interpretations. Be open to revising your review in response to new evidence, feedback, or insights gained from the literature. Maintain transparency and reflexivity in your approach, acknowledging the limitations and potential biases of your review (Boote & Beile, 2005).

By following these practical guidelines, researchers can conduct literature reviews in educational research that are systematic, rigorous, and informative. A well-executed literature review not only contributes to the advancement of knowledge in the field but also serves as a valuable resource for informing theory, practice, and policy in education.

Avoiding Plagiarism

Plagiarism is a serious ethical issue that can arise when conducting literature reviews in educational research. It involves the unauthorized use or reproduction of someone else's work, ideas, or words without proper attribution. In educational research, where originality and integrity are paramount, plagiarism can undermine the credibility of the research and erode trust within the academic community. Here are some strategies to avoid plagiarism while conducting literature reviews:

Use Proper Citation and Referencing: Whenever you directly quote or paraphrase ideas, concepts, or findings from another source, ensure that you provide proper citation and referencing. Follow the citation style recommended by your institution or publisher (e.g., APA, MLA, Chicago) and include accurate bibliographic details for each source cited (Purdue OWL, n.d.).

Paraphrase and Summarize with Attribution: When synthesizing information from multiple sources, paraphrase or summarize the ideas in your own words, while still attributing them to the original authors. Avoid simply rearranging or substituting a few words from the original text, as this can still constitute plagiarism. Instead, strive to rearticulate the ideas in a way that reflects your understanding and interpretation (Purdue OWL, n.d.).

Use Quotations Sparingly and Appropriately: Direct quotations should be used sparingly and only when the original wording is particularly significant or impactful. When quoting directly, use quotation marks to indicate the verbatim text and provide an accurate citation to the source. Avoid excessive reliance on quotations, as this can detract from your own voice and analysis (University of Wisconsin-Madison Writing Center, n.d.).

Maintain Clear Distinction Between Own Ideas and Others': Clearly distinguish between your own ideas, interpretations, and analyses, and those of other authors. Use signal phrases, such as "According to Smith (year)," or "Jones (year) argues that...," to indicate when you are referencing the work of others. This helps readers understand the source of each idea and ensures transparency in your writing (University of Wisconsin-Madison Writing Center, n.d.).

Keep Detailed Records and Notes: Keep detailed records and notes of all sources consulted during the literature review process. Record bibliographic information, page numbers, and direct quotations accurately to facilitate proper citation and referencing later. This also helps you keep track of which ideas and findings belong to which authors, reducing the risk of inadvertent plagiarism (Hart, 1998).

Utilize Plagiarism Detection Tools: Before submitting your literature review, utilize plagiarism detection tools such as Turnitin or Grammarly to check your document for potential instances of plagiarism. These tools can help identify any text that closely matches existing sources, allowing you to revise and correct any unintentional plagiarism before final submission (Turnitin, n.d.).

By following these strategies and maintaining a commitment to academic integrity, researchers can conduct literature reviews in educational research that are both rigorous and ethically sound.

Summary

The chapter discusses the importance and methods of reviewing literature in educational research. It highlights the significance of literature reviews in guiding research, identifying gaps, and contributing to knowledge development. The impact of the digital age on literature reviews is also explored, emphasizing the opportunities presented by digital technologies. The text outlines various literature review objectives, methods, writing styles, and conventions, providing a comprehensive guide for researchers. Further, the chapter emphasizes the significance of understanding various sources and addressing challenges such as information overload and bias. It outlines practical guidelines for conducting literature reviews effectively, including defining scope, developing search strategies, critically appraising literature, synthesizing findings, and avoiding plagiarism. Overall, this chapter serves as a resource for researchers seeking to navigate the complexities of literature review processes in educational research while upholding academic integrity.

Suggestions for Students

Key Questions

Use the following questions and prompts to check your understanding, discuss, and reflect upon the content of this chapter:

1. What are the key objectives of literature reviews in educational research, and why are they important for advancing knowledge within the field?

2. How has the digital age impacted the process of conducting literature reviews in educational research, and what opportunities does it present for researchers?

3. Describe three different methods or approaches for conducting literature reviews in educational research and explain when each method might be most appropriate.

4. What are some common writing styles and conventions used in literature reviews, and how do they contribute to the effectiveness of scholarly communication?

5. Can you provide an example of how a literature review in educational research might inform the development of a theoretical framework or research question?

6. What are some key sources commonly utilized in educational research literature reviews, according to the text?

7. Why is it important for researchers to use a combination of sources when conducting literature reviews?

8. What are some challenges associated with conducting literature reviews in educational research, as mentioned in the text?

9. How can researchers avoid plagiarism while conducting literature reviews, according to the text?

10. What are some practical guidelines provided in the text for conducting literature reviews effectively?

Suggestions for Instructors

Suggested Learning Activities

The following learning activities aim to engage students in active learning experiences that enhance their understanding of literature reviews in educational research and develop their research and writing skills.

Literature Review Workshop. Organize a workshop where students can practice conducting literature reviews in educational research. Provide them with a research question or topic, and guide them through the process of searching for relevant literature, critically analyzing sources, and synthesizing findings. Offer feedback and guidance as they develop their literature reviews.

Digital Literacy Exercise. Design an exercise to enhance students' digital literacy skills for conducting literature reviews in the digital age. Have students explore online databases, digital repositories, and academic search engines to locate scholarly sources related to a specific topic in educational research. Guide them in evaluating the credibility and relevance of the sources they find.

Methodological Debate. Divide students into groups and assign each group a different method or approach for conducting literature reviews in educational research (e.g., systematic reviews, narrative reviews, meta-analyses). Have each group research their assigned method and prepare a presentation

Suggestions for Instructors

debating the strengths, limitations, and applicability of their chosen approach.

Writing Styles Analysis. Provide students with excerpts from literature reviews written in different styles (e.g., narrative style, analytical style, argumentative style) and ask them to analyze the effectiveness of each style in communicating key ideas and synthesizing the literature. Encourage discussion on the advantages and disadvantages of each writing style.

Critical Review Activity. Assign students a published literature review in educational research and have them critically evaluate its quality and effectiveness. Prompt them to assess the clarity of the research question, the thoroughness of the literature search, the coherence of the synthesis, and the validity of the conclusions. Encourage students to identify strengths and weaknesses in the reviewed literature.

Literature Review Presentation. Have students select a literature review topic related to educational research and prepare a presentation summarizing the key objectives, methods, findings, and implications of their chosen topic. Encourage them to use visuals, such as charts or graphs, to enhance their presentations and facilitate understanding.

Peer Review Workshop. Organize a peer review workshop where students exchange drafts of their literature reviews and provide constructive feedback to their peers. Encourage students to focus on aspects such as clarity of writing, coherence of argumentation, and thoroughness of literature synthesis. Facilitate discussions on how feedback can be used to improve the quality of their literature reviews.

Literature Review Scavenger Hunt. Divide students into groups and provide them with a list of criteria for finding specific types of sources (e.g., peer-reviewed journal articles, conference proceedings). Have them search online databases and repositories to locate sources that meet the criteria, emphasizing the importance of varied sources.

Source Evaluation Exercise. Present students with a mix of credible and non-credible sources related to educational research. Have them work individually or in pairs to evaluate each source based on predefined criteria (e.g., credibility, relevance). Facilitate a discussion afterward to compare evaluations and discuss the importance of critical appraisal.

Plagiarism Awareness Workshop. Conduct a workshop on plagiarism, focusing on the ethical considerations and consequences of plagiarism in educational research. Provide examples of proper citation and referencing techniques and guide students through activities to practice paraphrasing and summarizing with attribution.

Literature Review Simulation. Assign students a research topic and ask them to conduct a mini-literature review following the practical guidelines provided in the text. Provide access to relevant sources and guide students through each step of the process, from defining the scope to synthesizing findings.

Peer Review and Feedback. Organize peer review groups where students exchange their literature review drafts for feedback. Provide a rubric or checklist based on the practical guidelines and learning objectives, focusing on aspects such as clarity, coherence, and adherence to ethical standards. Encourage constructive criticism and revision based on peer feedback.

References

Allen, M. P. (2016). The problem of information overload in business research: A review. International Journal of Business Research, 16(1), 33-42.

Introduction to Educational Research

Arksey, H., & O'Malley, L. (2005). Scoping studies: Towards a methodological framework. International Journal of Social Research Methodology, 8(1), 19-32.

Boote, D. N., & Beile, P. (2005). Scholars before researchers: On the centrality of the dissertation literature review in research preparation. Educational Researcher, 34(6), 3-15.

Booth, A., Sutton, A., & Papaioannou, D. (2016). Systematic approaches to a successful literature review. Sage.

Booth, A., Sutton, A., & Papaioannou, D. (2016). Systematic approaches to a successful literature review. Sage.

Boslaugh, S., & Watters, P. A. (2009). The Sage handbook of quantitative methods in psychology. Sage Publications.

Creswell, J. W. (2014). Research Design: Qualitative, Quantitative, and Mixed Methods Approaches. Sage Publications.

Denzin, N. K., & Lincoln, Y. S. (Eds.). (2018). The SAGE Handbook of Qualitative Research. Sage Publications.

Elbaz-Luwisch, F. (2018). No money, no access, no problem: a case study of open access publishing in education research. Information Development, 34(3), 328-334.

Fink, A. (2014). Conducting Research Literature Reviews: From the Internet to Paper. Sage Publications.

Gall, M. D., Borg, W. R., & Gall, J. P. (2003). Educational research: An introduction (7th ed.). Allyn and Bacon.

Grant, M. J., & Booth, A. (2009). A typology of reviews: An analysis of 14 review types and associated methodologies. Health Information & Libraries Journal, 26(2), 91-108.

Green, B. N., Johnson, C. D., & Adams, A. (2006). Writing narrative literature reviews for peer-reviewed journals: Secrets of the trade. Journal of Chiropractic Medicine, 5(3), 101-117.

Hannes, K., & Macaitis, K. (2012). A move to more systematic and transparent approaches in qualitative evidence synthesis: Update on a review of published papers. Qualitative Research, 12(4), 402-442.

Hart, C. (1998). Doing a Literature Review: Releasing the Social Science Research Imagination. Sage Publications.

Higgins, J. P. T., & Green, S. (Eds.). (2011). Cochrane handbook for systematic reviews of interventions. Wiley-Blackwell.

Kitchenham, B. (2004). Procedures for performing systematic reviews. Joint Technical Report, Software Engineering Group, Keele University, EBSE-2008-01.

Krippendorff, K. (2018). Content Analysis: An Introduction to Its Methodology. Sage Publications.

Noblit, G. W., & Hare, R. D. (1988). Meta-ethnography: Synthesizing qualitative studies. Sage Publications.

Introduction to Educational Research

Pawson, R., Greenhalgh, T., Harvey, G., & Walshe, K. (2004). Realist review--a new method of systematic review designed for complex policy interventions. Journal of Health Services Research & Policy, 9(Suppl 1), 21-34.

Purdue OWL. (n.d.). Avoiding plagiarism. Retrieved from https://owl.purdue.edu/owl/research_and_citation/conducting_research/academic_papers_and_citations/avoiding_plagiarism/index.html

Randolph, J. J. (2009). A guide to writing the dissertation literature review. Practical Assessment, Research & Evaluation, 14(13), 1-13.

Shamseer, L., Moher, D., Maduekwe, O., Turner, L., Barbour, V., Burch, R., ... & Shea, B. J. (2017). Potential predatory and legitimate biomedical journals: can you tell the difference? A cross-sectional comparison. BMC medicine, 15(1), 1-14.

Sutton, A., Clowes, M., & Preston, N. (2019). Open Access, Open Education, and Open Science: Foundations for the Digital Age. Springer.

Torraco, R. J. (2005). Writing integrative literature reviews. Guidelines and examples. Human Resource Development Review, 4(3), 356-367.

Tranfield, D., Denyer, D., & Smart, P. (2003). Towards a methodology for developing evidence-informed management knowledge by means of systematic review. British Journal of Management, 14(3), 207-222.

Turnitin. (n.d.). OriginalityCheck. Retrieved from https://www.turnitin.com/products/originality-check

University of Wisconsin-Madison Writing Center. (n.d.). Avoiding plagiarism. Retrieved from https://writing.wisc.edu/handbook/assignments/quotingsources/

Webster-Wright, A. (2009). Reframing Professional Development Through Understanding Authentic Professional Learning. Review of Educational Research, 79(2), 702-739

Chapter 4. Ethics in Educational Research

This chapter will address the following learning objectives:
• Discuss the importance of ethics in educational research.
• Define the concept of ethics in educational research.
• Define key ethical principles in educational research.
• Analyze examples of ethical and unethical practices in educational research and recognize the impact of these practices on participants and research integrity.
• Explain the importance of informed consent, confidentiality of research data, and protection from harm in research involving human participants.
• Summarize ethical considerations in conducting educational research involving children.
• Describe the role of Institutional Review Boards (IRBs) in regulating educational research and categorizing research proposals based on risk levels.
• Evaluate the ethical implications of academic dishonesty and plagiarism in educational research.
• Explore strategies for preventing and addressing academic dishonesty and plagiarism in educational settings.

Ethics in educational research is a critical component that ensures the protection of participants' rights, integrity, and well-being throughout the research process. In educational, ethics research refers to the principles, guidelines, and standards that govern the conduct of research involving human participants in the field of education. It encompasses ethical considerations related to the rights, welfare, and dignity of participants, as well as the integrity and transparency of the research process.

One comprehensive definition of ethics in educational research is provided by the American Educational Research Association (AERA) in their "Code of Ethics." According to AERA (2020), ethics in educational research involves "the rights, welfare, and dignity of people and of the animals with which researchers work; the social and moral values guiding the research; and the responsibilities of researchers to those they serve" (p. 1).

This definition highlights the multifaceted nature of ethics in educational research, emphasizing the importance of respecting the rights and well-being of participants, adhering to social and moral values, and fulfilling researchers' responsibilities to their participants and the broader community.

Researchers in the field of education face unique ethical challenges, particularly when working with vulnerable populations such as children, students with disabilities, or marginalized communities. Additionally, the increasing use of technology in educational research raises ethical concerns related to data privacy, consent, and digital surveillance.

Introduction to Educational Research

To navigate these complexities, educational researchers are encouraged to adhere to established ethical guidelines provided by professional associations such as the American Educational Research Association (AERA), the British Educational Research Association (BERA), and the Australian Association for Research in Education (AARE). These guidelines offer practical frameworks for ethical decision-making, including procedures for obtaining ethical approval from institutional review boards, conducting risk assessments, and ensuring transparency and accountability in research practices.

In summary, ethics in educational research is essential for upholding the rights and well-being of participants, maintaining the integrity of the research process, and fostering trust and credibility within the research community. By adhering to ethical principles and guidelines, researchers can conduct meaningful and responsible studies that contribute positively to the field of education.

Examples of Ethical and Unethical Practices in Educational Research:

Ethical Practices:
1. Ensuring that all participants understand the purpose of the research, what their participation will involve, and any potential risks or benefits before agreeing to take part.
2. Protecting the privacy of participants by keeping their personal information and responses confidential, using codes or pseudonyms when reporting data.
3. Treating participants with dignity and respect, acknowledging their autonomy, and honoring their right to withdraw from the study at any time without penalty.
4. Striving to maximize the benefits of the research while minimizing any potential harm to participants, including physical, psychological, or emotional harm.
5. Providing clear and accurate information about the research methods, data collection procedures, and any conflicts of interest that may exist.

Unethical Practices:
1. Conducting research without obtaining informed consent from participants or misrepresenting the purpose of the study to coerce participation.
2. Failing to protect the confidentiality of participants' identities or data, leading to potential harm or embarrassment.
3. Taking advantage of vulnerable populations, such as students or marginalized communities, for personal gain or without providing adequate support or benefits.
4. Manipulating or fabricating research data to support predetermined conclusions, compromising the integrity and validity of the study.
5. Presenting another researcher's ideas, words, or work as one's own without proper attribution, violating academic integrity and undermining trust in the research community.

These examples illustrate the importance of adhering to ethical principles and guidelines in educational research to uphold the rights and well-being of participants and maintain the integrity and credibility of the research process.

Ethical Principles in Educational Research

Ethical considerations in educational research are guided by principles such as respect for persons, beneficence, justice, and integrity, which are often adapted from broader ethical guidelines such as the

Introduction to Educational Research

Belmont Report (National Commission for the Protection of Human Subjects of Biomedical and Behavioral Research, 1979) and the Declaration of Helsinki (World Medical Association, 2013). These principles emphasize the importance of obtaining informed consent from participants, ensuring their voluntary participation, minimizing harm, maintaining confidentiality, and addressing potential conflicts of interest.

Ethical principles in educational research serve as guiding standards for researchers to ensure the protection of participants' rights, integrity in research practices, and the overall ethical conduct of studies. Several key principles are commonly emphasized in ethical guidelines and frameworks. Below are some of the most prominent ones, along with references for further reading:

1. **Respect for Persons**: This principle emphasizes treating individuals as autonomous agents and respecting their right to make informed decisions about their participation in research. It involves obtaining voluntary and informed consent from participants, acknowledging their autonomy, and ensuring their right to withdraw from the study at any time without repercussions (National Commission for the Protection of Human Subjects of Biomedical and Behavioral Research, 1979).

2. **Beneficence**: The principle of beneficence requires researchers to maximize the benefits of research while minimizing any potential harm to participants. This includes taking measures to protect participants' well-being, ensuring that risks are justified by potential benefits, and providing appropriate support and resources to mitigate any adverse effects of participation (National Commission for the Protection of Human Subjects of Biomedical and Behavioral Research, 1979).

3. **Justice**: Justice in research entails ensuring fairness in the distribution of both the burdens and benefits of research participation. It involves avoiding the exploitation of vulnerable populations, such as children, students with disabilities, or marginalized communities, and ensuring equitable access to research opportunities and benefits (National Commission for the Protection of Human Subjects of Biomedical and Behavioral Research, 1979).

4. **Integrity**: Integrity encompasses honesty, transparency, and accuracy in all aspects of the research process, including data collection, analysis, and reporting. Researchers are expected to adhere to high ethical standards, avoid conflicts of interest, and maintain the trust and credibility of the research community and the public (Shamoo & Resnik, 2015).

5. **Confidentiality and Privacy**: Protecting the confidentiality and privacy of participants' personal information and research data is crucial for maintaining trust and respect. Researchers should take measures to safeguard sensitive information, such as using anonymization techniques, secure data storage, and limited access to data (American Psychological Association, 2017).

These ethical principles provide a framework for researchers to navigate the complex ethical dilemmas and responsibilities inherent in educational research, ensuring that studies are conducted with integrity, respect, and consideration for the well-being of participants.

Protection from Harm

Protecting participants from harm in educational research is a fundamental ethical obligation that researchers must uphold throughout the entire research process. This involves identifying potential risks

Introduction to Educational Research

to participants' physical, psychological, or emotional well-being and taking proactive measures to minimize or mitigate these risks. Below is a description of the practice of protecting participants from harm, along with relevant references:

Risk Assessment: Researchers should conduct a thorough risk assessment to identify potential risks associated with the research, including physical, psychological, social, or legal risks. This assessment helps researchers anticipate and address potential harm to participants (National Commission for the Protection of Human Subjects of Biomedical and Behavioral Research, 1979).

Informed Consent: Obtaining informed consent from participants is crucial for ensuring that they understand the nature of the research, potential risks involved, and their rights as participants. Researchers should provide clear and detailed information about the study, allowing participants to make voluntary and informed decisions about their participation (American Psychological Association, 2017).

Minimization of Harm: Researchers should take proactive measures to minimize potential harm to participants. This may include implementing safeguards such as debriefing procedures, providing support services, ensuring confidentiality, and using appropriate research methods and techniques (American Educational Research Association, 2020).

Monitoring and Supervision: Researchers should monitor participants' well-being throughout the research process and be prepared to intervene if any adverse events or unexpected risks arise. This may involve regular check-ins with participants, establishing protocols for responding to distress, and involving qualified professionals when necessary (National Institutes of Health, n.d.).

Continual Ethical Review: Ethical considerations should be an ongoing concern throughout the research process. Researchers should regularly review and reassess the ethical implications of their study, particularly as new information emerges, or circumstances change (British Educational Research Association, 2018).

By implementing these practices, researchers can fulfill their ethical obligation to protect participants from harm and ensure that their research is conducted in a responsible and ethical manner.

Example of Unethical Educational Research Project
An example of an educational research project where participants are not adequately protected from harm might involve a study examining the effects of academic pressure on student mental health without implementing proper safeguards or support mechanisms. For instance, imagine a researcher conducting a longitudinal study on the impact of high stakes testing on student stress levels. In this study, the researcher administers surveys and interviews to students at various points throughout the academic year to assess their levels of anxiety, depression, and coping strategies in response to exam-related pressure. However, in this hypothetical scenario, the researcher fails to take appropriate measures to protect participants from harm: **Lack of Informed Consent**: The researcher does not fully inform participants about the potential risks of participating in the study, such as increased stress or anxiety levels, and fails to obtain informed consent. **Insufficient Debriefing**: After completing the surveys or interviews, participants are not provided with adequate debriefing or support to address any distress or negative emotions triggered by the research process. **Confidentiality Concerns**: The researcher does not guarantee the confidentiality of participants'

Introduction to Educational Research

Example of Unethical Educational Research Project
responses, leading to concerns about privacy and potential repercussions for disclosing sensitive information about their mental health. **No Referral to Support Services**: Despite identifying students experiencing significant distress or mental health issues during the study, the researcher does not provide referrals to counseling services or other support resources, leaving participants without access to necessary assistance. **Lack of Ethical Oversight**: The research project may not undergo ethical review by an institutional review board (IRB) or equivalent body, leading to oversight of potential risks and ethical concerns. In this example, the failure to adequately protect participants from harm can result in negative consequences for the well-being of students involved in the research, potentially exacerbating existing mental health issues, or causing unnecessary distress. It's crucial for researchers to prioritize the well-being of participants in educational research projects by implementing ethical safeguards, obtaining informed consent, providing appropriate support, and debriefing, ensuring confidentiality, and adhering to ethical guidelines and oversight mechanisms.

Informed Consent

Informed consent is crucial in educational research for several reasons:

Respect for Autonomy: Informed consent respects individuals' autonomy and their right to make voluntary and informed decisions about participating in research (American Psychological Association, 2017).

Ethical Obligation: Obtaining informed consent is an ethical obligation that ensures participants are fully aware of the purpose, procedures, potential risks, and benefits of the study before agreeing to participate (National Commission for the Protection of Human Subjects of Biomedical and Behavioral Research, 1979).

Protection of Participants: Informed consent helps protect participants from potential harm or discomfort by allowing them to make an informed decision about whether to participate in the study (American Educational Research Association, 2020).

Legal Requirement: In many jurisdictions, obtaining informed consent is a legal requirement for conducting research involving human participants, and failure to do so can have legal consequences (Shamoo & Resnik, 2015).

Trust and Credibility: Obtaining informed consent fosters trust and credibility between researchers and participants, enhancing the integrity and reliability of the research process (National Institutes of Health, n.d.).

Introduction to Educational Research

Procedure for Ensuring Informed Consent:

1. **Provide Information**: Before obtaining consent, provide participants with clear and comprehensive information about the purpose of the study, procedures involved, potential risks and benefits, confidentiality assurances, voluntary nature of participation, and contact information for the researcher and Institutional Review Board (IRB) (American Psychological Association, 2017).

2. **Opportunity to Ask Questions**: Allow participants the opportunity to ask questions and seek clarification about any aspects of the study before deciding whether to consent (American Educational Research Association, 2020).

3. **Written Consent Form**: Use a written consent form that summarizes the key information about the study and allows participants to indicate their voluntary agreement to participate by signing the form (National Institutes of Health, n.d.).

4. **Language and Literacy Considerations**: Ensure that the consent form and all verbal explanations are presented in language that is understandable to the participants and appropriate for their literacy level, using plain language and avoiding jargon or technical terms (National Institutes of Health, n.d.).

5. **Voluntary Participation**: Emphasize to participants that their participation is entirely voluntary, and they have the right to withdraw from the study at any time without penalty or consequence (American Psychological Association, 2017).

6. **Documentation**: Maintain documentation of informed consent, including signed consent forms, to demonstrate that participants were adequately informed and voluntarily agreed to participate in the study (American Educational Research Association, 2020).

By following these procedures, researchers can ensure that participants are fully informed about the research study and can make voluntary and informed decisions about their participation.

Example of Informed Consent Form
Title of Study: Examining the Impact of Technology Integration on Student Learning *Researcher:* [Researcher's Name] *Institution:* [Institution Name] *Purpose of the Study:* You are invited to participate in a research study that aims to explore the effects of technology integration in the classroom on student learning outcomes. The study seeks to understand how the use of technology influences student engagement, motivation, and academic achievement. *Procedures:* If you agree to participate, you will be asked to: • Complete a brief survey about your demographics, technology usage, and academic background. • Engage in classroom activities that involve the use of educational technology tools or applications.

Introduction to Educational Research

Example of Informed Consent Form

- Allow the researcher to observe your interactions with technology and academic performance in the classroom.
- Optionally participate in follow-up interviews or focus group discussions to provide additional insights into your experiences with technology integration.

Potential Risks:
Participation in this study involves minimal risk. However, you may experience minor discomfort or inconvenience associated with completing surveys, participating in classroom activities, or sharing your opinions during interviews or discussions.

Potential Benefits:
Your participation in this study may contribute to the advancement of knowledge in the field of education and inform efforts to enhance teaching and learning practices. Additionally, you may gain insights into the benefits and challenges of using technology in education.

Confidentiality:
All information collected during the study will be kept confidential to the fullest extent permitted by law. Your responses will be anonymized, and only the researcher will have access to the data. Any identifiable information will be securely stored and will not be disclosed without your explicit consent, except as required by law.

Voluntary Participation:
Participation in this study is entirely voluntary, and you have the right to withdraw at any time without penalty or consequence. Your decision to participate or withdraw will not affect your academic standing or relationship with the researcher or institution.

Contact Information:
If you have any questions or concerns about the study, you may contact the researcher, [Researcher's Name], at [Researcher's Contact Information]. If you have questions about your rights as a research participant or wish to report a research-related concern, you may contact the Institutional Review Board (IRB) at [Institution's IRB Contact Information].

Consent:
By signing below, you acknowledge that you have read and understood the information provided in this consent form, and you voluntarily agree to participate in the study.

Participant's Signature: _____

Date: _____

This example illustrates the key components of an informed consent form, including the purpose of the study, procedures, potential risks and benefits, confidentiality assurances, voluntary participation, and contact information for the researcher and Institutional Review Board (IRB). It's important to tailor the consent form to the specific requirements and ethical considerations of the research study and ensure that participants have the opportunity to ask questions and make an informed decision about their participation.

Confidentiality of Research Data

Ensuring the confidentiality of research data in educational research is of paramount importance for several reasons:

Protection of Privacy: Confidentiality safeguards the privacy of research participants by ensuring that their personal information and responses are kept confidential and secure (American Psychological Association, 2017).

Trust and Cooperation: Maintaining confidentiality fosters trust and cooperation between researchers and participants, encouraging honest and open communication and increasing the likelihood of obtaining accurate and reliable data (National Commission for the Protection of Human Subjects of Biomedical and Behavioral Research, 1979).

Ethical Obligation: Researchers have an ethical obligation to protect the confidentiality of participants' data as part of their commitment to respect participants' rights and welfare (American Educational Research Association, 2020).

Minimization of Risks: Protecting the confidentiality of research data helps minimize the risks of potential harm or negative consequences to participants, such as stigma, discrimination, or breaches of privacy (British Educational Research Association, 2018).

Compliance with Regulations: Maintaining confidentiality is often a legal requirement for researchers conducting studies involving human participants, and failure to do so can lead to legal and regulatory consequences (Shamoo & Resnik, 2015).

Data Integrity and Validity: Ensuring confidentiality enhances the integrity and validity of the research findings by reducing the likelihood of biases or distortions resulting from concerns about privacy or confidentiality breaches (National Institutes of Health, n.d.).

In summary, ensuring the confidentiality of research data in educational research is essential for protecting participants' privacy, fostering trust and cooperation, fulfilling ethical obligations, minimizing risks, complying with regulations, and maintaining the integrity and validity of research findings.

Example of Non-Confidential Research Data

A teacher conducted a study examining the experiences of students with learning disabilities in inclusive classrooms. The researcher collected data through interviews with students, teachers, and parents, aiming to explore challenges and successes in the inclusive education environment. She kept her notes in a file on her desk and then typed them on a computer in the school computer lab. In this example, the researcher failed to ensure the confidentiality of the data in several ways:

Lack of Anonymization: The researcher did not anonymize the data collected from participants, including their names, school names, and other identifying information. As a result, the confidentiality of participants' identities was compromised.

Inadequate Data Storage: The researcher stored the data on an unsecured computer without encryption or password protection, making it vulnerable to unauthorized access or breaches of confidentiality.

Insufficient Access Controls: The researcher did not establish adequate access controls to limit who could view or handle the data. This lack of control increased the risk of unauthorized individuals accessing sensitive information.

Example of Non-Confidential Research Data

Limited Data Handling Procedures: The researcher did not implement clear procedures for handling and sharing the data, increasing the likelihood of inadvertent disclosures or breaches of confidentiality.

Failure to Obtain Consent for Data Sharing: The researcher did not obtain informed consent from participants for sharing their data with other researchers or institutions, potentially exposing participants to risks of privacy violations.

As a result of these shortcomings, the confidentiality of participants' data was compromised, leading to concerns about privacy breaches, confidentiality breaches, and potential harm to participants.
It's essential for researchers to take proactive measures to ensure the confidentiality of research data, including anonymizing data, using secure data storage methods, implementing access controls, establishing clear data handling procedures, and obtaining informed consent for data sharing, to protect the privacy and confidentiality of participants in educational research projects.

Educational Research with Children

When conducting educational research with children, researchers must adhere to strict ethical considerations to ensure the protection of children's rights, well-being, and dignity. Several key ethical principles and procedures are essential in this context:

Ethical Considerations:

1. **Informed Consent**: Children should provide assent to participate in research, and researchers must obtain informed consent from parents or legal guardians. The consent process should be adapted to the child's age, maturity, and comprehension level, using language and explanations appropriate for their understanding (American Psychological Association, 2017).

2. **Respect for Autonomy**: Researchers should respect children's autonomy and right to make decisions about their participation in research. They should provide opportunities for children to withdraw from the study or decline participation without coercion or pressure (American Educational Research Association, 2020).

3. **Protection from Harm**: Researchers must take measures to minimize potential risks of harm to children, including physical, psychological, or emotional harm. This may involve obtaining approval from institutional review boards (IRBs), ensuring appropriate supervision and support during data collection, and prioritizing the well-being of participants (National Commission for the Protection of Human Subjects of Biomedical and Behavioral Research, 1979).

4. **Privacy and Confidentiality**: Researchers should protect the privacy and confidentiality of children's personal information and research data. They should use anonymization techniques, secure data storage methods, and limited access controls to safeguard sensitive information and prevent unauthorized disclosure (British Educational Research Association, 2018).

Procedures:

1. **Parental Consent**: Obtain informed consent from parents or legal guardians before involving children in research activities. Provide detailed information about the purpose of the study, procedures involved, potential risks and benefits, confidentiality assurances, and contact information for the researcher and IRB (American Psychological Association, 2017).

2. **Child Assent**: Seek assent from children to participate in the research, explaining the study in age-appropriate language and providing opportunities for them to ask questions or express concerns. Respect children's decisions and preferences regarding their participation (American Educational Research Association, 2020).

3. **Developmentally Appropriate Methods**: Use research methods and techniques that are developmentally appropriate for children's age, cognitive abilities, and communication skills. Adapt data collection tools, interview protocols, and survey instruments to ensure they are understandable and engaging for children (British Educational Research Association, 2018).

4. **Sensitive Topics and Emotional Support**: When researching sensitive topics or emotions, provide adequate support and resources to address any distress or discomfort experienced by children. Establish protocols for debriefing, referrals to counseling services, or additional support as needed (National Institutes of Health, n.d.).

By following these ethical considerations and procedures, researchers can conduct educational research with children in a responsible and respectful manner, ensuring the protection of children's rights and well-being.

Regulation of Educational Research

Regulating educational research from an ethics perspective is critically important for several reasons.

Protection of Human Participants: Ethical regulations ensure that the rights, welfare, and dignity of human participants are protected during the research process. By establishing guidelines for informed consent, confidentiality, and minimizing risks, regulatory bodies help prevent potential harm to participants and ensure their well-being (National Commission for the Protection of Human Subjects of Biomedical and Behavioral Research, 1979).

Maintenance of Trust and Integrity: Ethical regulations foster trust and integrity within the research community and society at large. By upholding ethical standards and ensuring transparency and accountability in research practices, regulatory oversight helps maintain public trust in the credibility and reliability of educational research findings (American Educational Research Association, 2020).

Promotion of Research Quality: Ethical regulations contribute to the quality and validity of educational research by promoting rigorous and responsible research practices. By requiring researchers to adhere to ethical principles and guidelines, regulatory bodies help prevent biases, conflicts of interest, and methodological flaws that could compromise the integrity and validity of research findings (American Psychological Association, 2017).

Respect for Diversity and Equity: Ethical regulations promote diversity, equity, and inclusion in educational research by ensuring that research practices are sensitive to the needs, perspectives, and experiences of diverse populations. By requiring researchers to consider issues of cultural competence, representation, and social justice, regulatory bodies help advance ethical research practices that respect the dignity and rights of all individuals (British Educational Research Association, 2018).

Legal and Professional Compliance: Ethical regulations provide legal and professional guidelines for researchers to follow in conducting educational research. By complying with ethical standards and regulatory requirements, researchers minimize the risk of legal liabilities, professional sanctions, and reputational damage associated with unethical conduct or violations of participants' rights (Shamoo & Resnik, 2015).

In summary, regulating educational research from an ethics perspective is essential for protecting human participants, maintaining trust and integrity, promoting research quality, respecting diversity and equity, and ensuring legal and professional compliance. By upholding ethical standards and oversight mechanisms, regulatory bodies play a vital role in promoting responsible and ethical conduct in educational research.

Institutional Review Boards

Institutional Review Boards (IRBs) play a crucial role in regulating educational research to ensure the protection of human participants' rights, welfare, and dignity. The process of regulating educational research through IRBs involves several key steps:

1. Submission of Research Proposals: Researchers seeking to conduct educational research involving human participants must submit a detailed research proposal to the IRB for review. The proposal typically includes information about the study's purpose, methodology, procedures, participant recruitment and selection criteria, informed consent process, potential risks and benefits, and data handling procedures (Shamoo & Resnik, 2015).

2. Ethical Review: The IRB conducts an ethical review of the research proposal to assess its compliance with ethical principles and guidelines, such as respect for persons, beneficence, justice, and integrity. The review process evaluates whether the proposed research adequately protects participants from harm, ensures informed consent, maintains confidentiality, and adheres to relevant ethical standards and regulatory requirements (National Commission for the Protection of Human Subjects of Biomedical and Behavioral Research, 1979).

3. Risk Assessment: The IRB assesses the potential risks associated with the research and determines whether they are justified by the potential benefits of the study. This involves evaluating the likelihood and severity of any physical, psychological, social, or legal risks to participants and ensuring that appropriate measures are in place to minimize or mitigate these risks (American Educational Research Association, 2020).

4. Informed Consent Process: The IRB reviews the proposed informed consent process to ensure that participants are fully informed about the nature of the research, potential risks and benefits, confidentiality assurances, and their rights as participants. The IRB may provide feedback on the consent form and recommend modifications to improve clarity and comprehensibility for participants, particularly in the case of vulnerable populations such as children or individuals with limited literacy (American Psychological Association, 2017).

5. Approval or Disapproval: Based on the review process, the IRB issues a decision to approve, approve with modifications, or disapprove the research proposal. Approval is contingent upon the researcher addressing any concerns or recommendations raised by the IRB and complying with any conditions or stipulations imposed by the board. If the research is approved, the researcher may proceed with data collection and analysis in accordance with the approved protocol. If the research is disapproved, the researcher may revise and resubmit the proposal for further review or reconsideration (Shamoo & Resnik, 2015).

6. Ongoing Oversight: Throughout the research process, the IRB provides ongoing oversight to ensure that the study is conducted in accordance with the approved protocol and ethical guidelines. This may involve periodic reviews of progress reports, monitoring of participant recruitment and consent procedures, addressing any adverse events or ethical concerns that arise during the study, and verifying compliance with regulatory requirements (National Institutes of Health, n.d.).

Institutional Review Boards (IRBs) classify research proposals into exempt, expedited, and full review categories based on the level of risk and the nature of the research. Exempt review applies to low-risk research meeting specific criteria, expedited review is for minimal risk research not eligible for exemption, and full review is required for research involving more than minimal risk or falling outside exemption or expedited review criteria. Below is a more detailed description of each category:

Exempt Review: Exempt review applies to research that poses no risk to participants and falls into specific categories outlined in federal regulations. These categories typically include research involving educational tests, educational practices or educational curriculums, passive observations of public behavior without the collection of identifying information, anonymous surveys, or interviews on non-sensitive topics. Exempt research is granted an exemption from full IRB review but still requires documentation and approval from the IRB to ensure compliance with ethical standards and regulatory requirements (National Institutes of Health, n.d.).

Expedited Review: Expedited review is appropriate for research that involves no more than minimal risk to participants but does not meet the criteria for exemption. Examples include studies on adult behavior that do not involve psychological intervention or deception, or studies where identifying information is collected. Expedited review is conducted by a designated member or subgroup of the IRB rather than the full board. The expedited review process allows for a quicker turnaround time compared to full board review while still ensuring that the research meets ethical standards and regulatory requirements (National Institutes of Health, n.d.).

Full Review: Full review is required for research that involves more than minimal risk to participants or falls outside the criteria for exempt or expedited review. The full board of the IRB conducts a comprehensive review of the research proposal, including the study's purpose, procedures, potential risks and benefits, informed consent process, data handling procedures, and safeguards for participant confidentiality and welfare. Examples of research that typically undergo full review include studies involving vulnerable populations, sensitive topics, or experimental interventions with potential risks to participants' physical or psychological well-being. Full review ensures thorough consideration of ethical issues and regulatory compliance to protect the rights and welfare of research participants (National Institutes of Health, n.d.).

In summary, the process of regulating educational research through IRBs involves thorough ethical review, risk assessment, informed consent, approval or disapproval of research proposals, ongoing oversight, and compliance with ethical standards and regulatory requirements. By ensuring that research involving human participants upholds ethical principles and protects participants' rights and welfare, IRBs play a critical role in promoting responsible and ethical research practices in education.

Academic Dishonesty and Plagiarism

A discussion about ethics in education must address the issue of academic dishonesty in general and plagiarism in particular. Academic dishonesty, including plagiarism, in educational research represents a serious ethical concern that undermines scholarly work's integrity, credibility, and trustworthiness. Below is a discussion of academic dishonesty and plagiarism from a moral perspective:

Academic Dishonesty. Academic dishonesty encompasses a range of unethical behaviors that violate the principles of honesty, integrity, and fairness in academic settings. It includes actions such as cheating on exams, fabricating data, falsifying research findings, and plagiarizing others' work (McCabe, Treviño, & Butterfield, 2001). Academic dishonesty undermines the core values of scholarship, including honesty, transparency, and intellectual integrity. It violates the trust placed in researchers, educators, and institutions and compromises the reliability and validity of research findings. From an ethical perspective, academic dishonesty not only undermines individual academic achievements but also erodes the foundation of knowledge production and dissemination in academia (Rest, 1986).

Plagiarism. Plagiarism is the act of using someone else's ideas, words, or work without proper attribution or acknowledgment. It can occur in various forms, including copying passages verbatim, paraphrasing without citation, and self-plagiarism (Pecorari, 2003). It represents a violation of intellectual property rights and ethical principles of attribution and credit. It undermines the principles of academic integrity, originality, and intellectual honesty. Plagiarism not only deprives the original author of recognition and credit for their work but also misleads readers and distorts the scholarly record. From an ethical perspective, plagiarism constitutes a form of academic fraud that undermines the integrity and credibility of educational research (Carroll, 2007).

Prevention and Mitigation

Preventing and addressing academic dishonesty and plagiarism requires proactive measures and a commitment to upholding ethical standards in research and scholarship. These may include:

- Educating researchers, students, and academic staff about ethical principles, including proper citation practices and the consequences of academic dishonesty.

- Implementing policies and procedures for detecting and addressing instances of plagiarism and academic misconduct.

- Encouraging a culture of academic integrity through mentorship, peer support, and role modeling by faculty and researchers.

- Providing resources and support for researchers and students to develop their research and writing skills ethically and responsibly.

By promoting a culture of academic integrity and ethical conduct, educational institutions and research communities can uphold the highest standards of scholarship and ensure the credibility and trustworthiness of educational research.

In conclusion, ethics serves as the cornerstone of educational research, guiding researchers in their pursuit of knowledge while upholding the rights, well-being, and dignity of participants. Throughout this exploration, it has become evident that ethical considerations are paramount at every stage of the research process. From the initial formulation of research questions to data collection, analysis, and dissemination of findings, ethical principles such as respect for persons, beneficence, justice, integrity, and confidentiality are fundamental.

Ultimately, the ethical conduct of educational research is essential not only for upholding the principles of fairness, integrity, and respect but also for advancing knowledge and contributing to positive societal change. By embracing ethical principles and practices, researchers can fulfill their moral obligation to conduct research that is rigorous, responsible, and ethical, thereby making meaningful contributions to the field of education and the betterment of society as a whole.

Summary

The chapter explores the significance of ethics in educational research, emphasizing its role in protecting participants' rights, integrity, and well-being throughout the research process. It defines ethics in educational research, highlighting principles such as respect for participants, beneficence, justice, integrity, and confidentiality, and discusses both ethical and unethical practices in educational research, providing examples to illustrate each. It covers the importance of informed consent, confidentiality of research data, protection from harm, and regulation of educational research, especially when involving vulnerable populations like children. The ethical considerations and procedures for conducting research with children are outlined, emphasizing the need for parental consent, child assent, developmentally appropriate methods, and sensitivity to emotional support. The chapter underscores the significance of regulatory oversight in maintaining trust, promoting research quality, and ensuring legal and professional compliance in educational research. It highlights the role of Institutional Review Boards (IRBs) in overseeing research and categorizes research proposals into exempt, expedited, and full review categories based on risk levels. Additionally, the text addresses academic dishonesty and plagiarism, underscoring their ethical implications and the need for prevention and mitigation strategies. The chapter underscores the vital role of ethics in upholding the integrity and credibility of educational research while ensuring the well-being of participants.

Suggestions for Students

Key Questions

Use the following questions and prompts to check your understanding, discuss, and reflect upon the content of this chapter:

1. How would you apply ethical principles and guidelines to hypothetical research scenarios, making decisions about ethical conduct and participant protection?

2. Provide examples of both ethical and unethical practices in educational research and explain the potential impact of each on participants and research integrity.

3. What are the procedures and considerations involved in obtaining informed consent from participants in educational research?

4. How can researchers ensure the confidentiality of research data and protect participants from

Suggestions for Students

potential harm in educational research?

5. What are some ethical challenges and considerations specific to conducting research with vulnerable populations, such as children, and how can researchers address these challenges?

6. Discuss the role of regulatory bodies and ethical guidelines in maintaining trust, promoting research quality, and ensuring legal and professional compliance in educational research.

7. How do Institutional Review Boards (IRBs) contribute to the regulation of educational research, and what are the key steps in their review process?

8. Describe the three categories of review (exempt, expedited, and full review) used by IRBs to assess research proposals. What types of research fall into each category?

9. What ethical concerns are associated with academic dishonesty and plagiarism in educational research? How do these behaviors undermine scholarly integrity?

10. What proactive measures can institutions take to prevent and address academic dishonesty and plagiarism among researchers and students?

Suggestions for Instructors

Suggested Learning Activities

The following learning activities aim to engage students in critical thinking about research ethics, promote discussion and collaboration, and enhance their understanding of ethical principles in educational research.

Ethical Case Studies: Provide students with hypothetical scenarios involving ethical dilemmas in educational research. Have them analyze the situations, identify the ethical principles at play, and propose solutions or courses of action.

Debate: Organize a debate where students argue for or against specific ethical practices in educational research, such as the use of deception, protection of vulnerable populations, or the balance between privacy and transparency.

IRB Simulation: Create a simulation activity where students take on the roles of Institutional Review Board (IRB) members. Provide them with research proposals to review and discuss, considering factors like risk assessment, informed consent, and ethical considerations.

Research Ethics Workshop: Conduct a workshop on research ethics, covering topics such as informed consent, confidentiality, data handling, and participant protection. Use interactive activities, case studies, and group discussions to reinforce key concepts.

Interview with Researcher: Invite a researcher experienced in navigating ethical issues in educational research for a guest lecture or interview session. Students can learn from real-world examples and ask questions about ethical decision-making in research.

Review of Ethical Guidelines: Assign students to review and analyze ethical guidelines and regulations relevant to educational research, such as those from professional organizations or government agencies. Have them identify key principles and considerations.

Ethical Reflection Paper: Ask students to reflect on their own ethical values and how they apply to educational research. Have them write a reflective paper discussing ethical challenges they may

Suggestions for Instructors

encounter as researchers and how they would address them.

Collaborative Ethical Analysis: Divide students into small groups and provide them with different research scenarios. Have each group analyze the ethical issues involved, discuss potential solutions, and present their findings to the class.

Ethics Training Modules: Develop interactive online modules or resources covering various aspects of research ethics in education. Students can complete these modules at their own pace, engaging with quizzes, case studies, and multimedia content.

Peer Review Exercise: Facilitate a peer review exercise where students exchange research proposals or manuscripts and provide feedback from an ethical perspective. Emphasize constructive criticism and the importance of ethical oversight in improving research quality.

References

American Educational Research Association. (2020). AERA Code of Ethics. Retrieved from https://www.aera.net/Professional-Opportunities-Funding/AERA-Funding-Opportunities/AERA-Research-Grants-Program/AERA-Code-of-Ethics

American Psychological Association. (2017). Ethical Principles of Psychologists and Code of Conduct. Retrieved from https://www.apa.org/ethics/code/ethics-code-2017.pdf

Australian Association for Research in Education. (2018). AARE Code of Ethics. Retrieved from https://www.aare.edu.au/publications/aare-code-of-ethics/

British Educational Research Association. (2018). Ethical guidelines for educational research. Retrieved from https://www.bera.ac.uk/publication/ethical-guidelines-for-educational-research-2018

Carroll, J. (2007). A handbook for deterring plagiarism in higher education. Oxford Centre for Staff and Learning Development.

McCabe, D. L., Treviño, L. K., & Butterfield, K. D. (2001). Cheating in academic institutions: A decade of research. Ethics & Behavior, 11(3), 219-232.

National Commission for the Protection of Human Subjects of Biomedical and Behavioral Research. (1979). The Belmont Report: Ethical principles and guidelines for the protection of human subjects of research. Retrieved from https://www.hhs.gov/ohrp/regulations-and-policy/belmont-report/index.html

National Institutes of Health. (n.d.). Protecting research participants. Retrieved from https://oir.nih.gov/sourcebook/ethical-conduct/protecting-research-participants

Pecorari, D. (2003). Good and original: Plagiarism and patchwriting in academic second-language writing. Journal of Second Language Writing, 12(4), 317-345.

Rest, J. R. (1986). Moral development: Advances in research and theory. Praeger.

Shamoo, A. E., & Resnik, D. B. (2015). Responsible Conduct of Research (3rd ed.). Oxford University Press.

World Medical Association. (2013). World Medical Association Declaration of Helsinki: Ethical principles for medical research involving human subjects. Retrieved from https://www.wma.net/policies-post/wma-declaration-of-helsinki-ethical-principles-for-medical-research-involving-human-subjects/

Chapter 5. Variables and Hypotheses

This chapter will address the following learning objectives:
• Define and classify variables used in educational research, including independent variables, dependent variables, mediator variables, moderator variables, and control variables.
• Compare and contrast different measurement scales (nominal, ordinal, interval, ratio) in educational research.
• Describe the role of hypotheses in educational research.
• Explain the distinction between null hypotheses and alternative hypotheses.
• Differentiate between directional and non-directional hypotheses.
• Discuss the importance of research questions and propositions in qualitative research.
• Analyze examples of variables and hypotheses in educational research studies to identify their characteristics and relationships.
• Evaluate the strengths and limitations of different types of hypotheses and variables in educational research contexts.
• Apply knowledge of variables and hypotheses to design research studies and formulate research questions in the field of education.
• Synthesize key concepts related to variables and hypotheses to critically analyze research literature and contribute to the advancement of knowledge in educational research.

Variables and hypotheses play crucial roles in educational research, providing a framework for inquiry and analysis. Educational researchers employ variables to measure, manipulate, and understand the relationships between different aspects of the educational process, while hypotheses serve as testable predictions or statements about these relationships. By clearly defining variables and formulating hypotheses, researchers can systematically investigate questions about teaching, learning, and educational outcomes.

Variables in educational research refer to any characteristic, attribute, or factor that can vary and be measured. These may include demographic variables such as age, gender, and socioeconomic status, as well as educational variables such as instructional methods, classroom environment, or academic achievement. Variables can be independent (the presumed cause) or dependent (the outcome or effect), and researchers often seek to identify relationships between these variables to better understand educational phenomena.

Hypotheses, on the other hand, are specific, testable predictions or statements about the expected relationship between variables. A hypothesis typically proposes a relationship between one or more independent variables and a dependent variable. For example, a hypothesis might predict that students who receive a certain teaching intervention will demonstrate higher levels of academic achievement compared to students who do not receive the intervention.

Introduction to Educational Research

Educational researchers use variables and hypotheses to design studies, collect data, and analyze findings. By formulating clear hypotheses and selecting appropriate variables, researchers can rigorously test theories and contribute to the advancement of knowledge in the field of education.

Variables

In educational research, variables are any measurable attributes or characteristics that can vary and are used to study relationships, differences, or effects. Variables can include both independent variables, which are manipulated or controlled by the researcher, and dependent variables, which are the outcomes or effects that are measured. For example, in a study examining the impact of teaching methods on student achievement, the teaching method would be the independent variable, while student achievement would be the dependent variable.

Types of Variables

Variables can be classified into different measurement scales based on the nature of the data they represent. The main measurement scales include nominal, ordinal, interval, and ratio scales.

1. **Nominal Scale.** Nominal variables are categorical variables that represent categories or groups with no inherent order or ranking. They are used to classify data into distinct categories without any numerical significance. Examples of nominal variables include gender, ethnicity, religion, and marital status. Nominal variables can only be classified into mutually exclusive categories, and mathematical operations such as addition or subtraction are not meaningful with nominal data.

   Example: Ethnicity

   In a study examining the academic achievement gap among students, researchers might categorize participants into different ethnic groups (e.g., Caucasian, African American, Hispanic, Asian) to investigate disparities in educational outcomes.

2. **Ordinal Scale.** Ordinal variables represent categories or groups with a natural order or ranking. While the categories have a meaningful order, the intervals between categories may not be equal or measurable. Ordinal variables allow for ranking but do not provide information about the magnitude of differences between categories. Examples of ordinal variables include educational attainment levels, and socioeconomic status categories.

   Example: Socioeconomic Status (SES)

   Researchers studying the impact of SES on student academic performance might categorize participants into ordinal groups based on socioeconomic indicators such as parental income or education level (e.g., low SES, middle SES, high SES).

3. **Interval Scale.** Interval variables represent data that have a meaningful order and equal intervals between consecutive points on the scale. Interval variables have no true zero point, meaning that zero does not represent the absence of the measured quantity but rather a point on the scale. Examples of interval variables include temperature measured in Celsius or Fahrenheit, where the difference between 10°C and 20°C is the same as the difference between 20°C and 30°C.

Introduction to Educational Research

Example: Scholastic Aptitude Test (SAT) Scores

SAT scores are measured on a scale typically ranging from 400 to 1600, with separate scores for the Evidence-Based Reading and Writing (EBRW) and Math sections. The intervals between consecutive points on the scale are equal, meaning that the distance between 1200 and 1300 is the same as the distance between 1300 and 1400. However, there is no true zero point on the SAT scale, indicating the complete absence of aptitude or knowledge. Even if a student scores a 0 on the SAT, it doesn't mean they have no aptitude or knowledge; it simply reflects a point on the scale. Researchers often use SAT scores as an interval variable to study various factors related to academic achievement, college admissions, and educational equity. They may analyze SAT scores to explore the effectiveness of preparation programs, examine demographic disparities in scores, or investigate the predictive validity of SAT scores for college success.

4. **Ratio Scale**. Ratio variables represent data with a meaningful order, equal intervals between points on the scale, and a true zero point that represents the absence of the measured quantity. Ratio variables allow for meaningful comparisons of magnitudes and ratios between values. Examples of ratio variables include height, weight, age, and test scores.

Example: Number of Books

An example of a ratio variable in educational research is the measurement of the number of books read by students within a specific time frame. In this scenario, each student's reading activity can be quantified as a count of the number of books they have read. The variable has a meaningful order (students can read more or fewer books), equal intervals between consecutive points on the scale (each additional book represents the same increase in reading activity), and a true zero point (indicating the absence of reading activity). For example, if one student reads 5 books in a month and another reads 10 books, it can be accurately stated that the second student reads twice as many books as the first student. Additionally, if a student reads zero books, it indicates a complete absence of reading activity. Researchers can use the number of books read as a ratio variable to investigate various aspects of reading habits, literacy development, and academic achievement. They may explore the relationship between reading volume and reading proficiency, assess the effectiveness of reading interventions, or examine differences in reading behavior across demographic groups.

In educational research, variables can also be classified into different types based on their characteristics and roles in the study. The main types of variables include independent variables, dependent variables, intervening variables, moderator variables, and control variables.

1. **Independent Variables**. Independent variables are manipulated or controlled by the researcher and are hypothesized to cause changes in the dependent variable. They represent the factors that are being studied to determine their effect on the outcome. In educational research, independent variables could include teaching methods, instructional strategies, or interventions. For example, a researcher might investigate the impact of peer tutoring (independent variable) on student academic performance (dependent variable).

2. **Dependent Variables**. Dependent variables are the outcomes or effects that are measured in response to changes in the independent variable. They represent the variables that are expected to be influenced by the independent variable. In educational research, dependent variables often include measures of student learning, achievement, attitudes, or behaviors. For instance, in a

study on the effects of classroom environment on student motivation, student motivation levels would be the dependent variable.

3. **Mediator Variables**. Intervening variables, also known as intervening variables, are variables that come between the independent and dependent variables in a causal chain. They help to explain the relationship between the independent and dependent variables by mediating the effects of the independent variable on the dependent variable. For example, in a study examining the relationship between teacher feedback (independent variable) and student achievement (dependent variable), self-efficacy could act as an intervening variable, mediating the impact of teacher feedback on student achievement. Mediating variables are often identified through statistical analysis techniques such as mediation analysis, which allows researchers to assess the indirect effects of the independent variable on the dependent variable through the mediator. By identifying and understanding mediating variables, researchers can gain insights into the underlying mechanisms through which interventions or treatments exert their effects on educational outcomes.

4. **Moderator Variables**. Moderator variables are variables that influence the strength or direction of the relationship between the independent and dependent variables. They can help to identify under what conditions or for whom the relationship between the variables is stronger or weaker. In educational research, moderator variables could include student characteristics such as gender, socioeconomic status, or prior knowledge. For example, in a study on the effects of a teaching intervention (independent variable) on student learning outcomes (dependent variable), the moderator variable of student motivation might influence the effectiveness of the intervention.

5. **Control Variables**. Control variables are variables that are held constant or controlled by the researcher to eliminate or minimize their potential influence on the relationship between the independent and dependent variables. They help to ensure that any observed effects can be attributed to the independent variable rather than to extraneous factors. In educational research, control variables could include factors such as age, gender, or prior academic achievement. For instance, in a study on the impact of technology integration on student learning outcomes, the researcher might control for student demographics to isolate the effects of technology integration.

6. **Extraneous variables**. Also known as confounding variables, extraneous variables are factors other than the independent variable that may influence the dependent variable and thus affect the results of an experiment or study. In educational research, controlling for extraneous variables is essential to ensure that any observed effects can be attributed to the independent variable rather than to other factors. For example, in a study examining the impact of a teaching intervention (independent variable) on student academic achievement (dependent variable), extraneous variables such as student motivation, prior knowledge, or socioeconomic status could potentially confound the results if not properly controlled. Controlling for extraneous variables can be achieved through various research design and statistical techniques, such as randomization, matching, or statistical regression. By minimizing the influence of extraneous variables, researchers can enhance the internal validity of their findings and draw more accurate conclusions about the effects of the independent variable on the dependent variable.

Hypotheses

In educational research, hypotheses are testable statements or predictions about the expected relationship between variables. Hypotheses are formulated based on theoretical frameworks, prior research findings, or observations, and they guide the research process by providing a clear focus for investigation.

Null and Alternative Hypotheses

There are two main types of hypotheses:

1. **Null Hypothesis (H0)**: The null hypothesis proposes that there is no significant relationship or difference between variables. It suggests that any observed effects are due to chance or random variation in the data. Null hypotheses are typically denoted as H0 and are tested against alternative hypotheses.

2. **Alternative Hypothesis (H1 or Ha)**: The alternative hypothesis proposes that there is a significant relationship or difference between variables. It represents the researcher's hypothesis of interest and suggests that any observed effects are not due to chance alone. Alternative hypotheses are typically denoted as H1 or Ha and are tested against null hypotheses.

   Educational researchers use hypotheses to structure their studies, design research questions, and make predictions about the outcomes of their research. By formulating clear hypotheses, researchers can systematically test theories, evaluate interventions, and contribute to the advancement of knowledge in the field of education.

Examples of null and alternative hypotheses in educational research:	
The following examples illustrate how null and alternative hypotheses are used in educational research to make predictions about the relationships between variables and guide the research process.	
Null Hypothesis (H0)	**Alternative Hypothesis (H1)**
There is no significant difference in math achievement scores between students who receive traditional instruction and students who receive computer-assisted instruction.	There is a significant difference in math achievement scores between students who receive traditional instruction and students who receive computer-assisted instruction.
Explanation: This null hypothesis proposes that any observed differences in math achievement scores between students who receive traditional instruction and those who receive computer-assisted instruction are due to chance or random variation in the data.	Explanation: This alternative hypothesis proposes that there is a meaningful relationship between the type of instruction (traditional vs. computer-assisted) and student math achievement scores. It suggests that any observed differences in math achievement scores between the two groups are not due to chance alone but are influenced by the type of instruction received.
There is no significant difference in math achievement scores between students who receive computer-assisted instruction and students who receive traditional instruction.	Students who receive computer-assisted instruction will achieve higher math scores compared to students who receive traditional instruction.
Explanation: This null hypothesis proposes that any observed differences in math achievement scores between students who receive computer-assisted instruction and those who receive traditional instruction are due to chance	Explanation: This alternative hypothesis suggests that there is a significant relationship between the type of instruction (computer-assisted vs. traditional) and student math achievement scores, with computer-assisted instruction leading to higher

Examples of null and alternative hypotheses in educational research:	
or random variation in the data. It suggests that there is no meaningful relationship between the type of instruction and student math achievement scores.	scores

Directional and Non-Directional Hypotheses

Directional and non-directional hypotheses represent different ways of formulating hypotheses in research, each implying different expectations about the direction of the effect being studied.

1. **Non-directional Hypotheses**: Non-directional hypotheses, also known as two-tailed hypotheses, do not specify the direction of the expected relationship between variables. Instead, they simply predict that there will be a difference or relationship between variables without indicating whether one variable is expected to be greater than or less than the other. Non-directional hypotheses are typically used when there is no specific theoretical basis or prior evidence to suggest the direction of the effect.

   Example:

   Non-directional Hypothesis: There is a difference in math achievement scores between students who receive traditional instruction and students who receive computer-assisted instruction. Explanation: This non-directional hypothesis predicts that there will be a difference in math achievement scores between the two groups of students but does not specify whether one group is expected to score higher or lower than the other.

2. **Directional Hypotheses**: Directional hypotheses, also known as one-tailed hypotheses, specify the direction of the expected relationship between variables. They predict that one variable will be greater than or less than the other variable based on theoretical reasoning or prior evidence. Directional hypotheses are used when there is a clear theoretical basis or previous research indicating the expected direction of the effect.

   Example:

   Directional Hypothesis: Students who receive computer-assisted instruction will achieve higher math scores compared to students who receive traditional instruction. Explanation: This directional hypothesis predicts that students who receive computer-assisted instruction will achieve higher math scores than students who receive traditional instruction, based on the assumption that computer-assisted instruction is more effective in improving math performance.

Propositions

In qualitative research, hypotheses are not usually formulated at the beginning of the study. Most often they emerge as the study progresses. In qualitative research, hypotheses are typically replaced by research questions and propositions. While hypotheses in quantitative research are often specific predictions about the relationships between variables, qualitative research tends to focus on exploring complex phenomena and generating theories rather than testing specific hypotheses.

Research Questions. Research questions in qualitative research serve as guiding inquiries that direct the research process. They are broad and open-ended, aiming to explore the complexities of a phenomenon rather than to test specific hypotheses. Research questions often emerge from the researcher's curiosity or the need to address gaps in knowledge. Qualitative researchers use various methods, such as interviews, observations, and document analysis, to collect rich, in-depth data that can help answer these questions.

Propositions. Propositions in qualitative research are tentative statements or assertions about the relationships between concepts or phenomena. Unlike hypotheses, which are formulated based on deductive reasoning and are intended for testing, propositions in qualitative research are often generated through inductive reasoning and are used to guide data collection and analysis. Propositions provide a framework for organizing and interpreting qualitative data, helping researchers make sense of the complexities of the phenomena under study.

For example, in a qualitative study exploring the experiences of teachers implementing a new teaching method, a proposition might be: "Teachers who receive ongoing support and training are more likely to successfully implement the new teaching method." This proposition guides the researcher's data collection and analysis by suggesting a potential relationship between teacher support/training and successful implementation.

Summary

The chapter provides a comprehensive overview of key concepts in educational research, focusing on the role of variables and hypotheses in guiding inquiry and analysis. It begins by defining variables as any measurable attributes or characteristics that can vary and be used to study relationships, differences, or effects. Variables are classified into different measurement scales, including nominal, ordinal, interval, and ratio scales, based on their characteristics and roles in the research process. The chapter then discusses various types of variables commonly used in educational research, such as independent variables, dependent variables, mediator variables, moderator variables, and control variables. Examples are provided to illustrate each type of variable and its significance in educational research. Next, the chapter explores the concept of hypotheses, which are testable predictions or statements about the expected relationship between variables. Hypotheses are categorized into null hypotheses, which propose no significant relationship or difference between variables, and alternative hypotheses, which propose a significant relationship or difference between variables. Examples of null and alternative hypotheses are presented to demonstrate their application in educational research. Furthermore, the chapter discusses directional and non-directional hypotheses, explaining how they differ in their implications for the expected direction of the relationship between variables. Examples are provided to illustrate how directional and non-directional hypotheses are formulated and tested in educational research. Finally, the chapter introduces propositions as an alternative to hypotheses in qualitative research. Propositions are tentative statements or assertions about the relationships between concepts or phenomena, generated through inductive reasoning to guide data collection and analysis. The chapter emphasizes the importance of research questions and propositions in qualitative research for exploring complex phenomena and generating theories. Overall, the chapter provides a comprehensive overview of variables and hypotheses in educational research, highlighting their significance in guiding research inquiry, formulating testable predictions, and advancing knowledge in the field of education.

Suggestions for Students

Key Questions

The following questions cover key concepts discussed in the chapter and can be used to assess one's understanding of variables, hypotheses, and their roles in educational research.

1. What is the role of variables in educational research, and why are they important?
2. Can you differentiate between independent variables, dependent variables, mediator variables, moderator variables, and control variables? Provide examples of each type.
3. Explain the significance of different measurement scales (nominal, ordinal, interval, ratio) in educational research. How do these scales influence the types of analyses that can be conducted?
4. What are hypotheses, and how do they differ from research questions? Provide examples of null and alternative hypotheses in educational research.
5. What is the difference between directional and non-directional hypotheses? How do researchers decide which type of hypothesis to use in their studies?
6. Describe the process of hypothesis testing in educational research. What are the steps involved, and how do researchers determine whether hypotheses are supported or rejected?
7. How do variables and hypotheses contribute to the design and interpretation of research studies in education? Provide examples to illustrate their significance.
8. Explain the importance of research questions and propositions in qualitative research. How do these elements guide inquiry and analysis in qualitative studies?
9. Can you identify variables and hypotheses in a given research study or scenario? How would you evaluate the clarity and relevance of the variables and hypotheses?
10. Reflect on the strengths and limitations of variables and hypotheses in educational research. How might researchers address these limitations in their studies?

Suggestions for Instructors
Suggested Learning Activities The following learning activities engage students in active learning and critical thinking about variables and hypotheses in educational research, helping them develop essential research skills and understanding of research methodology. **Variable Classification Activity**: Divide students into small groups and provide them with a set of scenarios or research studies. Ask each group to identify and classify the variables present in each scenario or study as independent, dependent, mediator, moderator, or control variables. Afterward, have each group present their classifications and reasoning to the class for discussion. **Hypothesis Formulation Exercise**: Provide students with research questions related to educational topics and ask them to formulate null and alternative hypotheses based on each research question. Encourage students to consider the directionality of the hypotheses and whether they can be tested empirically. Afterward, discuss the hypotheses as a class, highlighting the differences between null and alternative hypotheses. **Case Study Analysis**: Assign students a case study or research article from the field of education that includes variables and hypotheses. Ask students to read the case study/article and identify the variables and hypotheses present. Then, have them critically analyze the hypotheses in terms of their clarity, testability, and relevance to the research questions. Encourage students to discuss how the variables and hypotheses contribute to the overall research design and findings. **Research Proposal Development**: Divide students into small groups and provide them with a research topic or question related to education. Ask each group to develop a research proposal that includes variables, hypotheses, and a proposed research design. Students should articulate clear research questions, formulate hypotheses, identify relevant variables, and propose methods for data collection and analysis. Afterward, have each group present their research proposal to the class for feedback and discussion. **Qualitative Research Propositions Activity**: For students focusing on qualitative research, provide them with a qualitative research question related to education. Ask students to generate propositions based on the research question using inductive reasoning. Encourage students to consider the relationships between concepts or phenomena and articulate tentative assertions about these relationships. Afterward, facilitate a class discussion where students compare and contrast their propositions and discuss their implications for qualitative research design and analysis. **Research Ethics Discussion**: Organize a class discussion on the ethical considerations related to variables and hypotheses in educational research. Present students with ethical dilemmas or scenarios involving variables and hypotheses (e.g., issues of confidentiality, informed consent, bias in hypothesis formulation). Encourage students to reflect on the ethical implications of their research practices and discuss strategies for addressing ethical concerns in educational research.

References

Ary, D., Jacobs, L. C., Razavieh, A., & Sorensen, C. (2018). Introduction to Research in Education. Cengage Learning.

Baron, R. M., & Kenny, D. A. (1986). The moderator-mediator variable distinction in social psychological research: Conceptual, strategic, and statistical considerations. Journal of Personality and Social Psychology, 51(6), 1173–1182. https://doi.org/10.1037/0022-3514.51.6.1173

Creswell, J. W., & Poth, C. N. (2018). Qualitative Inquiry & Research Design: Choosing Among Five Approaches (4th ed.). Sage Publications.

Introduction to Educational Research

Fraenkel, J. R., Wallen, N. E., & Hyun, H. H. (2011). How to Design and Evaluate Research in Education (8th ed.). McGraw-Hill.

Gall, M. D., Gall, J. P., & Borg, W. R. (2006). Educational Research: An Introduction (8th ed.). Pearson.

Gay, L. R., Mills, G. E., & Airasian, P. (2018). Educational Research: Competencies for Analysis and Applications (12th ed.). Pearson.

Merriam, S. B. (2009). Qualitative Research: A Guide to Design and Implementation. Jossey-Bass.

Trochim, W. M. K., & Donnelly, J. P. (2008). The Research Methods Knowledge Base (3rd ed.). Atomic Dog Publishing.

Chapter 6. Sampling

This chapter will address the following learning objectives:
• Define sampling in educational research.
• Distinguish between populations and samples in educational research.
• describe various sampling techniques used in educational research.
• Outline the steps of random and non-random sampling methods.
• Evaluate the strengths and limitations of random and non-random sampling methods.
• Analyze examples of random and non-random sampling methods.
• Evaluate the appropriateness of different sampling techniques in educational research contexts.
• Justify the selection of a particular sampling technique based on research objectives, population characteristics, and resource constraints.
• Analyze the implications of the sample size.

Sampling in educational research is a crucial methodological process that involves selecting a subset of individuals or elements from a larger population to represent it accurately. Sampling allows researchers to draw inferences about a broader group of students, teachers, schools, or educational practices based on data collected from a smaller, more manageable sample. Sampling allows researchers to feasibly study a portion of the population while still making inferences about the whole (Cohen, et al. 2017).

The goal of sampling is to ensure that the selected subset is representative of the population of interest, enabling researchers to generalize their findings with confidence. Various sampling techniques, such as random sampling, stratified sampling, and cluster sampling, are employed in educational research to obtain diverse and unbiased samples. The choice of sampling method depends on factors such as the research objectives, the characteristics of the population, and the available resources. By employing rigorous sampling techniques, educational researchers can enhance the validity and reliability of their findings, thus contributing to the advancement of knowledge in the field of education.

Populationsversus Samples

In educational research, understanding the distinction between samples and populations is essential for designing studies, analyzing data, and drawing conclusions. The population refers to the entire group of individuals, entities, or elements that possess the characteristics of interest to the researcher. This population could encompass various groups within the educational context, such as students, teachers, schools, administrators, or educational programs. The population serves as the target for the research study, representing the broader group to which the findings are intended to apply. For example, if a researcher is interested in studying the effectiveness of a particular teaching method on elementary school students' math achievement, the population would consist of all elementary school students who might potentially benefit from or be affected by that teaching method.

Introduction to Educational Research

It's important to note that populations in educational research can vary depending on the research questions, objectives, and scope of the study. Researchers may define populations based on specific characteristics such as age, grade level, socio-economic status, geographical location, or other relevant factors that are pertinent to the research inquiry. Understanding the population under study is crucial for researchers to properly define their research questions, select appropriate sampling techniques, and ensure the generalizability and applicability of their findings to the broader educational context.

A sample, on the other hand, is a subset of the population that is selected for inclusion in the study. It is chosen in such a way that it represents the characteristics of the larger population. Sampling allows researchers to conduct studies more efficiently, economically, and feasibly, as it is often impractical or impossible to study an entire population due to its size, diversity, or logistical constraints. Understanding the relationship between samples and populations is crucial for assessing the validity and generalizability of research findings in educational research.

The goal of sampling is to obtain a group of participants or elements that is diverse and representative enough to allow researchers to draw valid conclusions about the population as a whole. Samples can vary in size and composition depending on the research design, objectives, and methodologies employed. Various sampling techniques, such as random sampling, stratified sampling, or convenience sampling, may be utilized to ensure that the sample accurately reflects the diversity and characteristics of the population. For example, if a researcher is conducting a study on the effectiveness of a new teaching method in urban high schools, they may select a sample of high schools from different neighborhoods within the city to ensure representation from various socio-economic backgrounds and demographics. Sampling is a critical aspect of educational research, as it allows researchers to gather data efficiently and make valid inferences about the population of interest. By carefully selecting representative samples, researchers can ensure the validity and reliability of their findings, ultimately contributing to the advancement of knowledge in the field of education.

Sample Sizes

Sample sizes in educational research play a crucial role in determining the validity, reliability, and generalizability of study findings. Here are some key points to consider when discussing sample sizes in educational research:

1. **Representativeness**: A sample size should be large enough to accurately represent the population of interest. This means that the characteristics of the sample should closely match those of the population to ensure the findings can be generalized.

2. **Statistical Power**: Statistical power refers to the likelihood of detecting a true effect if it exists. Larger sample sizes generally lead to higher statistical power, meaning researchers are more likely to detect significant differences or relationships between variables.

3. **Precision**: Larger sample sizes tend to result in more precise estimates of population parameters. A larger sample reduces the margin of error and increases confidence in the study's results.

4. **Cost and Resources**: Conducting research with larger sample sizes can be more expensive and time-consuming. Researchers must balance the need for a sufficient sample size with the available resources.

5. **Heterogeneity**: The desired sample size may vary depending on the level of heterogeneity within the population. If the population is highly diverse, a larger sample size may be necessary to capture this diversity adequately.

6. **Sampling Techniques**: Different sampling techniques may require different sample sizes to achieve the desired level of representativeness and statistical power. For example, cluster sampling may require larger sample sizes compared to simple random sampling.

7. **Research Design and Analysis**: The research design and analysis methods employed also influence the required sample size. Complex statistical analyses or multivariate models may require larger sample sizes to yield meaningful results.

8. **Effect Size**: The size of the effect being studied can influence the required sample size. Larger effect sizes may require smaller sample sizes to detect significant differences, while smaller effect sizes may necessitate larger sample sizes.

In summary, determining the appropriate sample size in educational research involves considering factors such as research design, representativeness, statistical power, precision, cost, heterogeneity, sampling techniques, analysis methods, and effect size. Researchers should carefully justify their chosen sample size based on these considerations to ensure the validity and reliability of their study findings.

Sampling Methods

Random and non-random sampling procedures are two primary methods used in educational research to select participants or elements for a study. Each method has its advantages and limitations, and the choice between them depends on the research objectives, research design, population characteristics, and practical considerations.

Random Sampling Methods

Random sampling procedures are often preferred in educational research because they provide a high degree of objectivity and allow researchers to generalize findings to the broader population with confidence. These sampling methods involve selecting participants or elements from the population in a purely random manner, where each member of the population has an equal chance of being selected. This method aims to minimize bias and ensure that the sample is representative of the population. Random sampling techniques include simple random sampling, systematic sampling, stratified random sampling, cluster sampling, and two-stage random sampling.

Simple Random Sampling. Simple random sampling involves randomly selecting participants from the population without any specific criteria. With this sampling method, every individual or element in the population has an equal chance of being selected. It is considered one of the most rigorous sampling techniques because it minimizes bias and ensures that the sample is representative of the population. Below are general steps for implementing random sampling:

1. **Define the Population:** Begin by identifying the entire population of interest. This could be students, teachers, schools, or any other relevant entities within the scope of the study.

2. **Determine Sample Size:** Decide on the desired sample size, which is the number of individuals or elements that will be included in the sample.

3. **Random Selection:** Use a random selection method to choose participants from the population. This can be done through various techniques such as random number generators, lottery methods, or drawing names from a hat. The key is to ensure that every member of the population has an equal chance of being selected for the sample.

4. **Select Sample:** Once the random selection method is applied, the selected individuals or elements constitute the sample for the study.

Example of Random Sampling in Educational Research

The following example demonstrates how random sampling can be applied in educational research to investigate the effects of interventions, programs, or teaching methods on student outcomes.

Research Objective: Investigate the impact of a new teaching method on student performance in mathematics.

Population: All students enrolled in a particular school district.

Sample Size: The researcher aims to select a sample of 200 students from the population.

Random Sampling Procedure:
1. **Population Identification:** Identify all students enrolled in the school district, including elementary, middle, and high school students.
2. **Assign Identifiers:** Assign a unique identifier (e.g., student ID numbers) to each student in the population.
3. **Random Selection:** Use a random number generator or a randomization method to select 200 student ID numbers from the population.
4. **Contact Selected Students:** Contact the selected students and their parents/guardians to inform them about the study and request their participation.
5. **Obtain Consent:** Obtain written consent from the selected students' parents/guardians, ensuring that they understand the study's purpose, procedures, and potential risks.
6. **Pre-Intervention Assessment:** Administer pre-test assessments to the selected students to establish their baseline mathematics performance levels.
7. **Intervention:** Implement the new teaching method in mathematics classes attended by the selected students.
8. **Post-Intervention Assessment:** After the intervention period, administer post-test assessments to the selected students to measure any changes in their mathematics performance.
9. **Data Analysis:** Analyze the pre-test and post-test assessment scores to evaluate the impact of the new teaching method on student performance in mathematics.

By using random sampling in this example, the researcher ensures that every student in the school district has an equal chance of being selected for the study. This approach helps minimize bias and increases the likelihood that the sample accurately represents the population, allowing for valid conclusions to be drawn about the impact of the new teaching method on student performance in mathematics.

Random sampling offers several advantages. It ensures that the sample is free from bias, as each member of the population has an equal chance of being included. This method also allows for the generalization of findings from the sample to the broader population with a high level of confidence. While random sampling is widely regarded as one of the most rigorous sampling techniques in educational research, it does have some disadvantages:

Introduction to Educational Research

Impracticality with Small Populations. Random sampling may not be feasible or practical when dealing with small populations, as it may result in a sample size that is too small to draw meaningful conclusions.

Resource Intensive. Random sampling can be resource-intensive, particularly when the population is large. It may require significant time, effort, and resources to generate random samples and collect data from a large number of participants.

Difficulty in Implementation. Random sampling requires a clear understanding of sampling techniques and may be challenging to implement correctly, especially in complex research designs or with limited access to the population.

Potential for Sampling Error. While random sampling aims to minimize bias, there is still a possibility of sampling error. Variability within the population may lead to differences between the sample and the population, impacting the generalizability of findings.

Underrepresentation or Overrepresentation. Despite efforts to ensure randomness, random sampling may still result in underrepresentation or overrepresentation of certain subgroups within the population, particularly if the population is not homogeneous.

Cost. Conducting random sampling can be expensive, especially if researchers need to cover a wide geographical area or if specialized equipment or personnel are required for data collection.

Loss of Control. Random sampling may lead to a loss of control over the characteristics of the sample. Researchers cannot guarantee that specific subgroups or characteristics will be adequately represented in the sample.

Systematic Sampling. Systematic sampling involves selecting every n^{th} element from the population after a random starting point is determined. This method ensures that the sample is selected in a systematic, orderly manner while maintaining a degree of randomness. Below are some general steps for implementing systematic sampling:

1. **Establish the Population:** Define the entire population of interest. This could be students, teachers, schools, or any other relevant entities within the scope of the study.

2. **Determine Sample Size:** Decide on the desired sample size, which is the number of elements that will be included in the sample.

3. **Calculate Sampling Interval:** Calculate the sampling interval (n) by dividing the total population size by the desired sample size. For example, if the population size is 1000 and the desired sample size is 100, the sampling interval would be $1000/100 = 10$.

4. **Random Starting Point:** Choose a random starting point between 1 and the sampling interval (n). This ensures that the sample selection process begins randomly within the population.

Select Sample: Begin at the random starting point and select every n^{th} element from the population until the desired sample size is reached. For example, if the random starting point is 7, then elements 7, 17, 27, 37, and so on would be selected until the sample size is achieved.

Example of Systematic Sampling in Educational Research
Suppose a researcher wants to investigate the study habits and academic performance of students in a large high school with a population of 1000 students. The researcher aims to select a representative sample of 100 students for the study using systematic sampling.

1. **Establish the Population:** The population consists of the 1000 students enrolled in the high school.
2. **Determine Sample Size:** The researcher decides on a sample size of 100 students for the study.
3. **Calculate Sampling Interval:** The sampling interval (*n*) is calculated by dividing the total population size by the desired sample size: 1000 students ÷ 100 = 10.
4. **Random Starting Point:** A random starting point between 1 and the sampling interval is chosen. Let's say the random starting point is determined to be the 5th student.
5. **Select Sample:** Starting from the 5th student, the researcher selects every 10th student thereafter until reaching the desired sample size of 100. The selected students would be the 5th, 15th, 25th, 35th, and so on until the 100th student is reached.

By using systematic sampling in this example, the researcher ensures that the sample is selected in an orderly and systematic manner while maintaining a degree of randomness. This approach allows for a representative sample of students from the high school population, enabling the researcher to generalize findings about study habits and academic performance to the broader student body.

Systematic sampling is a useful technique in educational research when it's essential to maintain randomness while also ensuring an orderly selection process. It strikes a balance between simplicity and representativeness, making it a valuable tool for researchers. This procedure offers several advantages, including simplicity, ease of implementation, and efficiency. It also ensures that the sample is spread evenly across the population, reducing the risk of bias compared to some other non-random sampling methods. However, systematic sampling may introduce bias if there is a periodic pattern or trend in the population that aligns with the sampling interval. Below is a list of advantages and disadvantages of systematic sampling:

Advantages:

1. **Simple Implementation.** Systematic sampling is straightforward to implement compared to other sampling methods. Once the sampling interval is determined, selecting participants involves a systematic process, making it relatively easy to execute.

2. **Efficiency.** Systematic sampling can be more efficient than simple random sampling, especially when dealing with large populations. It allows researchers to cover a wide range of individuals or elements in the population with fewer resources and less time.

3. **Uniform Coverage.** Systematic sampling ensures that the entire population is covered evenly, as every n^{th} element is selected from the population. This reduces the likelihood of bias compared to convenience sampling methods.

4. **Reduced Variability.** Systematic sampling tends to have lower variability compared to other sampling methods, such as convenience sampling. This can lead to more precise estimates and reliable research findings.

Disadvantages:

1. **Risk of Bias.** Systematic sampling may introduce bias if there is a systematic pattern or periodicity in the population that aligns with the sampling interval. For example, if the population is sorted in some systematic order, selecting every n^{th} element may not provide a representative sample.

2. **Lack of Flexibility.** Systematic sampling requires a predetermined sampling interval, which may not always be appropriate for the population under study. If the interval is not chosen carefully, it may lead to biased or unrepresentative samples.

3. **Limited Representation.** Systematic sampling may result in limited representation of certain subgroups or characteristics within the population. If the systematic selection process does not adequately capture diversity within the population, the sample may not be fully representative.

4. **Sensitive to Order.** Systematic sampling is sensitive to the order of elements in the population. If the population is sorted or arranged in a non-random order, the systematic selection process may not provide a representative sample.

Overall, while systematic sampling offers simplicity and efficiency, researchers must be cautious about its potential for bias and limited representation. Careful consideration of the sampling interval and its implications for the population under study is essential to ensure the validity and reliability of research findings.

Stratified Sampling. The stratified sampling method involves dividing the population into distinct subgroups based on specific characteristics (such as age, grade level, gender, ethnicity, or academic performance) and then selecting samples from each stratum in proportion to their representation in the population. The goal is to ensure that each subgroup is adequately represented in the sample, allowing for more precise analysis and comparison of the different groups. Below are general steps for implementing the stratifies sampling method:

1. **Identify Strata:** Determine the relevant characteristics or variables that define the subgroups within the population. For example, if studying student performance in a school, the researcher may identify grade levels (e.g., elementary, middle, high school) as the strata.

2. **Divide Population:** Divide the population into mutually exclusive and exhaustive strata based on the identified characteristics. Each individual or element in the population should belong to only one stratum.

3. **Calculate Sample Size:** Determine the desired sample size for each stratum based on its proportion in the population. The sample size for each stratum may be proportional to its size relative to the total population or based on specific research objectives.

4. **Random Sampling Within Strata:** Randomly select samples from each stratum using appropriate random sampling techniques (such as simple random sampling or systematic sampling). Ensure that the sample size from each stratum reflects its proportion in the population.

5. **Combine Samples:** Combine the samples from each stratum to create the final stratified sample for the study.

Stratified sampling allows researchers to ensure that each subgroup within the population is adequately represented in the sample, which can lead to more accurate and reliable research findings. This method is particularly useful when there are significant variations or differences between subgroups that need to be accounted for in the analysis, thereby enhancing the validity and reliability of research findings.

Example of Stratified Sampling in Educational Research
The following example demonstrates how stratified sampling can be effectively applied in educational research to ensure that important subgroups within the population are adequately represented in the sample, leading to more accurate and reliable research findings.

Introduction to Educational Research

Example of Stratified Sampling in Educational Research

Research Objective: Investigating the relationship between academic performance and socioeconomic status (SES) among high school students.

Population: All high school students enrolled in a particular school district.

Stratification Variable: Socioeconomic status (SES), categorized into three levels: low, medium, and high.

Stratified Sampling Procedure:

1. **Population Identification:** Identify all high school students in the school district.
2. **Stratification:** Divide the population into three strata based on SES levels: low, medium, and high. This stratification is based on socioeconomic indicators such as parental income, education level, and occupation.
3. **Determine Sample Sizes:** Determine the desired sample size for each SES stratum based on its proportion in the population. For example, if the population consists of 1000 students with 30% low SES, 50% medium SES, and 20% high SES, the sample sizes could be 30, 50, and 20 students, respectively.
4. **Random Sampling Within Strata:** Randomly select samples from each SES stratum using appropriate random sampling techniques (e.g., simple random sampling or systematic sampling). Ensure that the sample sizes from each stratum reflect their proportions in the population.
5. **Combine Samples:** Combine the samples from each SES stratum to create the final stratified sample for the study.
6. **Data Collection:** Administer surveys or assessments to the selected students to collect data on their academic performance and SES indicators.
7. **Data Analysis:** Analyze the data to investigate the relationship between academic performance and SES among high school students, stratified by SES level.

By using stratified sampling in this example, the researcher ensures that students from diverse socioeconomic backgrounds are represented in the sample. This allows for a more nuanced analysis of the relationship between academic performance and SES, accounting for variations across different socioeconomic groups.

Stratified sampling offers several advantages in terms of precision, efficiency, and comparability, but researchers must carefully consider its complexity and potential limitations when designing and implementing educational research studies. Below is a list of advantages and disadvantages of using stratified random sampling in educational research:

Advantages:

1. **Improved Precision.** Stratified sampling ensures that each subgroup or stratum within the population is adequately represented in the sample. By stratifying the population based on relevant characteristics (such as age, grade level, or socioeconomic status), researchers can increase the precision of their estimates within each subgroup, leading to more accurate and reliable results.

2. **Increased Efficiency.** Stratified sampling can be more efficient than simple random sampling, especially when there are significant differences or variations between subgroups within the population. By focusing sampling efforts on specific strata, researchers can achieve a more balanced representation of the population with a smaller overall sample size.

3. **Enhanced Comparisons.** Stratified sampling allows researchers to make meaningful comparisons between different subgroups or strata within the population. By ensuring that each

stratum is adequately represented in the sample, researchers can examine variations in outcomes or behaviors across different demographic or contextual factors, leading to richer insights and interpretations.

4. **Reduced Sampling Bias.** By stratifying the population based on relevant characteristics, stratified sampling can help reduce sampling bias and improve the external validity of research findings. This method ensures that each subgroup is proportionally represented in the sample, reducing the risk of underrepresentation or overrepresentation of certain groups.

Disadvantages:

1. **Complexity.** Implementing stratified sampling can be more complex and time-consuming than simple random sampling, particularly when there are numerous strata or when the population is heterogeneous. Researchers need to carefully identify relevant stratification variables and determine appropriate sample sizes for each stratum, which may require additional planning and resources.

2. **Inflexibility.** Stratified sampling requires researchers to predefine strata based on specific characteristics or variables, which may limit flexibility in sample selection. If new subgroups or strata emerge during the study, it may be challenging to incorporate them into the sampling framework, potentially leading to sampling biases or inaccuracies.

3. **Potential for Overstratification.** Overstratification can occur when researchers create too many strata or when certain strata have small sample sizes. This can result in inefficient sample selection and may lead to difficulties in data analysis and interpretation.

4. **Assumption of Homogeneity.** Stratified sampling assumes that each stratum within the population is homogeneous with respect to the variables being studied. However, in practice, there may be variability within strata that researchers need to account for to ensure the validity of their findings.

Cluster Sampling. Cluster sampling is a sampling technique commonly used in educational research, especially when the population of interest is large and geographically dispersed. In cluster sampling, the population is divided into clusters or groups, and a random sample of clusters is selected for inclusion in the study. Then, all individuals or elements within the selected clusters are included in the sample, rather than selecting individual participants directly from the population. Below are general steps for implementing cluster sampling in educational research:

1. **Identify Clusters:** Clusters are predefined groups within the population that share similar characteristics or are geographically proximate. Clusters could be schools, classrooms, districts, or any other naturally occurring groups.

2. **Random Selection of Clusters:** Randomly select a sample of clusters from the population. This can be done using a random number generator or a randomization method to ensure that each cluster has an equal chance of being selected.

3. **Include All Individuals in Selected Clusters:** Once clusters are selected, all individuals or elements within those clusters are included in the sample. This could involve all students in selected classrooms, all teachers in selected schools, or all schools in selected districts.

Example of Cluster Sampling in Educational Research

The following example illustrates how cluster sampling can be effectively applied in educational research to investigate the effects of interventions or programs at the group level, while still providing valuable insights into individual student outcomes.

Research Objective: Investigating the effectiveness of a new literacy program in improving reading comprehension among elementary school students.

Population: All elementary school students in a large school district comprising multiple schools.

Clusters: The schools within the school district serve as the clusters for this study.

Cluster Sampling Procedure:

1. **Identify Clusters:** Divide the population of elementary school students into clusters based on the schools they attend. Each school serves as a separate cluster.

2. **Random Selection of Clusters:** Randomly select a sample of schools (clusters) from the entire school district. This could involve using a random number generator to select a subset of schools from a list of all schools in the district.

3. **Include All Students in Selected Clusters:** Once clusters (schools) are selected, include all elementary school students enrolled in those selected schools in the sample. This means that every student in the selected schools is included in the study.

4. **Intervention:** Implement the new literacy program in the selected schools over a specified period, providing the program to all students within those schools.

5. **Pre- and Post-Intervention Assessment:** Administer pre- and post-intervention assessments to measure reading comprehension skills among students in the selected schools. These assessments may include standardized tests, reading passages, or other measures of reading proficiency.

6. **Data Analysis:** Analyze the pre- and post-intervention assessment scores to evaluate the effectiveness of the literacy program in improving reading comprehension among elementary school students in the selected schools.

By using cluster sampling in this example, the researcher ensures that the sample is representative of the entire population of elementary school students within the school district. Selecting entire schools as clusters simplifies the sampling process and allows for the implementation of the literacy program at the school level, rather than individually selecting students for participation.

Cluster sampling is a valuable sampling technique in educational research, particularly when dealing with large and dispersed populations. By selecting clusters and including all individuals within those clusters in the sample, researchers can obtain representative data while minimizing logistical challenges. This sampling method offers several advantages in educational research, but also has some limitations. Below is a list of advantages and disadvantages of cluster sampling:

Advantages:

1. **Efficiency:** Cluster sampling is more efficient than other sampling methods, especially when dealing with large and dispersed populations. By selecting clusters rather than individual participants, researchers can reduce the time and resources required for data collection.

2. **Logistical Convenience:** Cluster sampling is particularly useful in educational research settings where it may be impractical or costly to sample individuals directly from the population. For example, sampling all students in selected schools is often more feasible than attempting to sample students from every school in a district.

3. **Accounting for Group Effects:** Cluster sampling allows researchers to account for group-level effects or characteristics that may influence outcomes of interest. For example, studying student

achievement within schools allows researchers to examine school-level factors that may impact student performance.

Disadvantages:

1. **Increased Variability:** Due to the inclusion of entire clusters in the sample, cluster sampling may result in increased variability compared to other sampling methods. This can affect the precision of estimates and may require larger sample sizes to achieve similar levels of statistical power.

2. **Potential for Homogeneity:** Clusters selected for inclusion in the sample may be relatively homogenous, leading to limited variability in the sample. Researchers must carefully consider the representativeness of selected clusters to ensure the generalizability of findings.

Two-stage Random Sampling. Two-stage random sampling, also known as two-stage cluster sampling, is a sampling technique commonly used in educational research, especially when dealing with large and geographically dispersed populations. This method involves selecting clusters or groups from the population in the first stage and then randomly selecting individuals or elements from within those clusters in the second stage.

The two-stages random sampling are:

1. **Stage 1: Selection of Clusters:**

   - Divide the population into clusters or groups based on certain criteria (e.g., schools, classrooms, districts).

   - Randomly select a sample of clusters from the entire population using a random selection method. Each selected cluster represents a subset of the population.

2. **Stage 2: Selection of Individuals within Clusters:**

   - Within each selected cluster, randomly select individuals or elements to include in the sample. This can be done using simple random sampling, systematic sampling, or other randomization techniques.

   - Ensure that all individuals within the selected clusters have an equal chance of being selected for the sample.

Example of Two-Stage Sampling in Educational Research

The following example illustrates how two-stage sampling can be effectively applied in educational research to investigate the effects of interventions or programs across multiple clusters or groups while still providing valuable insights into individual student outcomes.

Research Objective: Investigating the effectiveness of a new teaching method on student performance in mathematics across different school districts.

Population: All students enrolled in elementary schools across multiple school districts.

Stage 1: Selection of Clusters (School Districts):

1. **Identify Clusters:** Divide the population into clusters based on school districts. Each school district represents a separate cluster.

2. **Random Selection of Clusters:** Randomly select a sample of school districts from the entire population of school districts. This could involve using a random selection method to choose a subset of districts from a list of all districts in the region.

Stage 2: Selection of Units within Clusters (Schools):

Example of Two-Stage Sampling in Educational Research

1. **Within Selected Clusters (School Districts):**
   - Identify all elementary schools within the selected school districts.
   - Randomly select a sample of elementary schools from each selected district.
2. **Within Selected Schools:**
   - Within each selected elementary school, randomly select a sample of students to participate in the study. This could involve selecting specific grade levels or classrooms within the selected schools.

Intervention and Data Collection:

1. Implement the new teaching method in the selected schools over a specified period.
2. Administer pre- and post-intervention assessments to measure student performance in mathematics.

Data Analysis:

Analyze the pre- and post-intervention assessment scores to evaluate the effectiveness of the new teaching method across different school districts.

By using two-stage sampling in this example, the researcher ensures that the sample is representative of elementary school students across multiple school districts. Selecting school districts as clusters in the first stage simplifies the sampling process and allows for efficient data collection, while random selection of schools and students within those districts ensures adequate representation of different schools and students within each district.

Overall, two-stage random sampling is a valuable sampling technique in educational research, allowing researchers to efficiently sample large and diverse populations while ensuring adequate representation of clusters and individuals within those clusters. Nevertheless, two-stage random sampling also has some limitations. Below is a list of advantages and disadvantages of this sampling method:

Advantages:

1. **Efficiency:** By selecting clusters in the first stage, researchers can reduce the time and resources required for sampling compared to sampling individual elements directly from the population.

2. **Logistical Convenience:** Two-stage sampling is particularly useful when dealing with large and dispersed populations, as it allows researchers to sample groups rather than individuals, simplifying the sampling process.

3. **Representation of Clusters:** Two-stage sampling ensures that clusters from different segments of the population are represented in the sample, increasing the generalizability of research findings.

Disadvantages:

1. **Complexity:** Implementing two-stage sampling can be more complex than single-stage sampling methods, as it involves multiple stages of selection and coordination.

2. **Potential for Cluster Effects:** The inclusion of entire clusters in the sample may introduce cluster effects or dependencies, which can affect the analysis and interpretation of results.

3. **Sample Design Considerations:** Researchers must carefully consider the sample design, including the selection of clusters and the allocation of sample sizes, to ensure that the sample is representative and unbiased.

Non-Random Sampling

Non-random sampling procedures, also known as non-probability sampling, involve selecting participants or elements from the population based on specific criteria or convenience. Unlike random sampling, non-random sampling techniques do not provide an equal chance of selection for all members of the population, which can introduce bias into the sample. Common non-random sampling techniques include convenience sampling, purposive sampling, and quota sampling. Convenience sampling involves selecting participants who are readily available or easily accessible to the researcher. Purposive sampling involves selecting participants based on specific characteristics or criteria relevant to the research objectives. Quota sampling involves selecting participants based on pre-defined quotas for certain characteristics, such as age, gender, or ethnicity. While non-random sampling procedures are often more practical and cost-effective, they may result in samples that are not representative of the population, limiting the generalizability of findings.

Convenience Sampling. Convenience sampling is a non-probability sampling technique widely used in educational research and other fields. In convenience sampling, participants are selected based on their convenient availability and accessibility to the researcher, rather than through a random selection process. This method is often employed due to its ease of implementation and practicality, particularly when researchers have limited time, resources, or access to the entire population of interest. The main characteristics of convenience sampling are:

1. **Selection of Participants Based on Availability.** Researchers select participants based on their convenient availability and accessibility. This could involve approaching individuals who are readily available in a specific location, such as students in a particular classroom, attendees at an event, or visitors to a website.

2. **Absence of Randomization.** Unlike probability sampling methods, convenience sampling does not involve random selection of participants from the population. Instead, participants are chosen based on convenience, proximity, or accessibility to the researcher.

3. **Sample Bias.** Convenience sampling may introduce bias into the sample, as individuals who are easily accessible to the researcher may not be representative of the entire population. This can lead to limitations in the generalizability of research findings to broader populations.

4. **Practicality.** Convenience sampling is often chosen for its practicality and ease of implementation, especially in situations where researchers have limited time, resources, or access to the entire population. It allows for quick data collection and may be suitable for exploratory or preliminary studies.

5. **Potential for Biased Results.** Due to its non-random nature, convenience sampling may result in biased estimates of population characteristics or relationships. The sample may overrepresent certain groups or characteristics while underrepresenting others, leading to skewed or inaccurate results.

6. **Limitations in Inference.** Researchers must exercise caution when making inferences or generalizations based on convenience samples, as they may not accurately reflect the characteristics or behaviors of the entire population. Findings derived from convenience samples should be interpreted with caution and may require further validation through additional research.

Example of Convenience Sampling in Educational Research

Research Objective: Exploring student attitudes towards online learning platforms during the COVID-19 pandemic.

Population: All high school students in a particular city.

Convenience Sampling Procedure:

1. **Selection of Participants:**
   - Researchers select participants based on their convenient availability within the school setting.
   - Rather than using a systematic or random selection process, researchers choose to survey students who are present in specific classes or school events during the data collection period.

2. **Location:**
   - Researchers conduct surveys in classrooms during breaks or after school hours.
   - Alternatively, researchers distribute online surveys to students via email or school communication platforms, making participation accessible to those who are connected to school networks.

3. **Sampling Process:**
   - Researchers approach students who are present in the selected classrooms or have access to the online survey link.
   - Students who voluntarily agree to participate in the survey are included in the convenience sample.

4. **Sample Composition:**
   - The convenience sample may include students from a limited number of classes or grade levels, as well as those who are more inclined to participate in surveys or have access to online platforms.
   - Students who are absent or not actively engaged in school activities during the data collection period are not included in the sample.

Data Collection:
- Researchers administer surveys to participating students, collecting information about their experiences, attitudes, and preferences regarding online learning platforms.
- Alternatively, researchers may conduct interviews or focus groups with a subset of students who agree to participate in qualitative data collection.

Data Analysis:
- Researchers analyze survey responses or qualitative data to identify common themes, patterns, and trends in student attitudes towards online learning platforms.
- Findings from the convenience sample are interpreted within the context of the specific groups of students surveyed and may not be generalizable to the entire population of high school students in the city.

Limitations:
- The convenience sample may not accurately represent the diversity of student attitudes towards online learning platforms, as it primarily includes students who are present and willing to participate during the data collection period.
- Findings from the convenience sample may be influenced by factors such as class schedules, student availability, and access to online surveys, potentially introducing bias into the research results.

In this example, convenience sampling allows researchers to collect data quickly and efficiently within the school setting, providing insights into student attitudes towards online learning platforms during a specific time period. However, researchers must be mindful of the limitations of convenience sampling and the potential impact on the generalizability of their findings.

Introduction to Educational Research

Convenience sampling is commonly used in educational research settings where researchers may have limited resources or access to the entire population of interest. While it offers practical advantages in terms of ease of implementation, researchers must be aware of its limitations and potential biases when interpreting the results.

Self-Selection Sampling. Self-selection sampling, also known as voluntary sampling, is a non-probability sampling technique commonly used in educational research where participants voluntarily choose to be part of the study. Unlike probability sampling methods where participants are randomly selected from the population, self-selected sampling relies on individuals' willingness or initiative to participate, often in response to invitations or announcements about the research.

In educational research, self-selection sampling can be advantageous in certain contexts where researchers aim to study specific groups or individuals with particular characteristics or experiences. For example, researchers investigating the effectiveness of an online learning platform might invite educators who have used the platform voluntarily to participate in a survey or interview. Similarly, studies examining the experiences of parents with homeschooling might recruit participants who have self-identified as homeschoolers through online forums or social media groups.

One of the primary advantages of self-selected sampling is its convenience and accessibility. Researchers can reach a large pool of potential participants quickly and at relatively low cost by posting recruitment notices in online forums, social media platforms, or community centers. Additionally, self-selected sampling allows researchers to study populations that may be difficult to access through traditional sampling methods, such as individuals with rare conditions or specific educational backgrounds.

However, self-selected sampling also has several limitations that researchers must consider when interpreting the findings:

1. **Sampling Bias**: Participants self-select to be part of the study, therefore the sample may not be representative of the broader population. Individuals who choose to participate may have unique characteristics or experiences that differ from those who do not participate, leading to sampling bias. For example, participants who have had particularly positive or negative experiences with a program may be more motivated to participate, skewing the results.

2. **Limited Generalizability**: Due to sampling bias, findings from studies using self-selected sampling may have limited generalizability to the broader population. Researchers must be cautious when extrapolating findings to other contexts or populations, as they may not accurately reflect the experiences or perspectives of non-participants.

3. **Difficulty Establishing Causality**: Self-selection sampling can make it challenging to establish causal relationships between variables. Without random assignment to treatment groups, researchers cannot control for potential confounding variables that may influence the outcomes of interest. As a result, researchers may need to rely on alternative study designs or statistical methods to strengthen causal inferences.

To mitigate some of the limitations associated with self-selection sampling, researchers can employ strategies such as:

- **Sensitivity Analysis**: Assessing the robustness of findings by comparing results obtained from self-selected samples with those from more representative samples or alternative study designs.

Introduction to Educational Research

- **Subgroup Analysis**: Examining differences in outcomes between participants with different characteristics or experiences to identify potential sources of bias or variability.

- **Triangulation**: Using multiple methods or sources of data to corroborate findings and enhance the validity of conclusions drawn from self-selected samples.

Despite its limitations, self-selected sampling can be a valuable tool in educational research, particularly in exploratory or qualitative studies where researchers seek to understand the experiences, perspectives, and behaviors of specific groups or individuals. By acknowledging and addressing the inherent biases associated with self-selected sampling, researchers can generate valuable insights that contribute to the broader understanding of educational phenomena.

Purposive Sampling. Purposive sampling, also known as judgmental or selective sampling, is a non-probability sampling technique commonly used in educational research, particularly in qualitative research. In purposive sampling, researchers deliberately select participants who possess specific characteristics or traits that are relevant to the research question or objectives. Unlike probability sampling methods, which rely on random selection to ensure representativeness, purposive sampling focuses on selecting participants based on their unique qualities, expertise, or relevance to the study. Below are the main features of purposive sampling:

1. **Definition of Sampling Criteria:** Researchers identify specific criteria or characteristics that are important for addressing research questions or objectives. These criteria may include demographic characteristics, expertise, experience, or other relevant factors.

2. **Selection of Participants:** Based on the predefined criteria, researchers purposively select participants who meet the desired characteristics or traits. This could involve selecting individuals with specific expertise, experiences, or perspectives that are relevant to the study.

3. **Subjective Judgment:** Purposive sampling relies on the subjective judgment of the researcher to identify and select participants who are deemed most suitable for the study. Researchers may use their knowledge, expertise, or prior experience to identify individuals who can provide valuable insights or perspectives on the research topic.

4. **Diverse Selection:** Purposive sampling allows researchers to select participants from diverse backgrounds, experiences, or perspectives, depending on the research objectives. This diversity enhances the richness and depth of data collected, providing a broader understanding of the research topic.

5. **Flexibility:** Purposive sampling offers flexibility in participant selection, allowing researchers to adapt their sampling strategy based on emerging findings or changes in research priorities. Researchers can refine their selection criteria or add new participants as needed to ensure comprehensive coverage of the research topic.

Purposive sampling is commonly used in educational research settings where researchers seek to gain insights from specific individuals or groups with specialized knowledge, experiences, or perspectives. Examples of purposive sampling include:

- **Expert Sampling:** Selecting experts or practitioners in a particular field or discipline who possess specialized knowledge or experience relevant to the research topic.

Introduction to Educational Research

- **Criterion Sampling:** Selecting participants who meet specific criteria or characteristics identified by the researcher as essential for addressing the research question.

- **Snowball Sampling:** Identifying initial participants who can then refer other individuals who meet the sampling criteria, leading to the recruitment of additional participants through referrals.

While purposive sampling offers advantages in terms of targeted participant selection and depth of insights, researchers must be mindful of potential limitations, such as sample bias and limited generalizability. It is essential to clearly define the sampling criteria and justify the selection of participants to ensure the validity and reliability of research findings.

Quota Sampling. Quota sampling is a non-probability sampling technique widely used in educational research to ensure that the sample reflects specific characteristics or proportions present in the population. In quota sampling, researchers select participants based on pre-defined quotas for certain characteristics, such as age, gender, ethnicity, or socioeconomic status, rather than through random selection. This method allows researchers to control the composition of the sample and ensure that it represents the diversity of the population on key variables of interest. Below are the main steps of the quota sampling method:

1. **Identify Quota Categories:** Researchers identify the key characteristics or variables of interest that they want to ensure are represented in the sample. These may include demographic factors (e.g., age, gender, ethnicity) or other relevant variables related to the research question.

2. **Establish Quotas:** Based on the characteristics identified, researchers establish quotas specifying the desired proportions of each category in the sample. For example, if the population is 60% female and 40% male, the researcher may set quotas to ensure that the sample reflects these proportions.

3. **Select Participants:** Researchers then select participants for the sample based on these quotas. They may use various methods, such as convenience sampling or purposive sampling, to recruit individuals who meet the quota requirements.

4. **Monitor Quotas:** Throughout the data collection process, researchers monitor the quotas to ensure that they are being met. If certain quota categories are underrepresented, researchers may adjust their sampling strategy to recruit additional participants from those categories.

5. **Data Analysis:** Once the sample is collected, researchers analyze the data, considering the quotas established for each category. This allows them to examine how different groups within the population respond to the variables of interest and make comparisons based on these characteristics.

Quota sampling offers several advantages in educational research:

- **Control over Sample Composition:** Quota sampling allows researchers to control the composition of the sample and ensure that it reflects the diversity of the population on key variables of interest.

- **Efficiency:** Quota sampling can be more efficient than probability sampling methods, as researchers can target specific groups or characteristics without the need for random selection.

- **Flexibility:** Quota sampling offers flexibility in participant selection, allowing researchers to adjust quotas and sampling strategies as needed to ensure adequate representation of different groups.

However, quota sampling also has limitations, including the potential for bias and lack of generalizability. Researchers must carefully consider these limitations and ensure that the sample accurately reflects the population's characteristics and diversity.

In summary, both random and non-random sampling procedures have their role in educational research, and researchers must carefully consider the advantages and limitations of each method when selecting the most appropriate sampling technique for their study. The choice of sampling method depends on various factors such as the research objectives, the research design, the characteristics of the population, and the available resources. Researchers must carefully consider their sampling approach and justify their choices based on the specific context of their study. By employing appropriate sampling techniques, researchers can enhance the validity of their findings and contribute to the advancement of knowledge in the field of education.

Summary

This chapter delves into the critical process of sampling in educational research. Sampling involves selecting a subset of individuals or elements from a larger population to accurately represent it, allowing researchers to draw conclusions about the broader group based on data collected from a manageable sample. The chapter emphasizes the importance of sampling in ensuring research findings are representative, valid, and generalizable to the larger population. It covers key concepts such as populations versus samples, sample size considerations, and various sampling methods. The chapter describes random sampling procedures including random sampling, systematic sampling, stratified sampling, cluster sampling, and two-stage sampling. Further, the chapter presents non-random sampling methods such as convenience sampling, purposive sampling, and quota sampling. Each sampling method has advantages and limitations, and researchers must carefully choose the appropriate technique based on their research objectives, population characteristics, and available resources to ensure the validity and reliability of their findings. The chapter concludes by stressing the significance of employing rigorous sampling techniques to enhance the validity and reliability of research findings in the field of education.

Suggestions for Students

Key Questions

1. What is the purpose of sampling in educational research, and why is it essential for the validity and generalizability of research findings?

2. How do populations and samples differ in educational research, and why is it important to understand this distinction when designing studies?

3. What are the various sampling techniques used in educational research, and how do researchers choose the most appropriate method for their study?

4. Can you provide examples of situations where stratified sampling would be more appropriate than random or systematic sampling in educational research?

5. Compare and contrast cluster sampling and two-stage random sampling, highlighting their differences and similarities.

6. How does purposive sampling differ from convenience sampling? Provide examples to illustrate the differences.

7. Explain quota sampling and its purpose in educational research. What are its key features?

8. What are some potential sources of bias in self-selection sampling, and how can researchers mitigate these biases to support the validity of their findings?

9. How do researchers determine the appropriate sample size for their study, and what factors influence this decision?

10. Suppose you are conducting a study on student attitudes towards online learning platforms. Which sampling technique would you choose, and why? Justify your selection based on the characteristics of the population and the research objectives.

Suggestions for Instructors

Suggested Learning Activities

Sampling Techniques Exploration: Divide students into small groups and assign each group a specific sampling technique discussed in the text (e.g., random sampling, systematic sampling, stratified sampling). Have each group research and prepare a short presentation explaining their assigned sampling technique, including its definition, steps for implementation, advantages, and disadvantages. After the presentations, facilitate a class discussion comparing and contrasting the different sampling techniques.

Case Study Analysis: Provide students with a case study or research scenario related to educational research. Ask them to identify the population, research objectives, and potential sampling methods that could be used in the study. Then, have students work individually or in pairs to outline a sampling plan, including the rationale for selecting a particular sampling method and the steps involved in its implementation. Encourage students to justify their choices based on the characteristics of the population and the research objectives.

Sampling Simulation Game: Develop a sampling simulation game where students act as researchers conducting a study in an educational setting. Provide them with a simulated population, research objectives, and constraints (e.g., budget, time). Students must choose a sampling method and design a sampling plan to gather data efficiently while ensuring the validity and representativeness of their

Suggestions for Instructors

findings. The game can involve scenarios with varying levels of complexity to challenge students' decision-making skills.

Sampling Bias Discussion: Present students with examples of sampling bias in educational research (e.g., volunteer bias, non-response bias, sampling frame bias). Divide students into groups and assign each group a specific type of sampling bias to research further. Have groups analyze how the bias could affect research findings and propose strategies to minimize or mitigate the bias in sampling. Encourage students to think critically about the implications of sampling bias for research validity and generalizability.

Real-world Sampling Analysis: Provide students with real-world examples of educational research studies that utilize different sampling techniques. Ask students to critically evaluate the sampling methods used in each study and assess their strengths and limitations. Facilitate a class discussion where students share their analyses and engage in debates about the appropriateness of the sampling techniques employed in the studies.

Sampling Plan Development: Task students with designing a sampling plan for a hypothetical educational research study of their choice. Students should identify the population, research objectives, and relevant variables to consider in sampling. They should then select a sampling method (e.g., random sampling, stratified sampling) and outline the steps for implementing the sampling plan. Encourage students to justify their decisions and consider potential challenges or limitations in their sampling approach.

Research Proposal Development: Have students develop research proposals for hypothetical studies in educational research. Require them to justify their choice of sampling technique based on the research objectives, population characteristics, and available resources. This activity allows students to apply their understanding of sampling methods in a practical context.

Research Ethics Workshop: Host a workshop on research ethics, focusing on the ethical considerations associated with different sampling techniques. Discuss issues such as informed consent, privacy, confidentiality, and potential harm to participants. Use case studies and real-world examples to illustrate ethical dilemmas in sampling and research conduct.

Field Observation: Arrange a field trip or virtual observation session where students can witness sampling techniques being used in educational research settings. This could involve visiting a school or educational institution where researchers are conducting studies, providing students with firsthand exposure to sampling methods in practice.

Guest Speaker Series: Invite guest speakers, such as experienced researchers or practitioners in educational research, to discuss their experiences with sampling techniques. Encourage students to ask questions and engage in dialogue with the speakers, gaining insights into real-world applications and challenges associated with sampling in educational research.

References

Babbie, E. (2016). The Practice of Social Research. Cengage Learning.

Cohen, L., Manion, L., & Morrison, K. (2017). *Research methods in education.* Routledge.

Creswell, J. W. (2014). *Research design: Qualitative, quantitative, and mixed methods approaches.* Sage publications.

Introduction to Educational Research

Fraenkel, J. R., Wallen, N. E., & Hyun, H. H. (2018). *How to design and evaluate research in education.* McGraw-Hill Education.

Gall, M. D., Gall, J. P., & Borg, W. R. (2007). *Educational research: An introduction.* Pearson.

Johnson, B., & Christensen, L. (2016). *Educational research: Quantitative, qualitative, and mixed approaches.* Sage Publications.

Neuman, W. L. (2013). Social Research Methods: Qualitative and Quantitative Approaches. Pearson.

Palinkas, L. A., Horwitz, S. M., Green, C. A., Wisdom, J. P., Duan, N., & Hoagwood, K. (2015). Purposeful sampling for qualitative data collection and analysis in mixed method implementation research. Administration and Policy in Mental Health and Mental Health Services Research, 42(5), 533-544.

Chapter 7. Instrumentation

This chapter will address the following learning objectives:
• Describe the instrumentation process in educational research.
• Explain the importance of instrumentation in educational research.
• Compare and contrast different data collection instruments used in educational research.
• Evaluate the advantages and disadvantages of different data collection methods.
• Select appropriate data collection methods based on research questions, objectives, resources, population characteristics, cultural sensitivity, language proficiency, or accessibility.
• Apply ethical considerations in the use of data collection instruments.
• Analyze the process of developing new data collection instruments.

Instrumentation in educational research refers to the tools, techniques, and methods used to collect data in studies aimed at understanding various aspects of education. These aspects can range from student learning outcomes and teacher effectiveness to educational policies and program evaluations. Effective instrumentation is crucial for ensuring the reliability and validity of research findings, as it directly impacts the accuracy and credibility of the data collected.

In educational research, instrumentation encompasses a wide array of instruments, including surveys, questionnaires, interviews, observations, tests and assessments, focus groups, and document analysis (Cohen, Manion, & Morrison, 2018). Each instrument serves a specific purpose and is designed to gather particular types of data relevant to the research objectives. Researchers must carefully select or design instruments that align with their research questions, objectives, and the characteristics of the population under study (Fraenkel, Wallen, & Hyun, 2019).

Moreover, the development and validation of instruments are essential steps in the research process (DeVellis, 2016). Researchers often conduct pilot studies or utilize established instruments with proven reliability and validity to ensure the quality of data collection. Additionally, considerations such as cultural sensitivity, language proficiency, and accessibility are vital in instrument design to ensure inclusivity and fairness in data collection (Gay, Mills, & Airasian, 2018).

Overall, instrumentation plays a fundamental role in educational research by providing researchers with the means to collect empirical evidence that informs decision-making, policy development, and educational practices. Understanding the fundamental concepts related to instrumentation is essential for researchers, educators, policymakers, and other stakeholders involved in improving educational outcomes and promoting evidence-based practices in education.

Data Collection Instruments

Data collection instruments in educational research refer to the tools used to gather information for the purpose of studying various aspects of education. These instruments are designed to systematically collect data from specific sources, such as students, teachers, administrators, to address research questions, evaluate interventions, or assess educational outcomes. In educational research, various types of data collection instruments are used to gather information about student learning, teacher practices, educational environments, and other relevant factors. Below are some common types:

Surveys and Questionnaires. Surveys and questionnaires are popular instruments for collecting self-reported data from participants, such as students, teachers, administrators, and parents. These instruments typically consist of structured sets of questions designed to measure attitudes, beliefs, behaviors, or demographic information (Cohen, Manion, & Morrison, 2018).

Interviews. Interviews involve direct interaction between the researcher and the participant, allowing for in-depth exploration of topics and perspectives. Interviews can be structured, semi-structured, or unstructured, depending on the level of guidance provided by the researcher (Brinkmann & Kvale, 2018).

Observations. Observations involve systematically watching and recording behaviors, interactions, or events within educational settings. Observational data can provide insights into classroom dynamics, teaching strategies, student engagement, and other aspects of the learning environment (Merriam & Tisdell, 2016).

Tests and Assessments. Tests and assessments are used to measure various aspects of student learning, including knowledge, skills, and abilities. These instruments can range from standardized tests to teacher-created quizzes and performance assessments (Nitko & Brookhart, 2019).

Document Analysis. Document analysis involves examining written or recorded materials, such as textbooks, lesson plans, student work samples, and institutional policies. Document analysis can provide contextual information and supplement other data collection methods (Bowen, 2009).

Focus Groups. Focus groups bring together a small group of participants to discuss specific topics or issues related to education. These group discussions allow researchers to explore shared experiences, perspectives, and opinions in a collaborative setting (Krueger & Casey, 2014).

Each type of data collection instrument has its strengths and limitations, and researchers often use a combination of methods to triangulate findings and enhance the validity and reliability of their research. When selecting data collection instruments, researchers typically consider several criteria to ensure that the chosen method aligns with the research questions, objectives, and the characteristics of the study population. Some common criteria include:

Relevance to Research Questions. The instrument should directly address the research questions and objectives of the study. It should be capable of capturing the data necessary to answer the research questions effectively (Creswell & Creswell, 2017).

Validity and Reliability. The instrument should be supported by evidence of validity, meaning it supports accurate inferences about the measured constructs. Further, the instrument should be reliable, providing consistent results over time and across different contexts or point in time. Researchers may use established measures with demonstrated validity and reliability or conduct pilot studies to assess the instrument's psychometric properties (DeVellis, 2016).

Feasibility: Researchers should consider the practicality and feasibility of using the instrument within the constraints of the study, including time, resources, and access to participants. The instrument should be feasible to administer and analyze given the available resources (Fraenkel, Wallen, & Hyun, 2019).

Appropriateness for Study Population: The instrument should be appropriate for the characteristics of the study population, including age, language proficiency, cultural background, and educational level. Consideration should be given to the readability, comprehensibility, and cultural relevance of the instrument (Gay, Mills, & Airasian, 2018).

Ethical Considerations: Researchers should ensure that the data collection instrument and procedures adhere to ethical standards, including informed consent, confidentiality, and protection of participants' rights. Ethical considerations are particularly important when working with vulnerable populations, such as children or individuals with disabilities (American Educational Research Association, 2011).

By carefully considering these criteria, researchers can select data collection instruments that are well-suited to their research goals and contribute to the validity, reliability, and ethical conduct of the study.

Surveys and Questionnaires

Surveys and questionnaires are widely used in educational research to gather self-reported information from participants. These instruments typically consist of a set of structured questions designed to collect data on various aspects such as attitudes, beliefs, behaviors, demographics, or experiences related to education. Surveys are administered through various means, including paper-and-pencil forms, online platforms, or interviews conducted by trained researchers. They can target different groups within the educational context, including students, teachers, parents, administrators, or other stakeholders.

Questionnaires are similar to surveys but are typically self-administered by participants without direct involvement from researchers. Participants are provided with a written or electronic form containing the survey questions, which they complete at their convenience and return to the researchers. Although they share similarities, such as their use in collecting self-reported data, there are also differences between the two methods.

Similarities:

Self-Reported Data. Both surveys and questionnaires rely on self-reported data, where participants provide responses to specific questions or prompts.

Structured Format. Surveys and questionnaires typically have a structured format, with predetermined questions and response options.

Quantitative and Qualitative Data. Depending on the nature of the questions, both methods can collect quantitative or qualitative data.

Differences:

Administration. Surveys can be administered through various means, including face-to-face interviews, telephone interviews, online forms, or paper-and-pencil formats. Questionnaires, on the other hand, are typically self-administered by participants without direct interaction with a researcher.

Introduction to Educational Research

Scope. Surveys often refer to a broader data collection process that may involve multiple methods and instruments, including questionnaires. Questionnaires, however, specifically refer to written or electronic forms containing a set of questions for participants to complete.

Length and Complexity. Surveys can vary in length and complexity, covering multiple topics or dimensions of a research study. Questionnaires are usually shorter and more focused, with a specific set of questions addressing a particular aspect of the research.

Response Rate. Surveys administered through interviews may have higher response rates compared to questionnaires, as the presence of an interviewer can encourage participation and clarify any ambiguities in the questions.

Flexibility. Surveys may offer more flexibility in adapting to the needs of participants or the research context, particularly in interviews where researchers can probe for additional information or adjust the sequence of questions. Questionnaires, being self-administered, offer less flexibility in this regard.

The questions included in surveys and questionnaires are often referred to as "items" and can be of different types. Below are some of the most common types of questions included in surveys and questionnaires:

Closed-Ended Questions. These questions provide respondents with a set of predefined response options to choose from. Closed-ended questions are often used to collect quantitative data and can include multiple-choice questions, dichotomous (yes/no) questions, and Likert scale items.

Open-Ended Questions. Open-ended questions allow respondents to provide their own answers in their own words. These questions are used to gather qualitative data and elicit detailed responses from participants. Open-ended questions are valuable for exploring complex topics and understanding participants' perspectives in depth.

Multiple-Choice Questions. Multiple-choice questions present respondents with a list of options, and they are instructed to select one or more responses that best apply to them. Multiple-choice questions are efficient for collecting data on categorical variables with predefined response categories.

Dichotomous (Yes/No) Questions. Dichotomous questions offer respondents only two response options, typically "yes" or "no." These questions are straightforward and easy to analyze but may lack nuance in capturing respondents' attitudes or opinions.

Likert Scale Questions. Likert scale questions measure the strength of respondents' agreement or disagreement with a statement using a scale of ordered response options, such as "strongly agree," "agree," "neutral," "disagree," and "strongly disagree." Likert scales are commonly used to assess attitudes, perceptions, or opinions.

Ranking or Rating Questions. Ranking questions ask respondents to prioritize or rank a set of items according to their preferences or importance. Rating questions require respondents to assign a value or rating to a specific attribute or statement, typically on a numerical scale.

Semantic Differential Questions. Semantic differential questions measure respondents' perceptions or attitudes toward a concept using bipolar adjectives or phrases anchored at opposite ends of a scale. Respondents indicate their position along the scale based on their perception of the concept.

Introduction to Educational Research

Matrix Questions. Matrix questions present a set of related statements or attributes in a tabular format, with a common set of response options for each row. Matrix questions are useful for assessing multiple items with similar response scales efficiently.

Sample Survey Used in Educational Research

The following survey aims to gather feedback from students about various aspects of their educational experience, including academic satisfaction, campus life, and suggestions for improvement. The questions are designed to elicit both quantitative and qualitative responses to provide a comprehensive understanding of students' perspectives.

Title: Student Satisfaction Survey

Introduction: Thank you for participating in this survey. Your feedback is valuable in helping us improve the quality of education provided at our institution. Please answer the following questions honestly and to the best of your ability.

1. Demographic Information:
   - What is your age?
     - Under 18
     - 18-24
     - 25-34
     - 35-44
     - 45 or older
   - What is your gender?
     - Male
     - Female
     - Non-binary
     - Prefer not to say
   - What is your current level of education?
     - High school
     - Undergraduate
     - Graduate
2. Academic Experience:
   - How satisfied are you with the variety of courses offered?
     - Very satisfied
     - Satisfied
     - Neutral
     - Dissatisfied
     - Very dissatisfied
   - How would you rate the quality of instruction provided by your professors?
     - Excellent
     - Good
     - Fair
     - Poor
     - Very poor
   - Are you satisfied with the resources available to support your learning (e.g., library, computer labs, tutoring services)?
     - Yes

Introduction to Educational Research

Sample Survey Used in Educational Research

- No
- How often do you engage in extracurricular activities related to your academic interests?
  - Daily
  - Weekly
  - Monthly
  - Rarely
  - Never

3. Campus Life:
   - How would you rate the overall campus environment (e.g., safety, cleanliness, facilities)?
     - Excellent
     - Good
     - Fair
     - Poor
     - Very poor
   - Are you satisfied with the availability of campus amenities (e.g., dining options, recreational facilities)?
     - Yes
     - No
   - Have you ever experienced discrimination or harassment based on your race, gender, ethnicity, or other factors at our institution?
     - Yes
     - No

4. Suggestions for Improvement:
   - What aspects of our institution do you believe need improvement?
     - Open-ended response

5. Additional Comments:
   - Is there anything else you would like to share about your experience at our institution?
     - Open-ended response

Thank you for taking the time to complete this survey. Your feedback is greatly appreciated.

By utilizing different types of survey questions, researchers can collect diverse types of data and gain comprehensive insights into various aspects of education. Surveys and questionnaires offer several advantages in educational research, including the ability to collect data from large samples efficiently, standardize data collection across participants, and facilitate quantitative analysis of responses. However, they also have limitations, such as potential response bias, reliance on self-reported data, and limited depth of information compared to qualitative data collection methods. The following list explains the advantages and disadvantages of using surveys and questionnaires in educational research:

Introduction to Educational Research

Advantages:

Efficiency. Surveys and questionnaires allow researchers to collect data from a large number of participants efficiently, making them suitable for studies with large sample sizes (Cohen, Manion, & Morrison, 2018).

Standardization. These instruments provide standardized sets of questions, ensuring consistency in data collection across participants and facilitating comparability of responses (Fraenkel, Wallen, & Hyun, 2019).

Anonymity and Confidentiality. Participants can complete surveys and questionnaires anonymously, which may encourage more honest and candid responses, particularly for sensitive topics (Gay, Mills, & Airasian, 2018).

Ease of Analysis. Data collected through surveys and questionnaires are often quantitative and can be analyzed using statistical methods, facilitating rigorous data analysis and interpretation (Cohen, Manion, & Morrison, 2018).

Accessibility. With advancements in technology, surveys and questionnaires can be administered online, making them accessible to a wide range of participants regardless of geographical location (Fraenkel, Wallen, & Hyun, 2019).

Disadvantages:

Response Bias. Participants may provide socially desirable responses or inaccurately recall information, leading to response bias and potentially compromising the validity of the data (Gay, Mills, & Airasian, 2018).

Limited Depth. Surveys and questionnaires often gather structured, closed-ended responses, which may limit the depth of information collected compared to qualitative methods like interviews or focus groups (Cohen, Manion, & Morrison, 2018).

Low Response Rates. Depending on the administration method, surveys and questionnaires may suffer from low response rates, particularly if participants perceive them as time-consuming or uninteresting (Fraenkel, Wallen, & Hyun, 2019).

Inability to Clarify. Unlike interviews where researchers can clarify questions or probe for additional information, surveys and questionnaires lack the opportunity for clarification, potentially leading to misunderstandings or incomplete responses (Gay, Mills, & Airasian, 2018).

Limited Representativeness. Surveys and questionnaires may not capture the perspectives of certain populations, such as individuals with limited literacy or access to technology, leading to sampling bias (Cohen, Manion, & Morrison, 2018).

While surveys and questionnaires offer numerous advantages, researchers should be mindful of their limitations and consider using complementary methods to ensure comprehensive data collection and analysis.

Introduction to Educational Research

Interviews

Interviews involve direct interaction between the researcher and the participant(s), where the researcher asks questions and the participant(s) respond(s) orally. Interviews can be conducted in various formats, including face-to-face, via telephone, video conferences, or even email exchanges, depending on the preferences and accessibility of participants.

Based on the flexibility of the questions asked, interviews can be structured, semi-structured, or unstructured:

1. **Structured Interviews**: In structured interviews, researchers ask predetermined questions in a fixed order to all participants. This format ensures consistency across interviews and facilitates quantitative analysis of responses.

2. **Semi-Structured Interviews**: Semi-structured interviews involve a set of core questions but allow for flexibility in probing for elaboration, clarification, or follow-up questions based on participants' responses. This format encourages deeper exploration of topics while maintaining some level of standardization.

3. **Unstructured Interviews**: Unstructured interviews are open-ended and free-flowing, with no predetermined set of questions. Researchers guide the conversation based on participants' responses, allowing for rich, detailed data but requiring strong interviewer skills to manage the interaction effectively.

Interviews offer a powerful means of collecting qualitative data in educational research, enabling researchers to gain deep insights into complex phenomena and contribute to a deeper understanding of educational practices, processes, and outcomes. However, when using interviews, researchers must consider a series of advantages and disadvantages:

Advantages:

Rich Data. Interviews allow researchers to gather detailed, nuanced data, providing insights into participants' experiences, perspectives, and contexts (Merriam & Tisdell, 2016).

Flexibility. Interview formats can be tailored to suit the research goals, the characteristics of participants, and the research context. Researchers can adapt their questions and probes dynamically during the interview (Brinkmann & Kvale, 2018).

Clarification and Probing. Interviews offer the opportunity for researchers to clarify questions, probe for deeper understanding, and explore unexpected topics or responses, enhancing the richness of the data collected (Merriam & Tisdell, 2016).

Disadvantages:

1. **Time and Resources**. Conducting interviews can be time-consuming and resource-intensive, especially when transcribing and analyzing the data. Recruiting and scheduling participants can also present logistical challenges (Brinkmann & Kvale, 2018).

2. **Interviewer Bias**. The presence and behavior of the interviewer can influence participants' responses, leading to interviewer bias. Researchers must be mindful of their own biases and strive to maintain neutrality and objectivity during the interview process (Merriam & Tisdell, 2016).

3. **Subjectivity**. Data collected through interviews are inherently subjective, reflecting participants' perceptions, interpretations, and experiences. Researchers should triangulate findings with other sources of data to enhance validity and reliability (Brinkmann & Kvale, 2018).

Observation

Observation is a valuable data collection method in educational research, providing researchers with firsthand insights into various aspects of educational settings, interactions, and behaviors. Observation involves systematically watching and recording behaviors, interactions, events, or phenomena within educational environments. Researchers may observe classrooms, playgrounds, workshops, meetings, or other educational settings to understand teaching practices, student behaviors, social dynamics, organizational processes, or the implementation of educational interventions.

Based on the role of the observer, observation can be classified as participatory or non-participatory:

Participant Observation: Researchers immerse themselves in the educational setting as active participants, engaging with participants and experiencing the context firsthand while also observing and recording behaviors and interactions (Merriam & Tisdell, 2016).

Non-participant Observation: Researchers observe the educational setting from an external standpoint without actively participating in the activities. This approach allows for more objective observation but may limit the depth of understanding compared to participant observation.

Based on the degree of structure, observations can be classified as structured or unstructured:

Structured Observations: Researchers use predefined observation protocols, checklists, or coding schemes to systematically document specific behaviors, events, or phenomena of interest. Structured observations facilitate standardized data collection and quantitative analysis of observations.

Unstructured Observations: Researchers engage in open-ended observation without predefined categories or coding schemes. Unstructured observations allow for flexible exploration of the context and emergence of unexpected themes or patterns but may require more subjective interpretation.

Researchers use observation protocols to outline the procedures and guidelines for systematically observing and recording behaviors, interactions, or events within educational settings. Below is an example of an observation protocol for studying classroom interactions:

Sample Observation Protocol Used in Educational Research

Observation Protocol: Classroom Interactions

Using the following observation protocol, researchers can systematically collect data on classroom interactions, informing insights into teaching practices, student engagement, and instructional effectiveness in mathematics education.

Research Objective: To observe and document teacher-student interactions during mathematics instruction in a middle school classroom.

Observers: Trained research assistants familiar with the research objectives and protocol.

Observation Schedule: Observations will be conducted during regular mathematics classes, three times a week, for a total of four weeks.

Observation Tools:

1. **Behavior Coding Sheet**: A structured form for recording specific teacher and student behaviors observed during the lesson.

   - Teacher behaviors:
     - Giving instructions
     - Asking questions
     - Providing feedback
     - Facilitating group work
   - Student behaviors:
     - Raising hand
     - Participating in discussion
     - Working independently
     - Seeking assistance

2. **Time Sampling Sheet**: A time-based grid for recording the occurrence and duration of different activities or interactions during the lesson.

   - Time intervals: 5 minutes
   - Activity categories:
     - Whole-class instruction
     - Small-group work
     - Independent work
     - Teacher-student interaction
     - Student-student interaction

Introduction to Educational Research

Sample Observation Protocol Used in Educational Research

Procedures:

1. **Pre-Observation Preparation**: Review observation protocol and tools. Familiarize observers with classroom layout, seating arrangements, and teacher-student roles.

2. **Observation**: Observers enter the classroom discreetly and begin recording observations according to the established schedule and tools. Observations focus on teacher-student interactions, instructional strategies, student engagement, and classroom dynamics.

3. **Data Collection**: Observers document behaviors, interactions, and activities observed during the lesson using the behavior coding sheet and time sampling sheet.

4. **Post-Observation Debriefing**: Observers meet to discuss observations, clarify any discrepancies, and ensure consistency in data collection. Researchers may review recorded data for accuracy and completeness.

5. **Data Analysis**: Recorded data are analyzed to identify patterns, trends, and themes related to teacher-student interactions, instructional strategies, and classroom dynamics.

Ethical Considerations:

- Obtain informed consent from the teacher and school administration.

- Ensure confidentiality and anonymity of students and teachers.

- Minimize disruption to the learning environment during observations.

Observation offers researchers a powerful means of collecting data in educational research, enabling them to explore complex phenomena, contexts, and interactions within educational settings. Nevertheless, when using this method, researchers must consider both its advantages and disadvantages:

Advantages:

1. **Naturalistic Data.** Observations provide naturalistic, real-time data, capturing behaviors and interactions as they naturally occur in the educational setting (Merriam & Tisdell, 2016).

2. **Contextual Understanding.** Observations allow researchers to gain an in-depth understanding of the context, culture, and dynamics of educational environments, providing insights that may not be captured through other data collection methods (Creswell & Creswell, 2017).

3. **Richness and Detail.** Observations yield rich, detailed data, including nonverbal cues, environmental factors, and contextual nuances, enhancing the depth and breadth of the research findings (Merriam & Tisdell, 2016).

Disadvantages:

1. **Observer Bias**. Researchers' interpretations and observations may be influenced by their own biases, perspectives, or preconceptions, potentially leading to observer bias. Researchers should employ reflexivity and triangulation to mitigate bias (Creswell & Creswell, 2017).

2. **Time and Resource Intensive**. Conducting observations can be time-consuming and resource-intensive, requiring careful planning, training of observers, and extensive data collection and analysis efforts (Merriam & Tisdell, 2016).

3. **Ethical Considerations**. Observations may raise ethical considerations related to privacy, confidentiality, and informed consent, particularly when observing sensitive behaviors or vulnerable populations. Researchers must ensure ethical conduct throughout the observation process (Creswell & Creswell, 2017).

Tests and Assessments

Tests and assessments are widely used in educational research to measure various aspects of student learning, performance, and achievement. They involve administering standardized or customized assessments to students to evaluate their knowledge, skills, abilities, or competencies in specific subject areas or domains. These instruments can take various forms, including multiple-choice tests, essay exams, performance assessments, portfolios, and standardized achievement tests. Tests and assessments can serve several purposes in educational research:

Diagnostic Assessment: Assessing students' prior knowledge, skills, or misconceptions to inform instructional planning and differentiation.

Formative Assessment: Monitoring students' progress and understanding throughout instruction to provide feedback and guide instructional decisions.

Summative Assessment: Evaluating students' overall learning outcomes or achievement at the end of a unit, course, or academic year.

Program Evaluation: Assessing the effectiveness of educational programs, interventions, or curricula in achieving desired learning outcomes.

Norm Referenced and Criterion Referenced Assessments. Norm-referenced instruments and criterion-referenced instruments are two distinct types of assessment tools used in educational settings to measure students' performance or achievement. Norm-referenced instruments focus on comparing individuals to their peers, while criterion-referenced instruments focus on measuring individual achievement against specific criteria or standards. Therefore, norm-referenced assessments provide information about how individuals rank relative to one another, whereas criterion-referenced assessments provide information about whether individuals have achieved specific learning objectives.

Norm-Referenced Instruments. Norm-referenced instruments compare an individual's performance against the performance of a group of peers, known as the norm group. The purpose of norm-referenced assessments is to rank individuals relative to one another and determine their position within the group. The norm group is typically a representative sample of the population for which the assessment is intended. Key characteristics of norm-referenced instruments include:

1. **Standardization**: Norm-referenced assessments are standardized to ensure consistency in administration, scoring, and interpretation across all test-takers.

2. **Ranking**: Scores on norm-referenced assessments are often reported as percentile ranks, stanines, lexiles, etc. indicating the percentage of test-takers in the norm group who scored lower or at the same level as the individual.

3. **Comparative Interpretation**: Interpretation of scores focuses on how an individual's performance compares to that of their peers. Common interpretations include classifications such as "below average," "average," or "above average."

Examples of norm-referenced instruments include standardized achievement tests like the SAT, ACT, and IQ tests.

Criterion-Referenced Instruments. Criterion-referenced instruments measure an individual's performance against predetermined criteria or standards, rather than comparing it to the performance of peers. The purpose of criterion-referenced assessments is to determine whether an individual has achieved specific learning objectives or mastered particular skills. Key characteristics of criterion-referenced instruments include:

Objective Standards. Criterion-referenced assessments are aligned with specific learning objectives or performance standards, providing clear criteria for evaluating student achievement.

Absolute Interpretation. Scores on criterion-referenced assessments are interpreted in absolute terms, indicating the extent to which an individual has met the established criteria or standards.

Diagnostic Feedback. Criterion-referenced assessments often provide detailed feedback on students' strengths and weaknesses relative to the learning objectives, allowing for targeted instruction and remediation.

Examples of criterion-referenced instruments include end-of-course exams, competency-based assessments, and proficiency tests.

In summary, norm-referenced and criterion-referenced instruments serve different purposes in educational assessment, with norm-referenced assessments emphasizing comparative performance and criterion-referenced assessments emphasizing mastery of specific skills or knowledge. Both types of assessments play important roles in evaluating student learning and informing instructional decisions.

Tests and assessments play a crucial role in educational research, providing researchers with valuable data to evaluate student learning, inform instructional practices, and assess the effectiveness of educational interventions and programs. However, researchers should be mindful of the limitations and potential biases associated with these methods and consider using a variety of assessment tools and approaches to obtain a comprehensive understanding of student learning and achievement. Below is a list of advantages and disadvantages that researchers should consider when using tests and assessments as data collection methods in educational research:

Advantages:

1. **Objective Measurement**. Tests and assessments provide standardized, objective measures of student performance, allowing for quantitative analysis and comparison across individuals or groups.

2. **Reliability**. Well-designed tests and assessments demonstrate reliability, providing consistent results across different administrations.

3. **Validity**. Valid tests and assessments accurately measure the intended learning objectives, ensuring that they assess what they purport to assess thus supporting accurate inferences.

4. **Efficiency**. Tests and assessments allow researchers to collect data from large samples of students efficiently, making them suitable for studies with large sample sizes.

Disadvantages:

1. **Limited Scope**. Tests and assessments may only measure certain types of knowledge, skills, or abilities, potentially overlooking other important aspects of learning, such as creativity, critical thinking, or problem-solving.

2. **Context Dependency**. Assessment conditions, such as testing environment, time constraints, or test format, may influence students' performance, leading to context-dependent results.

3. **Test Bias**. Tests and assessments may contain biases that disadvantage certain groups of students, such as cultural or linguistic biases, affecting the validity and fairness of the results.

4. **Overemphasis on Testing**. Overreliance on standardized tests or high-stakes assessments may narrow the curriculum, encourage teaching to the test, and neglect other important educational goals and outcomes.

Document Analysis

Document analysis is a valuable data collection method in educational research that involves the systematic examination and interpretation of written or recorded materials relevant to the research topic. These materials can include a wide range of documents, such as textbooks, curriculum guides, lesson plans, policy documents, student work samples, assessment instruments, meeting minutes, or archival records. Document analysis allows researchers to explore educational phenomena, policies, practices, and outcomes by analyzing existing written or recorded materials. Researchers examine documents to uncover patterns, themes, trends, and insights that contribute to a deeper understanding of the research topic.

The main steps of document analysis are:

1. **Document Selection**: Researchers identify relevant documents related to the research topic or question. Documents may be obtained from educational institutions, government agencies, professional organizations, online databases, or archival collections.

2. **Document Review**: Researchers systematically review and familiarize themselves with the selected documents. They read through the documents carefully, noting key themes, concepts, and information relevant to the research objectives.

3. **Data Coding and Analysis**: Researchers analyze the documents using coding schemes or thematic analysis techniques to identify patterns, recurring themes, or trends. They may categorize information, extract relevant data, and organize findings into meaningful categories or themes.

4. **Interpretation**: Researchers interpret the findings from document analysis, drawing conclusions, and generating insights about the research topic. They consider the context, significance, and implications of the documented information for educational theory, practice, or policy.

Document analysis offers researchers a valuable approach to studying educational phenomena, policies, and practices, complementing other data collection methods, and providing rich insights into the complexities of education; however, when using document analysis, researchers must evaluate this method's advantages and disadvantages:

Advantages:

Rich Data. Document analysis yields rich, detailed data, providing insights into educational policies, practices, and outcomes over time (Bowen, 2009).

Access to Historical Data. Researchers can access historical documents and archival records to study educational trends, changes, and developments over time (Bowen, 2009).

Non-intrusive. Document analysis is non-intrusive and does not require direct interaction with participants, making it suitable for studying sensitive topics or historical phenomena (Bowen, 2009).

Disadvantages:

Potential Bias. Document analysis may be subject to bias introduced by document creators or archivists. Researchers should critically evaluate the credibility, reliability, and representativeness of the documents (Bowen, 2009).

Limited Depth. Documents may provide limited insight into individuals' perspectives, motivations, or experiences compared to qualitative methods like interviews or observations (Bowen, 2009).

Access Challenges. Accessing certain documents, particularly confidential or restricted materials, may pose challenges for researchers, limiting the scope of document analysis (Bowen, 2009).

Focus Groups

Focus groups are a qualitative data collection method commonly used in educational research to gather insights, perceptions, and experiences from participants regarding specific topics or issues. They are facilitated group discussions with a small number of participants, typically ranging from six to twelve individuals, who share common characteristics or experiences relevant to the research topic. The discussions are guided by a trained facilitator using a semi-structured interview protocol, allowing participants to express their views, exchange ideas, and interact with one another. The process of conducting focus groups involves the following steps:

1. **Participant Selection**: Participants are purposefully selected based on criteria relevant to the research question or objectives. They may include students, teachers, parents, administrators, or other stakeholders with firsthand experience or knowledge related to the research topic.

2. **Focus Group Design**: Researchers design a semi-structured interview guide with open-ended questions or prompts to guide the discussion. The questions are designed to elicit participants' perspectives, experiences, and opinions on the research topic while allowing flexibility for exploration of emerging themes.

3. **Facilitation**: A trained facilitator leads the focus group discussion, encouraging participation, maintaining group dynamics, and ensuring that all participants have an opportunity to contribute. The facilitator uses active listening, probing, and summarization techniques to deepen the discussion and clarify participants' responses.

4. **Data Collection**: Focus group discussions are audio or video-recorded, with participants' consent, to capture the richness of the conversation. Researchers may also take field notes to document non-verbal cues, group dynamics, and key observations during the discussion.

5. **Data Analysis**: Recorded focus group transcripts are transcribed verbatim and analyzed using qualitative analysis techniques, such as thematic analysis or content analysis. Researchers identify patterns, themes, and recurring ideas across focus groups to generate insights and interpretations.

Focus groups offer researchers a dynamic and interactive approach to exploring educational phenomena, perspectives, and experiences, providing valuable insights for informing policy, practice, and research. When using focus groups as a data collection method, researchers should consider this method's advantages and disadvantages:

Advantages:

Depth and Richness. Focus groups generate rich, detailed data by tapping into participants' collective experiences, perspectives, and insights on the research topic (Krueger & Casey, 2014).

Group Dynamics. The interactive nature of focus group discussions allows participants to build on each other's ideas, share diverse viewpoints, and stimulate discussion, leading to deeper exploration of the research topic (Krueger & Casey, 2014).

Exploration of Complex Issues. Focus groups are well-suited for exploring complex, multifaceted issues or phenomena that benefit from diverse perspectives and group interactions (Krueger & Casey, 2014).

Disadvantages:

Group Dynamics. Group dynamics, including dominant voices, social desirability bias, or conformity pressures, may influence participants' responses and limit the diversity of perspectives shared (Krueger & Casey, 2014).

Data Analysis Complexity. Analyzing focus group data can be time-consuming and labor-intensive, requiring careful transcription, coding, and interpretation of the discussion content (Krueger & Casey, 2014).

Sample Representativeness. Focus group findings may not be generalizable to broader populations due to the small, purposive nature of the sample and the exploratory nature of the method (Krueger & Casey, 2014).

Developing New Data Collection Instruments

Developing new data collection instruments may be necessary when existing tools do not directly align with the research objectives or may not provide all the information needed to adequately address the research questions. The development of new data collection instruments typically follows a systematic process to provide evidence of validity, reliability, and relevance to the research objectives. Below is an overview of the key steps involved in the instrument development process:

1. Identify Research Objectives:
- Define the research questions, objectives, and variables of interest that the new instrument will address.
- Clarify the specific constructs or phenomena the instrument should measure or assess.

2. Review Existing Instruments:
- Conduct a thorough literature review to identify existing instruments relevant to the research topic.
- Evaluate the strengths, weaknesses, and appropriateness of existing instruments for the current study.

3. Determine Measurement Needs:
- Determine the type of data (quantitative, qualitative, or mixed methods) required to address the research questions.
- Decide on the format and structure of the new instrument (e.g., surveys, questionnaires, interviews, observations, etc.)

4. Develop Initial Instrument Items:
- Generate a pool of potential items, questions, or prompts based on the identified constructs and research objectives.
- Ensure that items are clear, concise, and relevant to the research context.

5. Expert Review and Revision:
- Seek feedback from experts in the field (e.g., researchers, practitioners, methodologists) to evaluate the content validity of the instrument.
- Revise and refine the instrument based on expert feedback to improve clarity, comprehensiveness, and relevance.

6. Pilot Testing:
- Conduct pilot testing of the instrument with a small sample of participants representative of the target population.
- Assess the feasibility, acceptability, and understandability of the instrument.
- Identify any issues with item wording, response options, or instructions and make necessary revisions.

7. Validation and Reliability Testing:
- Administer the instrument to a larger sample to assess its validity and reliability.
- Use statistical techniques (e.g., factor analysis, correlation analysis) to examine the internal consistency, construct validity, and criterion validity of the instrument.
- Test the instrument's reliability through measures such as test-retest reliability and inter-rater reliability.

8. Finalization and Documentation:
- Finalize the instrument based on the results of validation and reliability testing.
- Prepare clear and comprehensive documentation, including instructions for administration, scoring procedures, and guidelines for interpretation.

9. Dissemination and Use:
- Publish the instrument and related documentation to facilitate its use by other researchers and practitioners.
- Provide guidance on appropriate applications and interpretations of the instrument to ensure its effective use in diverse contexts.

In conclusion, instrumentation plays a crucial role in educational research by providing researchers with the tools and methods needed to collect data, measure variables, and explore complex phenomena within educational settings. Whether using surveys, questionnaires, interviews, observations, standardized tests, or newly developed instruments, researchers must carefully select and design their instruments to ensure validity, reliability, and relevance to their research objectives. By employing rigorous methods for instrument development, validation, and implementation, researchers can generate robust data that contribute to a deeper understanding of educational practices, processes, and outcomes. Additionally, ongoing advancements in technology and methodological approaches continue to expand the range of instruments available to educational researchers, offering new opportunities for innovative data collection and analysis. Ultimately, thoughtful consideration of instrumentation is essential for producing meaningful insights and informing evidence-based decision-making in education.

Summary

The chapter discusses the importance of instrumentation in educational research, which refers to the tools, techniques, and methods used to collect data for understanding various aspects of education. It delves into the specifics of data collection instruments such as surveys and questionnaires, interviews, observation, tests and assessments, focus groups, and document analysis outlining the advantages and disadvantages of each data collection method. Surveys and questionnaires are efficient for collecting data from large samples but may suffer from response bias and limited depth of information. Interviews offer rich, qualitative data but are time-consuming and subject to interviewer bias. Observation provides naturalistic data and contextual understanding but requires extensive time and resources and raises ethical considerations. Tests and assessments serve various purposes such as diagnostic, formative, summative assessment, and program evaluation, with norm-referenced and criterion-referenced assessments being prominent types. Document analysis involves systematically examining written materials to uncover patterns and insights, offering rich historical data but also facing potential biases. Focus groups gather qualitative insights from small groups, providing depth but also posing challenges in data analysis and sample representativeness. Overall, each method offers unique advantages and considerations, contributing to meaningful insights that inform educational practices and policies. The chapter also discusses the development of new data collection instruments, which is a systematic process aiming to support validity and reliability, enabling researchers to gather robust data aligned with research objectives. Overall, understanding the principles of instrumentation is essential for researchers, educators, policymakers, and stakeholders involved in improving educational outcomes and promoting evidence-based practices in education.

Suggestions for Students

Key Questions

1. What are the primary purposes of tests and assessments in educational research, and how do norm-referenced and criterion-referenced assessments differ?

2. When is the use of interviews as a data collection method most appropriate in educational research?

3. What are some advantages and limitations of using surveys and questionnaires?

4. How are tests and assessments useful in educational research?

5. Describe research scenarios where the use of surveys is preferable to interviews or observations.

6. Compare and contrast the benefits and limitations of interviews and observations. When should researchers select one versus the other?

7. What are the main steps involved in document analysis as a data collection method in educational research, and what are its advantages and disadvantages?

8. How are focus groups conducted as a qualitative data collection method in educational research, and what are their strengths and limitations?

9. What is the systematic process involved in developing new data collection instruments, and why is it important for ensuring validity and reliability?

10. What role does instrumentation play in educational research, and how can researchers use various instruments to collect robust data and inform evidence-based decision-making?

Suggestions for Instructors

Suggested Learning Activities

Instrument Selection Simulation. Divide students into small groups and assign each group a hypothetical educational research scenario. Provide a list of research questions and objectives related to each scenario. Ask each group to select the most appropriate data collection instrument(s) from a provided list (e.g., surveys, interviews, observations) and justify their choices based on the scenario's characteristics. Have groups present their selections and reasoning to the class, followed by a discussion on the suitability of each instrument for different research contexts.

Data Collection Instrument Design Project. Assign students to design a data collection instrument (e.g., survey, interview guide) for a specific educational research topic of their choice. Provide guidelines for instrument development, including considerations for clarity, relevance, cultural sensitivity, and alignment with research objectives. Have students present their designed instruments to the class, explaining their rationale behind question selection, wording, and format. Encourage peer feedback and discussion on the strengths and potential improvements of each instrument.

Advantages and Disadvantages Debate. Divide the class into two groups, with one group representing the advantages of surveys and questionnaires in educational research and the other

Suggestions for Instructors

group representing the disadvantages. Provide time for each group to research and prepare arguments supporting their assigned position. Conduct a debate where each group presents their arguments and counters the opposing group's points. Encourage critical thinking and analysis of the strengths and limitations of surveys and questionnaires, followed by a class discussion on the key takeaways from the debate.

Ethical Dilemma Case Study. Present students with a case study involving an ethical dilemma related to the use of a data collection instrument in educational research (e.g., obtaining informed consent from minors, protecting participant confidentiality). Divide students into small groups to analyze the case study, identify ethical considerations, and discuss potential courses of action. Have each group present their analysis and proposed solutions, followed by a class discussion on the ethical principles involved and the implications for research practice.

Field Observation Experience. Organize a field trip or virtual observation session to an educational setting (e.g., classroom, school, community center) where students can observe teaching practices, student interactions, or educational programs. Provide students with observation guidelines or protocols to focus their observations on specific aspects of interest (e.g., teacher-student interactions, student engagement). After the observation, facilitate a reflective discussion where students share their observations, insights, and any challenges encountered during the observation process. Encourage students to relate their observations to the concepts and principles discussed in the chapter, emphasizing the value of firsthand experiences in educational research.

References

American Educational Research Association, American Psychological Association, & National Council on Measurement in Education. (2014). Standards for educational and psychological testing. American Educational Research Association.

Bowen, G. A. (2009). Document analysis as a qualitative research method. Qualitative Research Journal, 9(2), 27-40.

Brinkmann, S., & Kvale, S. (2018). InterViews: Learning the craft of qualitative research interviewing. Sage Publications.

Cohen, L., Manion, L., & Morrison, K. (2018). Research methods in education. Routledge.

Creswell, J. W., & Creswell, J. D. (2017). Research design: Qualitative, quantitative, and mixed methods approaches. Sage Publications.

DeVellis, R. F. (2016). Scale development: Theory and applications (4th ed.). Sage Publications.

Fraenkel, J. R., Wallen, N. E., & Hyun, H. H. (2019). How to Design and Evaluate Research in Education. McGraw-Hill Education.

Gay, L. R., Mills, G. E., & Airasian, P. (2018). Educational Research: Competencies for Analysis and Applications. Pearson.

Gronlund, N. E., & Waugh, C. K. (2009). Assessment of Student Achievement (9th ed.). Pearson.

Krueger, R. A., & Casey, M. A. (2014). Focus groups: A practical guide for applied research. Sage Publications.

Krueger, R. A., & Casey, M. A. (2014). Focus groups: A practical guide for applied research. Sage Publications.

Merriam, S. B., & Tisdell, E. J. (2016). Qualitative research: A guide to design and implementation. Jossey-Bass.

Nitko, A. J., & Brookhart, S. M. (2019). Educational Assessment of Students. Pearson.

Robson, C. (2011). Real World Research (3rd ed.). Wiley.

Chapter 8. Reliability and Validity

This chapter will address the following learning objectives:
• Explain the importance of reliability and validity in educational research and their roles in ensuring the credibility of research findings.
• Analyze various types of reliability measures used in educational research.
• Explain the procedures and techniques for assessing internal consistency reliability, such as Cronbach's alpha, split-half method, and factor analysis.
• Evaluate test-retest reliability by outlining the steps involved in administering tests on two separate occasions and interpreting the correlation coefficients obtained.
• Describe parallel forms reliability and alternate forms reliability in educational research.
• Define the concept of validity in educational research.
• Differentiate between different types of validity, including content validity, construct validity, criterion validity, concurrent validity, and predictive validity.
• Analyze the process of evaluating content validity.
• Analyze the process of evaluating construct validity.
• Define the concepts of internal, external, and consequential validity.
• Analyze factors that may impact the internal, external, and consequential validity of educational research studies.
• Synthesize interrelationships between reliability and validity in educational research.

In educational research, ensuring the quality and integrity of data is paramount for drawing meaningful conclusions and making informed decisions. Central to this endeavor are the concepts of reliability and validity, which serve as key indicators of the trustworthiness and accuracy of research findings. Reliability refers to the consistency, stability, and precision of measurement tools or instruments used to collect data, while validity pertains to the extent to which an instrument accurately measures the intended construct or phenomenon of interest. Understanding and addressing reliability and validity are essential for researchers in education to design sound methodologies, interpret results accurately, and draw valid conclusions. This introduction provides an overview of reliability and validity in educational research, highlighting their significance, implications, and applications in ensuring the rigor and credibility of research studies.

Reliability

Reliability refers to the consistency, stability, and precision of measurement tools or instruments used to collect data. It reflects the extent to which the instrument produces consistent results when applied repeatedly under similar conditions. A reliable measurement tool yields consistent results across different administrations, observers, or time points, allowing researchers to have confidence in the accuracy and stability of their findings. In educational research, reliability is crucial for ensuring that the data collected accurately represent the underlying constructs or phenomena of interest. Several types of reliability exist, each assessing different aspects of measurement consistency: internal consistency, test-retest reliability, inter-rater reliability, and parallel forms reliability.

Internal Consistency

Internal consistency examines the similarity of responses across items within a measurement instrument. It assesses whether all items in a scale or questionnaire are measuring the same underlying construct. Measuring internal consistency in educational research involves assessing the degree of correlation between different items within a single measurement instrument, such as a questionnaire or test. Common methods for assessing internal consistency include Cronbach's alpha, the split-half reliability, or factor analysis.

Cronbach's alpha quantifies the extent to which items in the instrument are measuring the same underlying construct. Below are the main steps for measuring internal consistency using Cronbach's alpha coefficient:

1. Administer the measurement instrument to a sample of participants.

2. Collect responses to all items in the instrument.

3. Calculate the correlation between each item and the total score of all other items.

4. Compute the average of these correlation coefficients to obtain an overall index of internal consistency.

5. Interpret the Cronbach's alpha coefficient, with values closer to 1 indicating higher internal consistency reliability.

The split-half method is a technique used to assess internal consistency reliability by splitting a measurement instrument into two halves and comparing the scores obtained on each half. The steps for measure internal consistency using the split-half method are as follows:

1. Splitting the Instrument: Divide the measurement instrument into halves. This can be done randomly, by splitting the items in half, or systematically, by dividing the instrument based on content or item difficulty.
2. Scoring Each Half: Score the responses for each half of the instrument separately. For example, if the instrument is a questionnaire with Likert-scale items, sum the scores for each half.
3. Calculating the Correlation: Calculate the correlation coefficient (e.g., Pearson's correlation) between the scores obtained on the two halves of the instrument. This correlation coefficient reflects the degree of consistency or agreement between the two halves.
4. Adjusting for Reliability: Since splitting the instrument reduces the number of items and may decrease reliability, it's common to adjust the obtained correlation coefficient using a reliability

correction formula. The most widely used formula is the Spearman-Brown prophecy formula, which estimates the reliability of the full instrument based on the correlation of the halves.

5. Interpreting the Results: A higher correlation coefficient indicates greater internal consistency reliability. Typically, correlation coefficients above 0.70 are considered acceptable for research purposes, but this may vary depending on the context and the intended use of the instrument.

By using the split-half method, researchers can gain insights into the internal consistency of their measurement instrument and make informed decisions about its reliability and suitability for use in educational research.

Factor analysis is a statistical technique commonly used in educational research to assess the internal consistency of measurement instruments by examining the underlying structure of the data. The steps below describe the process of using factor analysis for measuring internal consistency:

1. **Data Collection**: Gather responses from participants on the measurement instrument, such as a questionnaire or survey.

2. **Factor Analysis**: Conduct factor analysis on the collected data. Factor analysis explores the relationships among variables and identifies underlying dimensions or factors that explain the patterns of correlations among the variables.

3. **Examine Factor Loadings**: Examine the factor loadings, which indicate the strength of the relationship between each item and the underlying factor. Items with high factor loadings on the same factor measure the same underlying construct.

4. **Assess Internal Consistency**: Calculate measures of internal consistency reliability based on factor analysis results. Common measures include Cronbach's alpha, which estimates the average correlation among items, and composite reliability, which considers both the factor loadings and measurement error.

5. **Interpretation**: Interpret the results of factor analysis and internal consistency measures to assess the reliability of the measurement instrument. Higher values of Cronbach's alpha or composite reliability indicate greater internal consistency.

Factor analysis provides valuable insights into the structure of the measurement instrument and the relationships among its items, helping researchers understand the underlying constructs being measured and assess the instrument's reliability.

Test-Retest Reliability

Test-retest reliability measures the consistency of results over time by administering the same test to the same group of participants on two separate occasions. The correlation between the scores obtained at the two time points indicates the extent to which the measurement is stable over time. The following steps summarize the process of measuring test-retest reliability:

1. **Administer the Test**: First, administer the test to a group of participants at the initial time point. Ensure that the testing conditions are consistent and that participants understand the instructions.

2. **Time Interval**: Determine the appropriate time interval between the initial test administration and the retest. The interval should be long enough to minimize the likelihood of participants

remembering their previous responses but short enough to prevent significant changes in the construct being measured.

3. **Re-administer the Test**: After the specified time interval has elapsed, re-administer the same test to the same group of participants under identical conditions as the initial administration.

4. **Calculate the Correlation**: Once data from both administrations are collected, calculate the correlation coefficient between the scores obtained at the two time points. The correlation coefficient (e.g., Pearson's r) measures the strength and direction of the linear relationship between the scores. A high correlation indicates high test-retest reliability.

5. **Interpretation**: Interpret the correlation coefficient to determine the extent of test-retest reliability. Generally, correlation coefficients above 0.70 are considered acceptable for most research purposes, although this threshold may vary depending on the context.

6. **Considerations**: Be mindful of potential sources of error or variability between the two administrations, such as practice effects, participant characteristics, or changes in the construct being measured. Minimizing these factors can enhance the reliability of the test-retest measurement.

Example. In educational research, test-retest reliability could be measured by administering a mathematics assessment to a group of high school students on two separate occasions with a two-week interval between administrations. The assessment would consist of a set of standardized math problems covering various topics such as algebra, geometry, and calculus. During the first administration, students would complete the assessment under controlled conditions in their classrooms. Two weeks later, the same assessment would be administered to the same group of students using the same instructions and testing environment. After collecting the data from both administrations, the scores obtained by each student on the two occasions would be compared using a correlation coefficient, such as Pearson's r. A high correlation between the scores from the first and second administrations would indicate strong test-retest reliability, suggesting that the assessment consistently measures students' mathematical abilities over time. By ensuring consistency in test administration procedures and minimizing external factors that could influence students' performance, researchers can assess the extent to which the assessment yields stable and consistent results across repeated administrations.

Inter-Rater Reliability

Interrater reliability in educational research refers to the consistency and agreement among different raters or observers when assessing the same phenomenon or data. It indicates whether multiple raters or observers interpret and score the data in a similar manner, thus reducing the potential for subjective bias or variability in the assessment process.

For example, in a study evaluating classroom behavior using an observation checklist, interrater reliability would assess whether different observers consistently provide similar scores when observing student behavior. High interrater reliability indicates that different observers are scoring the behaviors similarly, while low interrater reliability suggests inconsistency or disagreement among observers.

Interrater reliability is crucial in educational research, particularly in studies involving observations, assessments, rubrics, or other scoring systems with subjective components. Researchers often use statistical measures such as Cohen's kappa coefficient or intraclass correlation coefficient (ICC) to

Introduction to Educational Research

quantify interrater agreement and ensure the reliability of their data. Measuring interrater reliability in educational research involves several steps:

1. **Define Clear Criteria**: Clearly define the criteria or behaviors that raters will assess. This ensures that all raters have a common understanding of what they are evaluating.

2. **Train Raters**: Provide training to all raters to familiarize them with the assessment criteria and procedures. Training helps minimize individual biases and ensures consistency in rating decisions.

3. **Pilot Testing**: Conduct pilot testing with a small sample of data to assess interrater reliability before full-scale data collection. This allows researchers to identify and address any discrepancies or misunderstandings among raters.

4. **Select a Reliability Measure**: Choose an appropriate reliability measure based on the nature of the data and assessment method. Common measures include Cohen's kappa coefficient, intraclass correlation coefficient (ICC), or percent agreement.

5. **Calculate Reliability Coefficients**. Apply the selected reliability measure to the data collected by different raters. Calculate the coefficient to determine the level of agreement or consistency among raters.

6. **Interpret Results**: Interpret the reliability coefficients to assess the degree of agreement among raters. High coefficients indicate strong interrater reliability, while lower coefficients may signal the need for further training or clarification of assessment criteria.

7. **Address Discrepancies**: If discrepancies are identified, address them through additional training, clarification of criteria, or consensus-building discussions among raters. Repeat the reliability assessment process as needed until satisfactory agreement is achieved.

By following these steps, researchers can effectively measure interrater reliability in educational research, ensuring the consistency and accuracy of data collected by multiple observers or raters.

Example. Researchers are assessing the quality of student essays using a rubric. The rubric has specific criteria for evaluating aspects such as content, organization, language usage, and mechanics. To measure interrater reliability, two independent raters are assigned to evaluate the same set of student essays using the rubric. After training the raters on the rubric's criteria and scoring procedures, they independently evaluate a sample of student essays. Once all essays have been scored, the researchers calculate the interrater reliability coefficient, such as Cohen's kappa or intraclass correlation coefficient (ICC), to determine the level of agreement between the raters. For instance, if Cohen's kappa coefficient is calculated to be 0.80, it indicates strong agreement between the raters regarding the quality of the essays. Conversely, if the coefficient is lower, such as 0.60, it suggests moderate agreement and may prompt further investigation into discrepancies or areas of ambiguity in the rubric criteria. Through this process, researchers can assess the consistency of scoring among raters and ensure that the assessment of student essays is reliable.

Parallel Forms Reliability

Parallel forms reliability, also known as alternate forms reliability, evaluates the consistency of scores obtained from two different versions of the same test that are designed to measure the same construct.

Introduction to Educational Research

Both forms are administered to the same group of participants, and the correlation between their scores indicates the degree of equivalence between the two forms. The steps below describe the process of measuring parallel forms reliability:

1. **Development of Parallel Forms**: Two equivalent forms of the test are created, with each form containing items that measure the same construct but are phrased differently or have different content. It's essential to ensure that both forms are equivalent in difficulty and content.

2. **Administration of Parallel Forms**: Both forms of the test are administered to the same group of participants under similar conditions. Participants are randomly assigned to take one of the two forms to avoid bias.

3. **Data Collection**: Responses from both forms of the test are collected from the participants.

4. **Calculation of Reliability**: Parallel forms reliability is calculated by correlating the scores obtained from one form of the test with the scores obtained from the other form using a correlation coefficient, such as Pearson's r. The correlation coefficient indicates the degree of association between the two sets of scores.

5. **Interpretation**: A high correlation coefficient indicates strong agreement between the two forms of the test, suggesting high parallel forms reliability. Conversely, a low correlation coefficient suggests poor agreement between the forms, indicating low reliability.

Parallel forms reliability is particularly useful when researchers want to minimize practice effects or when repeated administration of the same test is not feasible due to fatigue or learning effects.

Example of Measuring Parallel Forms Reliability in Educational Research:

Scenario: A researcher is developing two equivalent forms of a mathematics achievement test to assess students' understanding of basic arithmetic operations. Each form consists of 50 multiple-choice questions covering addition, subtraction, multiplication, and division. The questions on both forms are carefully constructed to have similar difficulty levels and content coverage.
Procedure:

1. Development of Parallel Forms: The researcher creates Form A and Form B of the mathematics achievement test. The items on each form are designed to measure the same construct (mathematical proficiency) but are phrased differently or use different numerical examples.

2. Administration of Parallel Forms: The researcher administers both Form A and Form B of the test to a sample of 100 students from the target population. The students are randomly assigned to take one of the two forms to avoid order effects or bias.

3. Data Collection: After completing the tests, the researcher collects the responses from all participants for both Form A and Form B.

4. Calculation of Reliability: The researcher calculates the correlation coefficient between the scores obtained on Form A and Form B using statistical software. For example, Pearson's correlation coefficient (r) is computed to quantify the degree of association between the scores on the two forms.

5. Interpretation: The correlation coefficient obtained is 0.85, indicating a strong positive correlation between the scores on Form A and Form B. This high correlation suggests that the two forms of the test are consistent and reliable measures of students' mathematical proficiency.

Conclusion: Based on the results, the researcher concludes that the mathematics achievement test demonstrates high parallel forms reliability, indicating that both forms of the test are equally effective in assessing students' understanding of basic arithmetic operations. This finding provides evidence of

Example of Measuring Parallel Forms Reliability in Educational Research:
the reliability of the test and supports its use in educational assessment contexts. By employing parallel forms reliability analysis, researchers can ensure that assessment instruments yield consistent and dependable results across different test versions, enhancing the validity and trustworthiness of educational measurements.

Parallel Forms and Alternate Forms Reliability. Parallel forms reliability and alternate forms reliability are two methods used in educational research to assess the consistency of measurement between different versions of a test or assessment instrument. While these terms are often used interchangeably, they represent slightly different approaches to achieving the same goal of estimating the reliability of test scores. Nevertheless, parallel forms reliability refers to the consistency of measurement between two or more parallel forms of a test that are constructed to be equivalent in terms of content, format, and difficulty level. The key characteristic of parallel forms is that they are developed simultaneously to ensure comparability. This method involves creating multiple versions of the same test, with each version containing different items that measure the same construct or skill. Participants are randomly assigned to one of the parallel forms to complete, thereby minimizing the potential for practice effects or item familiarity to influence the results. The correlation between scores obtained on the different forms is then calculated to assess the degree of consistency in measurement.

Alternate forms reliability, on the other hand, is a broader concept that encompasses the use of multiple versions of a test or assessment instrument, regardless of whether they are developed simultaneously or not. While alternate forms reliability may involve the use of parallel forms, it can also include forms that are developed at different times or by different means. The primary focus of alternate forms reliability is to evaluate the consistency of measurement across different versions of the test, regardless of their construction process. Like parallel forms reliability, the correlation between scores obtained on the alternate forms is used to gauge reliability.

In summary, parallel forms reliability specifically refers to the consistency of measurement between simultaneously developed equivalent versions of a test, while alternate forms reliability encompasses the broader concept of consistency across multiple versions, regardless of their construction process. Both methods are valuable for assessing the reliability of test scores in educational research, providing researchers with confidence in the consistency and dependability of their measurement instruments.

In conclusion, measuring different forms of reliability in educational research is essential for ensuring the consistency and dependability of measurement instruments. By establishing high levels of reliability, researchers can have confidence in the accuracy and consistency of their data, thereby enhancing the validity and credibility of their research findings. However, it's crucial for researchers to carefully select the appropriate reliability method based on their research design, objectives, and measurement needs. Overall, robust reliability assessment contributes to the overall quality and rigor of educational research, ultimately advancing our understanding of educational phenomena and informing evidence-based practices in the field.

Validity

Validity in educational research refers to the degree to which a study accurately measures the concepts of interest and allows for accurate inferences. It ensures that the conclusions drawn from the research are meaningful and appropriate. Validity is crucial because it determines the trustworthiness and relevance of research findings for informing educational practices and policies. There are several types of validity that researchers consider when assessing the quality of their studies.

Content Validity

This type of validity refers to the extent to which a measurement instrument adequately covers the content domain it claims to measure. Content validity ensures that the items or questions included in the instrument represent the full range and depth of the content (Trochim & Donnelly, 2006). The process of measuring content validity involves several steps:

1. **Define the Domain:** Clearly define the domain that the measurement instrument is intended to assess. This involves identifying the key concepts, skills, or attributes that define the domain of interest.

2. **Develop Item Pool:** Generate a pool of items or questions that represent the various aspects of the defined domain. These items should cover a broad range of content areas and should be relevant to the content being measured.

3. **Expert Review:** Subject the item pool to review by a panel of experts in the field. Experts evaluate each item for its relevance, clarity, and representativeness of the domain. They may also provide feedback on item wording, formatting, and appropriateness for the target population.

4. **Item Analysis:** Conduct statistical analyses, such as item difficulty and discrimination indices, to identify items that perform poorly and may need to be revised or eliminated. This helps ensure that the final set of items adequately represents the content domain and provides reliable measurement.

5. **Pilot Testing:** Administer the measurement instrument to a small sample of participants to assess its clarity, comprehensibility, and relevance. Collect feedback from participants regarding their understanding of the items and any difficulties encountered.

6. **Revision:** Based on the feedback from expert review and pilot testing, revise the measurement instrument as needed to improve clarity, relevance, and representativeness of the content domain.

7. **Final Evaluation:** Once the measurement instrument has been refined, conduct a final evaluation of its content validity. This involves revisiting the initial definition of the domain and assessing the extent to which the final set of items adequately represents that domain.

8. **Documentation:** Document the process of content validation, including the criteria used to assess content validity, the results of expert review and item analysis, and any revisions made to the measurement instrument. This documentation helps establish the credibility and validity of the instrument for future users.

By following these steps, researchers can ensure that their measurement instruments have strong content validity, meaning they accurately represent the content domain they are intended to measure.

Example of Measuring Content Validity in Educational Research
Objective:
Develop a new mathematics assessment for middle school students.
Steps:
1. **Defining the Domain:** The researchers define the domain as mathematical problem-solving

Example of Measuring Content Validity in Educational Research

skills relevant to the middle school curriculum, including topics such as algebra, geometry, and arithmetic.

2. **Item Pool Development:** They generate a pool of math problems covering various content areas, difficulty levels, and problem-solving strategies. These problems are aligned with the curriculum standards and are reviewed by subject matter experts to ensure representativeness of the domain.

3. **Expert Review:** A panel of mathematics educators and assessment specialists review the item pool to evaluate each problem's relevance, clarity, and alignment with the intended domain. They provide feedback on item wording, mathematical correctness, and appropriateness for the target grade level.

4. **Item Analysis:** Statistical analyses, such as item difficulty and discrimination indices, are conducted to identify poorly performing items. Items with low difficulty or discrimination may be revised or eliminated to improve the instrument's content validity.

5. **Pilot Testing:** The assessment is administered to a sample of middle school students, and their responses are collected and analyzed. Participants are also asked to provide feedback on the clarity and relevance of the problems.

6. **Revision:** Based on the feedback from expert review and pilot testing, the researchers revise the assessment items to address any identified issues with clarity, relevance, or alignment with the domain.

7. **Final Evaluation:** The final set of assessment items is reviewed by the expert panel to ensure that it adequately represents the intended domain of mathematical problem-solving skills for middle school students.

8. **Documentation:** The researchers document the process of content validation, including the criteria used to assess content validity, the results of expert review and item analysis, and any revisions made to the assessment items. This documentation helps establish the credibility and validity of the assessment for use in middle school mathematics education.

This example demonstrates how content validity can be assessed and ensured in the development of educational assessments to accurately measure the intended domain of knowledge or skills.

Construct Validity

Construct validity assesses the extent to which a measurement instrument accurately measures the theoretical construct or concept it intends to measure. It involves examining the relationships between the measured variables and other variables as predicted by theory (Cook & Campbell, 1979). The process of measuring construct validity involves several steps:

1. **Theory Formulation:** Researchers start by clearly defining the theoretical construct they aim to measure. This could be a concept like "mathematical ability," "reading comprehension," or "critical thinking skills."

2. **Hypothesis Generation:** Based on the theoretical framework, researchers generate hypotheses about how the construct should manifest in observable behaviors or responses. For example, if the construct is "mathematical ability," hypotheses might include expectations about performance on math problems of varying complexity.

3. **Instrument Development:** Researchers design an assessment instrument (e.g., a test, survey, or questionnaire) that includes items or tasks intended to measure the construct of interest. The items should align with the theoretical framework and hypotheses.

4. **Data Collection:** The assessment is administered to a sample of participants representative of the target population. Data collected from the assessment include participants' responses to the instrument items.

5. **Statistical Analysis:** Statistical techniques are employed to analyze the relationship between the scores obtained on the assessment instrument and other variables that are theoretically related to the construct. These analyses might include correlational analyses, factor analyses, or regression analyses.

6. **Convergent Validity:** Researchers examine whether scores on the assessment instrument correlate positively with scores from other measures that are theoretically expected to assess the same construct. This demonstrates that the new instrument converges with existing measures of the same construct.

7. **Divergent Validity:** Researchers also assess whether scores on the assessment instrument correlate less strongly with measures of different constructs. This demonstrates that the new instrument diverges from measures of unrelated constructs.

8. **Criterion-Related Validity:** Researchers evaluate whether scores on the assessment instrument predict scores on other measures or outcomes that are theoretically related to the construct of interest. This could involve comparing assessment scores to academic performance, standardized test scores, or other relevant criteria.

9. **Cross-Validation:** The validity of the assessment instrument is further confirmed by replicating the findings across different samples, contexts, or methods. This helps establish the generalizability of the instrument's validity.

10. **Interpretation and Conclusion:** Based on the results of these analyses, researchers draw conclusions about the construct validity of the assessment instrument. If the data support the hypotheses and demonstrate consistent relationships with other variables, it provides evidence for the construct validity of the instrument.

By following these steps, researchers can systematically evaluate the construct validity of their assessment instruments, ensuring that they accurately measure the intended theoretical constructs in educational research.

Example of Measuring Construct Validity in Educational Research

Objective:

Develop a new assessment designed to measure "problem-solving skills" in high school students.

Steps:

1. **Theory Formulation:** The theoretical construct, "problem-solving skills," is defined as the ability to analyze, evaluate, and solve complex problems effectively.

2. **Hypothesis Generation:** Based on the theory, hypotheses are formulated. For example:
   - Students with higher problem-solving skills scores are expected to perform better academically in subjects like mathematics and science.
   - Scores on the problem-solving skills assessment should correlate positively with scores on existing measures of critical thinking and analytical reasoning.

3. **Instrument Development:** A new assessment instrument is designed with items that require students to apply problem-solving strategies to various scenarios or tasks. These items are reviewed by experts in education and psychometrics to ensure they align with the theoretical construct.

Example of Measuring Construct Validity in Educational Research

4. **Data Collection:** The assessment is administered to a sample of high school students, along with other relevant measures such as standardized test scores and academic grades.

5. **Statistical Analysis:** Statistical analyses are conducted to assess the relationship between scores on the problem-solving assessment and other variables:
    - **Convergent Validity:** Scores on the problem-solving assessment are positively correlated with scores on existing measures of critical thinking and analytical reasoning.
    - **Divergent Validity:** Scores on the problem-solving assessment show weaker correlations with measures of unrelated constructs, such as vocabulary or memory.
    - **Criterion-Related Validity:** Scores on the problem-solving assessment predict academic performance in math and science classes, as well as success on standardized tests known to assess problem-solving abilities.

6. **Cross-Validation:** The study's findings are replicated with a different sample of high school students or in different educational settings to confirm the validity of the assessment instrument across diverse populations.

7. **Interpretation and Conclusion:** If the data support the hypotheses and demonstrate consistent relationships with other variables, it provides evidence for the construct validity of the problem-solving assessment. Researchers can conclude that the assessment effectively measures students' problem-solving skills as intended.

Through this example, researchers can systematically evaluate the construct validity of the problem-solving assessment, ensuring its usefulness in educational research and practice.

Criterion Validity

Criterion validity examines the degree to which the scores obtained from a measurement instrument correlate with scores from a criterion measure that assesses the same construct. It involves comparing the scores obtained from the new instrument with those from an established measure to determine their level of agreement (Cook & Campbell, 1979).

Measuring criterion validity in educational research involves assessing whether scores obtained from a particular assessment instrument accurately predict performance on a criterion or outcome that is theoretically related to the construct being measured. Below is a step-by-step process:

1. **Selection of Criterion:** Researchers begin by identifying a criterion or outcome variable that represents the construct being measured by the assessment instrument. This criterion could be academic performance, job performance, or some other relevant measure.

2. **Administration of Assessment Instrument:** The assessment instrument is administered to a sample of participants, and scores are obtained from their responses. This step ensures that there is data to correlate with the criterion.

3. **Collection of Criterion Data:** Data on the criterion variable are collected from the same participants or a separate sample. For example, if the criterion is academic performance, researchers might collect students' grades or standardized test scores.

4. **Correlational Analysis:** Statistical techniques, such as Pearson's correlation coefficient or Spearman's rank correlation coefficient, are used to examine the relationship between scores obtained from the assessment instrument and scores on the criterion measure.

5. **Interpretation of Correlation:** The strength and direction of the correlation coefficient indicate the degree to which scores on the assessment instrument are related to performance on the criterion. A strong, positive correlation suggests good criterion validity, indicating that the assessment instrument accurately predicts performance on the criterion variable.

6. **Validity Coefficients:** Researchers may calculate validity coefficients, such as sensitivity, specificity, positive predictive value, or negative predictive value, to provide additional information about the accuracy of the assessment instrument in predicting performance on the criterion.

7. **Cross-Validation:** To ensure the robustness of the findings, researchers may replicate the analysis using different samples or criterion measures. This helps establish the generalizability of the criterion validity evidence.

8. **Interpretation and Conclusion:** Based on the results of the correlational analysis and validity coefficients, researchers draw conclusions about the criterion validity of the assessment instrument. If the data support a significant and meaningful relationship between scores on the instrument and performance on the criterion, it provides evidence for criterion validity.

By following these steps, researchers can systematically evaluate the criterion validity of their assessment instruments, ensuring that they accurately predict performance on relevant outcomes in educational research.

Example. Let's consider a scenario where researchers are developing a new mathematics assessment tool for high school students. To establish criterion validity, they decide to compare scores on their new assessment with scores from an established standardized mathematics test that is widely used and accepted as a measure of mathematical ability. First, the researchers administer both the new assessment and the standardized mathematics test to a sample of high school students from diverse backgrounds. They ensure that the administration conditions for both tests are standardized to minimize any extraneous factors that could affect students' performance. Next, they analyze the correlation between the scores obtained on the new assessment and those obtained on the standardized mathematics test. A high correlation coefficient would indicate that the new assessment is measuring the same construct (mathematical ability) as the established test, thus providing evidence of criterion validity. For example, if the correlation coefficient between the scores on the new assessment and the standardized mathematics test is found to be 0.85, this suggests a strong positive relationship between the two measures, providing support for the criterion validity of the new assessment as a measure of mathematical ability in high school students. By demonstrating a strong correlation with an established measure of the same construct, researchers can confidently assert the criterion validity of their new assessment tool in the context of educational research.

Concurrent Validity

Concurrent validity is a specific type of criterion validity that assesses the extent to which the scores obtained from a new measurement instrument correlate with scores from a criterion measure administered at the same time. It involves comparing the new instrument's scores with those from an established measure concurrently (Anastasi & Urbina, 1997).

Example. Suppose researchers are developing a new self-esteem questionnaire for adolescents. To establish concurrent validity, they administer both their new questionnaire and an established self-esteem scale to a sample of adolescents at the same time. By analyzing the correlation between scores on the new questionnaire and scores on the established scale, researchers can determine whether the new questionnaire accurately measures self-esteem in adolescents relative to the existing measure. If the scores on the new questionnaire demonstrate a strong positive correlation with scores on the established self-esteem scale, it suggests that the new questionnaire has concurrent validity—it is effectively measuring the same construct as the established scale. Conversely, a weak or non-existent correlation would indicate a lack of concurrent validity, suggesting that the new questionnaire may not accurately assess self-esteem in adolescents compared to the established measure.

Overall, concurrent validity provides valuable evidence of the extent to which a new assessment tool accurately measures the intended construct at the same time as an established measure, thus enhancing the credibility and usefulness of the new instrument in educational research.

Predictive Validity

Predictive validity evaluates the extent to which the scores obtained from a measurement instrument can accurately predict future performance or outcomes on a criterion measure. It involves administering the new instrument to a group of participants and assessing their performance on a criterion measure at a later time (Anastasi & Urbina, 1997). This can be done by administering the measure to a group of individuals and then tracking their performance or outcomes over time. The correlation between the scores on the measure and the subsequent performance or outcomes serves as an indicator of predictive validity.

Example. An example of measuring predictive validity in educational research could involve assessing the predictive power of a college admissions test, such as the SAT or ACT, on students' academic performance during their first year of college. Researchers would administer the admissions test to a group of high school seniors and then track their academic performance (e.g., GPA) during their first year of college. By calculating the correlation between the test scores and subsequent academic performance, researchers can determine the extent to which the admissions test accurately predicts students' success in college.

Overall, validity ensures that the findings of educational research accurately represent the phenomena being studied and can be generalized to other contexts or populations. By establishing validity, researchers enhance the credibility and usefulness of their research findings for informing educational practices and policies.

The types of validity described so far refer to the instrumentation process. Nevertheless, validity is a broad concept and can refer to the trustworthiness of an entire research study and its findings. In this context, researchers discuss concepts such as internal and external validity, or consequential validity.

Internal Validity

Internal validity refers to the extent to which a study accurately establishes relationships between the variables it investigates, without the influence of extraneous factors or confounding variables. In simpler terms, it's about ensuring that the results of a study can be attributed to the variables being studied rather than to some other factors. Several factors can affect internal validity:

Introduction to Educational Research

Research Design. The design of the study should be such that it allows for the manipulation of independent variables and the measurement of their effects on dependent variables while controlling for other factors.

Control Groups. Including control groups helps in comparing the outcomes of different experimental conditions, ensuring that any observed effects can be attributed to the manipulation of the independent variable.

Randomization. Random assignment of participants to different experimental conditions helps in minimizing the effects of individual differences and ensures that any differences observed between groups are likely due to the treatment.

Elimination of Confounding Variables. Researchers need to control for any variables other than the independent variable that could potentially influence the dependent variable, either through experimental design or statistical techniques.

Validity of Measures. Ensuring that the measures used to assess the dependent variable are valid and reliable helps in accurately capturing the effects of the independent variable.

Researcher Bias. Researchers should be cautious to avoid biases in conducting the study, analyzing the data, and interpreting the results, which could potentially influence the internal validity of the study.

Threats to internal validity in educational research are factors or conditions that can lead to erroneous conclusions about the relationships between variables being studied. These threats can compromise the researcher's ability to confidently attribute changes in the dependent variable to the independent variable. It's essential to identify and mitigate these threats to ensure the validity of research findings. Here are some common threats to internal validity in educational research:

History. Events occurring during the course of a study, other than the experimental treatment, that may influence the dependent variable. These events could be external to the study but occur within the same time frame.

Maturation. Natural changes or developments within participants that could affect their responses over time. This is particularly relevant in longitudinal studies where participants may change due to aging or other developmental processes.

Testing. Repeated testing of participants may lead to changes in their behavior or responses due to increased familiarity with the test or task rather than the experimental treatment itself.

Instrumentation. Changes in the measurement instruments or procedures used to assess the dependent variable over the course of the study can introduce bias or inconsistency in the data collection process.

Selection Bias. Systematic differences between groups of participants that are not due to the experimental treatment but rather to how participants are selected or assigned to different conditions.

Mortality. Attrition or dropout of participants from the study, which may result in a non-random sample and bias the results, particularly if certain types of participants are more likely to drop out.

Regression to the Mean. Extreme scores on a measure are likely to be less extreme upon retesting due to natural variability, rather than the effects of the experimental treatment.

Experimental Arrangements. Aspects of the experimental setting or procedures that unintentionally influence participants' responses, such as experimenter bias or the presence of demand characteristics.

By carefully designing studies and implementing appropriate controls, researchers can minimize these threats and enhance the internal validity of their research findings. Maintaining high internal validity is crucial for drawing accurate conclusions about causal relationships in educational research. However, it's essential to recognize that achieving high internal validity sometimes involves trade-offs with external validity (the generalizability of the findings to other settings or populations).

External Validity

External validity in educational research refers to the extent to which the findings of a study can be generalized to other populations, settings, or contexts beyond the specific conditions under which the study was conducted. It's about the applicability and relevance of the study's results to the broader real-world situations or diverse groups. Key considerations for assessing external validity include:

Population Representativeness. The extent to which the participants in the study represent the broader population of interest. A study with a diverse and representative sample is more likely to have high external validity.

Ecological Validity. This refers to the extent to which the study's findings apply to real-world settings and situations. Studies conducted in controlled laboratory environments may lack ecological validity compared to those conducted in naturalistic settings.

Contextual Variability. Educational interventions or treatments may have different effects depending on the specific characteristics of the educational settings, such as school culture, teaching methods, and resources available. Understanding how context influences the outcomes of a study is essential for assessing external validity.

Time Stability. The stability of the study's findings over time is also crucial for external validity. Educational practices and policies may change over time, so it's essential to consider whether the study's findings are likely to remain relevant and applicable in the future.

Cross-Cultural Validity. If the study involves participants from different cultural backgrounds, it's essential to assess whether the findings can be generalized across cultures or whether cultural factors may influence the results.

Ensuring high external validity is important for making meaningful and applicable conclusions in educational research. However, achieving high external validity often involves trade-offs with internal validity, as increasing the generalizability of the findings may require sacrificing some control over the research conditions.

Consequential Validity

Consequential validity in educational research refers to the ethical and practical implications of the study's findings and the potential consequences for individuals, educational systems, and society. It goes beyond the traditional notions of internal and external validity by considering the broader impact and ethical considerations of the research. Key aspects of consequential validity include:

Introduction to Educational Research

1. **Ethical Considerations**. Researchers must consider the potential ethical implications of their study, including the rights and well-being of participants, the potential harm that could result from the research, and the ethical use of research findings.

2. **Social Justice**. Consequential validity involves examining how the research findings may impact different groups within society, including marginalized or disadvantaged populations. Researchers should consider whether their research contributes to or mitigates existing inequalities in education.

3. **Policy and Practice Implications**. Educational research often informs policy decisions and educational practices. Consequential validity involves assessing how the research findings may influence policy development, educational interventions, curriculum design, and teaching practices.

4. **Long-Term Effects**. Researchers should consider the potential long-term consequences of their research findings on individuals' educational outcomes, career opportunities, and overall well-being.

5. **Stakeholder Perspectives**. Consequential validity requires engaging with stakeholders, including educators, policymakers, students, parents, and community members, to understand their perspectives and concerns regarding the research and its implications.

By considering consequential validity, researchers can ensure that their work not only produces valid and reliable findings but also contributes positively to the improvement of education and society.

Example: Considering Consequential Validity in the Development of a Research Study

The following example describes a research study examining the effectiveness of a new teaching method aimed at improving literacy skills among elementary school students. In this example, we'll explore how researchers might consider consequential validity throughout the research process:

1. **Research Design**: Before conducting the study, researchers would consider the potential consequences of the research design on various stakeholders. They might choose a mixed-methods approach, combining quantitative measures of literacy skills with qualitative data on student engagement and teacher experiences. This approach could provide a more comprehensive understanding of the intervention's effects and address the concerns of both educators and policymakers.

2. **Participant Selection**: Researchers would carefully select participants to ensure that the study includes a diverse range of students from different socioeconomic backgrounds, language abilities, and learning styles. By doing so, they can better understand how the intervention might impact various student populations and avoid exacerbating existing inequalities in education.

3. **Implementation**: Throughout the implementation of the teaching intervention, researchers would monitor its effects on students' literacy skills, as well as any unintended consequences, such as changes in student motivation or attitudes towards learning. They would also collect feedback from teachers and students to assess the intervention's acceptability and feasibility within real-world classroom settings.

4. **Data Analysis**: During data analysis, researchers would consider not only the statistical significance of the intervention's effects but also the practical significance and potential implications for educational practice. They might use qualitative data to identify underlying mechanisms of change and explore how the intervention aligns with broader educational

goals, such as promoting critical thinking skills or fostering a love of reading.

5. **Dissemination of Findings**: When disseminating the study findings, researchers would consider how to communicate the results in a way that is accessible and relevant to different stakeholders, including teachers, school administrators, policymakers, and parents. They would highlight both the benefits and limitations of the intervention and provide recommendations for its implementation based on the evidence collected.

Throughout the research process, researchers would continuously reflect on the ethical implications of their work and strive to minimize harm while maximizing the potential benefits for students, educators, and society. By considering consequential validity, researchers can ensure that their research contributes positively to the improvement of educational practice and policy.

Reliability versus Validity

Reliability and validity are two essential concepts in educational research, and they are closely related but distinct from each other. Reliability refers to the consistency, stability, or repeatability of measurements or observations. In other words, a reliable measurement tool produces consistent results over time or across different administrations when the phenomenon being measured remains unchanged. On the other hand, validity refers to the accuracy, truthfulness, or appropriateness of a measurement tool in assessing the intended construct or phenomenon. In essence, validity addresses whether a measurement tool measures what it is supposed to measure.

The relationship between reliability and validity lies in their interdependence. While reliability is a prerequisite for validity, a reliable measurement does not necessarily guarantee validity. A measurement tool can be reliable but not valid if it consistently produces consistent results that are consistently incorrect or unrelated to the construct being measured. Conversely, a measurement tool must be reliable to be valid because inconsistent or unstable measurements undermine the accuracy and trustworthiness of the assessment.

In educational research, researchers aim to develop measurement tools that are both reliable and valid to ensure that their findings accurately reflect the phenomena under investigation. Achieving both reliability and validity requires careful attention to the design, development, and validation of measurement instruments, as well as rigorous data collection and analysis procedures. By establishing the reliability and validity of their measurement tools, researchers can enhance the credibility and integrity of their research findings and draw meaningful conclusions about the educational phenomena they study.

Summary

The chapter delves into the crucial concepts of reliability and validity in educational research. Reliability refers to the consistency, stability, and precision of measurement tools, ensuring that results are dependable over time and across different conditions. Various types of reliability measures exist, including internal consistency reliability, test-retest reliability, inter-rater reliability, and parallel forms reliability. Validity in educational research emphasizes the importance of ensuring that studies accurately measure the concepts of interest and allow for meaningful inferences. Validity determines the trustworthiness and relevance of research findings for informing educational practices and policies. Several types of validity are discussed, including content validity, construct validity, criterion validity, concurrent validity, and predictive validity. In addition to instrumentation validity, the chapter discussed validity in reference to the overall design and findings of research studies. It explains the concept of internal, external, and consequential validity and discussed the factors that may impact them. Additionally, the chapter emphasizes that reliability and validity are closely related but distinct concepts. Both reliability and validity are essential for ensuring the credibility and integrity of research findings in educational research.

Suggestions for Students

Key Questions

1. What is the difference between reliability and validity in educational research?
2. Why is reliability important in educational research, and how does it impact the credibility of research findings?
3. Can you explain the concept of internal consistency reliability and provide examples of techniques used to measure it?
4. How do researchers assess test-retest reliability, and why is it essential in educational research?
5. What is inter-rater reliability, and why is it crucial in studies involving observations or assessments with subjective components?
6. Could you explain the process of measuring parallel forms reliability and provide an example?
7. What is the difference between parallel forms reliability and alternate forms reliability?
8. How do reliability assessments contribute to the overall quality and rigor of educational research?
9. What are some potential sources of error or variability that researchers need to consider when assessing reliability?
10. What is validity in the context of educational research, and why is it essential for ensuring the trustworthiness of research findings?
11. Can you explain the difference between content validity and construct validity? Provide examples of each type of validity in educational research.
12. Describe the steps involved in assessing content validity. Why is each step important, and how does it contribute to ensuring the validity of measurement instruments?
13. How is construct validity evaluated in educational research? Discuss the key components of the process and the types of analyses used to establish construct validity.
14. Why are criterion validity, concurrent validity, and predictive validity important in educational research? Provide examples of how each type of validity is applied in assessing the effectiveness of measurement instruments.
15. How does internal validity impact the overall quality and rigor of educational research?
16. Explain what researchers can do to ensure the internal validity of a study. Provide examples of threats to internal validity.
17. Can you explain the concept of external validity?
18. Explain the trade-off between internal and external validity and provide examples.
19. Why is consequential validity important in educational research? Provide at least one example.
20. Can educational assessments be reliable without being valid? Can they be valid without being reliable? Please explain and provide examples.

Suggestions for Instructors

Suggested Learning Activities

Reliability Analysis Exercise. Provide students with a dataset containing responses to a questionnaire. Ask them to calculate Cronbach's alpha coefficient to assess the internal consistency

Suggestions for Instructors

reliability of the questionnaire items. Students should interpret the alpha coefficient and discuss the implications of their findings.

Test-Retest Reliability Assessment. Have students design a study to assess the test-retest reliability of an educational assessment tool. They should plan the administration of the test to a sample population at two different time points, determine the appropriate time interval, and analyze the correlation between the scores obtained at each time point.

Inter-Rater Reliability Practice. Present students with video clips depicting classroom interactions. Divide them into groups and assign each group to independently rate the behavior observed in the videos using a provided rubric. Afterward, have groups compare their ratings and calculate inter-rater reliability using Cohen's kappa coefficient or intraclass correlation coefficient.

Parallel Forms Reliability Experiment. Create two versions of a mathematics test with different sets of questions but equivalent difficulty levels. Randomly assign students to take one of the two forms. After administering the tests, calculate the correlation between the scores obtained from both forms to evaluate parallel forms reliability. Discuss the implications of the correlation coefficient on the reliability of the test.

Internal/External Validity Analysis Exercise. Provide students with a set of research studies. Ask them to analyze each study and evaluate the internal and external validity. Encourage students to discuss the strengths and limitations of each study's validity assessment.

Measurement Instrument Critique. Present students with a sample measurement instrument used in educational research (e.g., a questionnaire, test, or assessment). In small groups, have students critique the instrument's validity by examining its alignment with theoretical constructs, the clarity of its items, and the appropriateness of its scoring methods. Each group can then present their findings and recommendations for improving validity.

Validity Case Studies. Assign students to read case studies involving validity issues in educational research. These case studies could include scenarios where researchers encounter challenges in establishing validity or where validity concerns lead to revisions in research designs. After reading each case study, students can engage in group discussions to identify the validity issues, propose solutions, and reflect on the implications for research practice.

Validity Assessment Project. Divide students into small research teams and assign each team a specific educational topic or concept (e.g., reading comprehension, student motivation). Task each team with developing a research study that includes the design of a measurement instrument with strong validity. Students should outline the steps they would take to establish validity, including defining the construct, developing items, conducting pilot testing, and analyzing validity evidence.

Validity Debate. Organize a debate where students take on the roles of researchers advocating for consequential validity approaches in educational research. Assign each group a specific perspective to argue and provide them with supporting evidence from the literature. After the debate, facilitate a discussion where students compare and contrast consequential validity perspectives and reflect on the implications for educational research and practice.

References

American Educational Research Association, American Psychological Association, & National Council on Measurement in Education. (2014). Standards for educational and psychological testing. American Educational Research Association.

Introduction to Educational Research

Anastasi, A., & Urbina, S. (1997). Psychological Testing (7th ed.). Prentice Hall.

Babbie, E. (2016). The Practice of Social Research. Cengage Learning.

Brown, T. A. (2015). Confirmatory Factor Analysis for Applied Research (2nd ed.). Guilford Press.

Campbell, D. T., & Stanley, J. C. (1963). Experimental and quasi-experimental designs for research. Houghton Mifflin.

Carmines, E. G., & Zeller, R. A. (1979). Reliability and Validity Assessment (Quantitative Applications in the Social Sciences). SAGE Publications, Inc.

Cohen, R. J., & Swerdlik, M. E. (2017). Psychological Testing and Assessment: An Introduction to Tests and Measurement (9th ed.). McGraw-Hill Education.

Cook, D. A., & Beckman, T. J. (2006). Current concepts in validity and reliability for psychometric instruments: Theory and application. The American journal of medicine, 119(2), 166-e7.

Cronbach, L. J. (1951). Coefficient alpha and the internal structure of tests. Psychometrika, 16(3), 297-334.

DeVellis, R. F. (2016). Scale development: Theory and applications (Vol. 26). Sage publications.

Downing, S. M. (2003). Validity: On the meaningful interpretation of assessment data. Medical education, 37(9), 830-837.

Gay, L. R., Mills, G. E., & Airasian, P. (2011). Educational research: Competencies for analysis and applications. Pearson.

Guba, E. G., & Lincoln, Y. S. (1989). Fourth generation evaluation. Sage Publications.

Kline, T. J. (2013). Handbook of psychological testing. Routledge.

Kuncel, N. R., Hezlett, S. A., & Ones, D. S. (2001). A comprehensive meta-analysis of the predictive validity of the Graduate Record Examinations: Implications for graduate student selection and performance. Psychological Bulletin, 127(1), 162–181.

Marshall, C., & Rossman, G. B. (2015). Designing qualitative research. Sage Publications.

Messick, S. (1989). Validity. In R. L. Linn (Ed.), Educational measurement (3rd ed., pp. 13–103). American Council on Education and Macmillan.

Morrow, J. (2005). Ethical issues in educational research. In K. Kempf-Leonard (Ed.), Encyclopedia of Social Measurement (Vol. 1, pp. 757-762). Academic Press.

Niu, L., Behling, S., & Du, Y. (2011). Assessing the predictive validity of the SAT: A meta-analysis and comparison with the ACT. Journal of Educational Measurement, 48(1), 1–18.

Nunnally, J. C., & Bernstein, I. H. (1994). Psychometric theory (3rd ed.). McGraw-Hill.

Powers, D. E., & Rock, D. A. (1999). Effects of coaching on SAT I: Reasoning Test scores. Journal of Educational Measurement, 36(2), 93–118.

Shadish, W. R., Cook, T. D., & Campbell, D. T. (2002). Experimental and quasi-experimental designs for generalized causal inference. Houghton Mifflin.

Introduction to Educational Research

Stake, R. E. (2010). Qualitative research: Studying how things work. Guilford Press.

Tabachnick, B. G., & Fidell, L. S. (2013). Using Multivariate Statistics (6th ed.). Pearson.

Trochim, W. M. (2006). Research methods: The concise knowledge base. Atomic Dog Publishing.

Yin, R. K. (2017). Case study research and applications: Design and methods. Sage Publications.

Zwick, R., & Schlemer, L. (2004). SAT validity for linguistic minorities at selective colleges. Educational Testing Service.

Zwick, R., Brown, M. A., & Sklar, J. C. (2013). Fair game? The predictive validity of the SAT for black and Latino freshmen. Educational Measurement: Issues and Practice, 32(4), 5–14.

Chapter 9. Quantitative Research Designs

This chapter will address the following learning objectives:
• Identify the key components and methodologies of quantitative research designs in educational research.
• Explain the significance of quantitative research methods in understanding educational phenomena and informing policy and practice decisions.
• Describe the characteristics and applications of experimental designs.
• Compare and contrast different experimental designs in terms of their advantages, disadvantages, and suitability for investigating causal relationships in educational research.
• Evaluate the practical constraints and challenges of implementing experimental designs in educational research.
• Discuss the advantages and limitations of quasi-experimental designs compared to experimental designs in educational research.
• Analyze the applications of causal-comparative research designs in educational research and their implications for understanding relationships between variables.
• Summarize the fundamental principles of correlational research designs and their significance in educational.
• Identify the distinguishing characteristics of descriptive research designs and their role in providing snapshots of educational phenomena.
• Explain the process and importance of meta-analysis in synthesizing findings from multiple studies to draw more robust conclusions and identify patterns across diverse research literature in education.
• Analyze the key features of longitudinal research designs and their utility in tracking developmental changes over time, including cohort effects and the assessment of causal relationships.
• Evaluate the essential components of cross-sectional research designs and their application in comparing different groups at a single point in time to explore variations in educational phenomena across diverse populations.

Quantitative research methods play a vital role in educational research by providing systematic approaches to gather, analyze, and interpret numerical data to understand educational phenomena. These methods employ structured instruments, statistical techniques, and standardized procedures to investigate educational issues, assess interventions, and inform policy and practice decisions. From examining the effectiveness of teaching strategies to identifying factors influencing student achievement, quantitative research offers valuable insights into the complex dynamics of education.

Quantitative research in education often involves large-scale surveys, experimental studies, quasi-experimental designs, and statistical analyses to explore relationships between variables, test hypotheses, and make predictions. By employing rigorous methodologies and statistical analyses, researchers can generate reliable and generalizable findings that contribute to the advancement of knowledge in the field of education. Key components of quantitative research in education include specific research designs, sampling techniques, data collection methods, data analysis procedures, and interpretation of results.

Researchers must carefully plan and execute each stage of the research process to ensure the validity, reliability, and credibility of their findings.

Types of Quantitative Research Designs

Quantitative research designs encompass various methodologies used to investigate relationships between variables, test hypotheses, and analyze numerical data in educational research. These designs offer systematic approaches to collecting and analyzing data, allowing researchers to draw valid and reliable conclusions. Below we describe some common quantitative research designs.

Experimental Design

Experimental designs involve manipulating an independent variable to observe its effects on a dependent variable while controlling for other variables. Random assignment of participants to experimental and control groups helps ensure internal validity. These designs are used to establish causal relationships between variables by systematically varying the conditions under which participants are exposed to the independent variable. Here are some common experimental designs used in educational research:

Pretest-Posttest Control Group Design: In this design, participants are randomly assigned to either an experimental group or a control group. Both groups are assessed on the dependent variable before and after the intervention, but only the experimental group receives the treatment or intervention. Any differences in posttest scores between the groups can be attributed to the intervention.

Posttest-Only Control Group Design: Similar to the pretest-posttest design, participants are randomly assigned to experimental and control groups. However, in this design, participants are only assessed on the dependent variable after the intervention. This design is less susceptible to threats such as testing effects and regression to the mean but may lack baseline data for comparison.

Solomon Four-Group Design: This design combines elements of both the pretest-posttest control group and posttest-only control group designs to control for testing effects and interaction effects. It includes two experimental groups (one with pretests and one without) and two control groups (one with pretests and one without), allowing researchers to assess the impact of the intervention while also accounting for preexisting differences between groups.

Factorial Design: Factorial designs involve manipulating two or more independent variables to examine their main effects and interaction effects on the dependent variable. This design allows researchers to investigate how different factors interact to influence outcomes, providing a more comprehensive understanding of the relationships between variables.

Randomized Controlled Trial (RCT): RCTs are considered the gold standard for evaluating the effectiveness of educational interventions. Participants are randomly assigned to either an experimental group receiving the intervention or a control group receiving no intervention or a placebo. RCTs minimize bias and maximize internal validity by ensuring that any differences in outcomes between groups can be attributed to the intervention.

Example of Experimental Study in Educational Research

Research Question: Does the use of a mindfulness intervention improve students' concentration levels in the classroom?

Experimental Design:

1. **Participants**: The participants are 60 elementary school students from two classes within the same school.

2. **Random Assignment**: The students are randomly assigned to either the experimental group or the control group. Each class is randomly divided into two groups: one experimental group and one control group.

3. **Intervention**: The experimental group participates in a mindfulness intervention for 10 minutes at the beginning of each school day for eight weeks. The intervention consists of guided mindfulness exercises led by a trained instructor.

4. **Control Group**: The control group continues with their regular classroom activities without participating in the mindfulness intervention.

5. **Data Collection**:

    - Pretest: Before the intervention begins, all students complete a concentration assessment, such as a sustained attention task or a concentration questionnaire.

    - Posttest: After the eight-week intervention period, all students complete the concentration assessment again.

6. **Data Analysis**: The pretest and posttest scores of the experimental and control groups are compared to determine if there are any significant differences in concentration levels between the two groups. Statistical analysis, such as independent samples t-tests or analysis of covariance (ANCOVA), is used to assess the effectiveness of the mindfulness intervention.

7. **Results**: If the experimental group shows a significant improvement in concentration levels compared to the control group, it can be concluded that the mindfulness intervention had a positive effect on students' concentration levels in the classroom.

This experimental research design allows researchers to investigate whether the mindfulness intervention leads to improvements in students' concentration levels while controlling for potential confounding variables. Random assignment helps ensure that any differences between the experimental and control groups can be attributed to the intervention rather than other factors.

Experimental designs offer a powerful method for determining causality in educational research. By carefully manipulating variables and controlling for potential confounding factors, researchers can draw meaningful conclusions about the effectiveness of educational interventions and instructional strategies. While experimental research offers valuable insights into causal relationships in educational research, researchers must carefully consider its advantages and disadvantages when designing and interpreting studies.

Advantages:

Causal Inference. Experimental research allows researchers to establish causal relationships between variables by manipulating the independent variable and observing its effects on the dependent variable. This enables researchers to determine the effectiveness of educational interventions and instructional strategies.

Introduction to Educational Research

Controlled Conditions. Experimental designs allow researchers to control extraneous variables that may influence the results, thus increasing the internal validity of the study. Random assignment of participants to different conditions helps ensure that any differences between groups are due to the intervention rather than other factors.

Replication and Generalizability. Experimental studies can be replicated in different settings or with different populations to assess the generalizability of the findings. Replication enhances the reliability and validity of research findings and allows for the identification of consistent effects across diverse contexts.

Quantitative Analysis. Experimental research generates quantitative data that can be analyzed using statistical techniques to assess the magnitude and significance of treatment effects. This allows for precise measurement and comparison of outcomes between groups.

Disadvantages:

Ethical Concerns: Some experimental manipulations may raise ethical concerns, particularly when they involve random assignment to treatment and control groups or when the intervention may have potential risks or harm to participants. Researchers must ensure that ethical guidelines are followed to protect participants' rights and well-being.

External Validity: Experimental research designs may sacrifice external validity in favor of internal validity. Strict control over experimental conditions and random assignment may limit the generalizability of findings to real-world educational settings or diverse populations.

Practical Constraints: Conducting experimental research in educational settings can be challenging due to logistical constraints, such as limited resources, time constraints, and cooperation from participants. Implementing interventions and controlling for extraneous variables in complex educational environments may be difficult.

Demand Characteristics and Hawthorne Effect: Participants in experimental studies may alter their behavior or responses due to awareness of being studied (demand characteristics) or simply because they are part of a research study (Hawthorne effect), which can confound the results.

Quasi-Experimental Design

Quasi-experimental research designs are used in educational research when random assignment of participants to different conditions is not feasible or ethical. These designs share similarities with experimental designs but lack the strict control over variables that characterize true experiments. Quasi-experimental designs are valuable for investigating causal relationships in real-world educational settings where researchers may not have full control over the conditions of the study. Below are some common quasi-experimental research designs used in educational research:

Non-equivalent Control Group Design. In this design, participants are assigned to either an experimental group or a control group, but without random assignment. The groups may be selected based on pre-existing characteristics, such as different classrooms or schools. Pre-test and post-test measures are used to assess changes in the dependent variable over time, allowing researchers to compare outcomes between groups.

Introduction to Educational Research

Time-Series Design. Time-series designs involve collecting data on the dependent variable at multiple time points before and after the implementation of an intervention. By examining changes in the dependent variable over time, researchers can assess the effects of the intervention while controlling for temporal trends and other extraneous variables.

Interrupted Time-Series Design. This design combines elements of the time-series design with the addition of an intervention or treatment at a specific point in time. Data are collected before and after the intervention, allowing researchers to compare the pre-intervention and post-intervention trends in the dependent variable. The interruption (intervention) serves as a quasi-experimental manipulation, but random assignment is typically not feasible.

Regression Discontinuity Design. In this design, participants are assigned to different groups based on a cutoff score on a continuous variable (e.g., a standardized test score). Participants just above or below the cutoff score are treated differently, allowing researchers to compare outcomes between the two groups. This design exploits the natural discontinuity in assignment to approximate the effects of an experimental manipulation.

Matched Groups Design. In this design, participants in the experimental group are matched with participants in the control group based on pre-existing characteristics, such as age, gender, or academic performance. Matching helps ensure that the groups are similar on relevant variables, reducing the risk of confounding.

Example of Quasi-Experimental Study in Educational Research

Research Question: Does the implementation of a new teaching method improve students' math achievement in a middle school classroom?

Quasi-Experimental Design:

1. **Participants**: The participants are 60 students from two different classes in the same middle school.
2. **Non-Equivalent Control Group**: The first class (Class A) serves as the experimental group, while the second class (Class B) serves as the control group. Participants are not randomly assigned to groups due to logistical constraints.
3. **Intervention**: In Class A, the teacher implements a new teaching method focused on interactive problem-solving activities and peer collaboration. The teacher receives training and support to implement the new method effectively. In Class B, the teacher continues with their usual teaching practices.
4. **Pretest-Posttest Measures**: Both classes are assessed on their math achievement using a standardized math test at the beginning of the school year (pretest) and again at the end of the school year (posttest).
5. **Data Analysis**: The pretest and posttest scores of both classes are compared to determine if there are any significant differences in math achievement between Class A (experimental) and Class B (control). Statistical analysis, such as analysis of covariance (ANCOVA) or propensity score matching, is used to control for pre-existing differences between the groups.
6. **Results**: If Class A demonstrates a significant improvement in math achievement compared to Class B after controlling for pre-existing differences, it can be concluded that the new teaching method had a positive effect on students' math achievement.

In this quasi-experimental study, the researcher cannot randomly assign students to different classes due to practical constraints. Instead, they leverage the existing differences between classes to approximate the conditions of a true experiment. By carefully controlling for pre-existing differences and comparing outcomes between groups, the researcher can still draw meaningful conclusions about the effectiveness of the new teaching method in improving students' math achievement.

Introduction to Educational Research

Quasi-experimental research designs offer valuable alternatives to experimental designs in educational research, allowing researchers to investigate causal relationships in real-world settings where random assignment may not be feasible or ethical. Nevertheless, researchers must be aware that in addition to several advantages quasi-experimental designs also have some disadvantages.

Advantages:

1. **Practicality**. Quasi-experimental designs are often more practical than true experimental designs, especially in educational settings where random assignment may be challenging or unethical. Quasi-experiments allow researchers to investigate causal relationships in real-world contexts where full experimental control is not feasible.

2. **Ecological Validity**. Quasi-experimental designs tend to have higher ecological validity than laboratory-based experiments because they are conducted in naturalistic settings. This increases the generalizability of findings to real-world educational environments and enhances the relevance of research for educational practice.

3. **Ethical Considerations**. Quasi-experimental designs may be more ethical than true experiments, particularly when random assignment to treatment conditions could have adverse consequences for participants. Quasi-experiments allow researchers to study interventions and educational practices in a way that minimizes harm to participants while still providing valuable insights.

4. **Longitudinal Analysis**. Quasi-experimental designs, such as interrupted time-series or longitudinal designs, allow researchers to examine changes in educational outcomes over time. These designs are well-suited for studying the long-term effects of interventions and educational programs.

Disadvantages:

1. **Internal Validity**. Quasi-experimental designs often have lower internal validity than true experiments because they lack random assignment. Without random assignment, it is more challenging to rule out alternative explanations for observed effects, such as selection bias or pre-existing differences between groups.

2. **Threats to Validity**. Quasi-experimental designs are susceptible to various threats to validity, such as history, maturation, and selection bias. These threats can compromise the accuracy and reliability of research findings, particularly if not adequately controlled for.

3. **Causal Inference**. While quasi-experimental designs can provide evidence of associations between variables, they cannot establish causality as definitively as true experiments. Researchers must exercise caution when interpreting causal claims based on quasi-experimental data, as alternative explanations may exist for observed effects.

4. **Limited Control**. Quasi-experimental designs offer less control over extraneous variables compared to true experiments. Researchers must carefully consider and address potential confounding variables to ensure the validity of their findings.

Causal-Comparative Designs

Causal-comparative research designs, also known as ex post facto designs, are used in educational research to explore relationships between variables and infer causality based on pre-existing differences or conditions. Unlike experimental designs, causal-comparative designs do not involve random assignment of participants to different groups or manipulation of the independent variable. Instead, researchers observe and compare groups that naturally differ in terms of the independent variable of interest. Below is a description of causal-comparative designs in educational research:

Purpose: The primary goal of causal-comparative designs is to examine the effects of an independent variable that cannot be manipulated for ethical or practical reasons. Researchers aim to identify potential causal relationships between variables by comparing groups that differ in terms of the independent variable.

Nature of the Study: Causal-comparative designs are typically retrospective and observational in nature. Researchers collect data on variables of interest after the fact, often using archival records, surveys, or standardized tests. They then compare groups based on their pre-existing differences in the independent variable.

Group Comparison: In causal-comparative designs, researchers compare groups that differ in terms of the independent variable but are similar in other respects. For example, researchers may compare groups of students from different socioeconomic backgrounds to examine the effects of socioeconomic status on academic achievement.

Control Variables: Researchers control for potential confounding variables that may influence the relationship between the independent and dependent variables. By statistically controlling for these variables, researchers can isolate the effects of the independent variable and draw more accurate conclusions about causality.

Data Analysis: Statistical techniques such as analysis of covariance (ANCOVA) or regression analysis are commonly used to analyze data in causal-comparative designs. These techniques help researchers assess the relationship between the independent and dependent variables while controlling for covariates.

Limitations: Causal-comparative designs have several limitations, including the inability to establish causality definitively. Because researchers cannot manipulate the independent variable, they cannot rule out alternative explanations or infer causality with certainty. Additionally, causal-comparative designs are vulnerable to threats to internal validity, such as selection bias or history effects.

Despite their limitations, causal-comparative designs are valuable for exploring relationships between variables in educational research and generating hypotheses for further investigation. By carefully controlling for potential confounding variables and drawing on existing data sources, researchers can gain insights into the factors that influence educational outcomes.

Introduction to Educational Research

Example of Causal-Comparative Study in Educational Research

Research Question: Does the type of school attended (public vs. private) affect students' academic achievement in mathematics?

Causal-Comparative Design:

1. **Participants**: The participants are 200 high school students, with 100 students attending public schools and 100 students attending private schools.

2. **Measurement of Variables**:
   - Type of School: Students' school type (public or private) serves as the independent variable. This variable is categorical and cannot be manipulated by the researcher.
   - Academic Achievement: Students' academic achievement in mathematics serves as the dependent variable. Achievement is measured using students' scores on a standardized math achievement test administered at the end of the school year.

3. **Data Collection**: Researchers collect data on students' school type and math achievement scores from school records or surveys. Students' math scores are obtained from the standardized test administered by both public and private schools.

4. **Data Analysis**: Statistical analysis, such as independent samples t-tests or analysis of covariance (ANCOVA), is used to compare the math achievement scores of students from public and private schools. Researchers control for potential confounding variables, such as socioeconomic status or prior academic achievement, to isolate the effects of school type on academic achievement.

5. **Results**: If students from private schools demonstrate significantly higher math achievement scores compared to students from public schools, it suggests that school type may have a causal effect on academic achievement in mathematics. Conversely, if there is no significant difference in math scores between public and private school students, it may indicate that school type does not influence academic achievement in mathematics.

In this causal-comparative study, researchers investigate the effects of school type on students' academic achievement in mathematics by comparing groups of students from public and private schools. By controlling for potential confounding variables and drawing on existing data sources, researchers can gain insights into the factors that contribute to differences in academic achievement between students from different types of schools.

Causal-comparative research designs offer several advantages and disadvantages in educational research.

Advantages:

1. **Examination of Pre-existing Differences**. Causal-comparative designs allow researchers to examine relationships between variables that cannot be manipulated for ethical or practical reasons. By comparing groups that naturally differ in terms of the independent variable, researchers can explore the effects of pre-existing differences on educational outcomes.

2. **Use of Existing Data**. Causal-comparative designs often utilize existing data sources, such as archival records, surveys, or standardized test scores. This makes these designs cost-effective and efficient, as researchers do not need to collect new data for their study.

3. **Generalizability**. Findings from causal-comparative research designs may have high external validity, as they are based on observations of naturally occurring differences in educational settings. This increases the generalizability of findings to broader populations or contexts.

4. **Control of Confounding Variables**. Researchers can control for potential confounding variables that may influence the relationship between the independent and dependent variables. By

statistically controlling for these variables, researchers can isolate the effects of the independent variable and draw more accurate conclusions about causality.

Disadvantages:

1. **Limited Causality**. Causal-comparative designs cannot establish causality definitively, as researchers cannot manipulate the independent variable. Instead, they must rely on observed differences between groups to infer causality, which may be subject to alternative explanations or confounding variables.

2. **Potential for Bias**. Causal-comparative designs are vulnerable to selection bias, where differences between groups may be influenced by factors other than the independent variable of interest. Researchers must carefully control for potential biases to ensure the validity of their findings.

3. **Validity Concerns**. Causal-comparative designs may lack internal validity compared to experimental designs, as they do not involve random assignment or manipulation of variables. Without experimental control, researchers cannot rule out alternative explanations for observed differences between groups.

4. **Difficulty Establishing Temporality**. Because causal-comparative designs are retrospective in nature, researchers may have difficulty establishing the temporal sequence of events. It can be challenging to determine whether differences in the independent variable preceded differences in the dependent variable or vice versa.

Despite these limitations, causal-comparative research designs are valuable for exploring relationships between variables in educational research and generating hypotheses for further investigation. By carefully controlling for potential confounding variables and drawing on existing data sources, researchers can gain insights into the factors that influence educational outcomes.

Correlational Design

Correlational research designs are commonly used in educational research to examine the relationships between variables without manipulating them. These designs focus on identifying associations, patterns, and trends among variables of interest. Correlational studies provide valuable insights into the complex dynamics of educational phenomena, informing theory development, program evaluation, and policy decisions. Below are several purposes of using correlational research designs in educational research:

Identifying Relationships. Correlational research allows researchers to explore the relationships between variables, such as academic achievement, socioeconomic status, and parental involvement. By measuring these variables and analyzing their associations, researchers can identify factors that may influence educational outcomes.

Predictive Validity. Correlational studies can assess the predictive validity of educational assessments and interventions. For example, researchers may examine the correlation between students' scores on standardized tests and their performance in college to determine the predictive accuracy of the tests.

Program Evaluation. Correlational research can be used to evaluate the effectiveness of educational programs and interventions. Researchers may measure variables such as program participation,

Introduction to Educational Research

instructional practices, and student outcomes to determine whether there is a relationship between program implementation and desired outcomes.

Identifying Risk and Protective Factors. Correlational studies help identify risk and protective factors that contribute to student success or failure. For instance, researchers may investigate the correlation between factors such as school climate, teacher support, and student engagement to understand their impact on academic achievement and well-being.

Survey Research. Correlational research often involves survey methods to collect data from large samples of students, teachers, parents, or other stakeholders. Surveys can measure attitudes, beliefs, behaviors, and other variables relevant to education, allowing researchers to examine correlations between different constructs.

Longitudinal Studies. Correlational research designs can be longitudinal, involving the collection of data at multiple time points to track changes in variables over time. Longitudinal studies help researchers understand the trajectory of educational outcomes and identify factors that contribute to developmental changes.

Correlational research designs offer valuable insights into the multifaceted nature of educational phenomena, providing a foundation for evidence-based decision-making in education. Below is an example of a correlational study in educational research.

Example of Correlational Study in Educational Research
Research Question: Is there a relationship between students' self-efficacy beliefs and their academic performance in mathematics?

Correlational Design:
 1. **Participants**: The participants are 200 high school students from diverse socioeconomic backgrounds.
 2. **Measurement of Variables**:
     • Self-Efficacy Beliefs: Students' self-efficacy beliefs in mathematics are assessed using a self-report questionnaire that measures their confidence in their ability to perform math tasks, overcome challenges, and succeed in mathematics.
     • Academic Performance: Students' academic performance in mathematics is measured using their scores on a standardized math achievement test administered at the end of the semester.
 3. **Data Collection**: Data on students' self-efficacy beliefs and academic performance are collected simultaneously or at different time points, depending on the research design. Students complete the self-efficacy questionnaire, and their math scores are obtained from school records.
 4. **Data Analysis**: Statistical analysis, such as Pearson's correlation coefficient or Spearman's rank correlation coefficient, is used to examine the relationship between students' self-efficacy beliefs and their academic performance in mathematics. The correlation coefficient indicates the strength and direction of the relationship between the two variables.
 5. **Results**: If the correlational analysis reveals a significant positive correlation between students' self-efficacy beliefs and their academic performance in mathematics, it suggests that students with higher self-efficacy beliefs tend to achieve higher math scores. Conversely, a non-significant or negative correlation would indicate a weaker or inverse relationship between the variables.

In this correlational study, the researcher does not manipulate students' self-efficacy beliefs or academic performance but rather examines how these variables naturally co-vary in a high school setting. By identifying the strength and direction of the relationship between self-efficacy beliefs and

Example of Correlational Study in Educational Research
academic performance, the study provides valuable insights into factors that may influence students' achievement in mathematics.

While correlational research designs offer valuable insights into relationships between variables in educational research, researchers must be mindful of their limitations and exercise caution when interpreting findings.

Advantages:

Identifying Relationships. Correlational designs allow researchers to identify relationships between variables without manipulating them. This enables researchers to explore naturally occurring patterns or associations in educational settings, providing valuable insights into potential factors influencing educational outcomes.

Predictive Ability. Correlational studies can help predict future behavior or outcomes based on the strength and direction of the relationship between variables. For example, if a positive correlation is found between students' attendance and academic performance, educators can use attendance records to predict which students may be at risk of falling behind academically.

Exploratory Research. Correlational designs are well-suited for exploratory research, where researchers aim to generate hypotheses or identify potential relationships between variables for further investigation. Correlational studies can lay the groundwork for future experimental or intervention studies by highlighting areas of interest or concern.

Ecological Validity. Correlational research is often conducted in naturalistic settings, enhancing the ecological validity of findings. By examining relationships between variables in real-world educational contexts, correlational studies provide insights that are directly applicable to educational practice and policy.

Disadvantages:

Causality. One of the main limitations of correlational designs is their limited ability to establish causality. Correlation does not imply causation, meaning that the observed relationship between variables may be due to other unmeasured variables or third variables. Without experimental manipulation, researchers cannot determine the direction of causality or rule out alternative explanations for observed associations.

Third-Variable Problem. Correlational studies are vulnerable to the third-variable problem, where the observed relationship between variables may be influenced by a third variable that has not been accounted for. Without controlling for potential confounding variables, researchers cannot establish a causal relationship between variables.

Limited Inferences. Correlational research designs can only provide information about the strength and direction of relationships between variables. They cannot explain why these relationships exist or provide evidence of causal mechanisms. As such, correlational findings should be interpreted cautiously and complemented with other research methods to gain a deeper understanding of educational phenomena.

Descriptive Design

Descriptive research designs in educational research aim to describe characteristics, behaviors, attitudes, or phenomena within educational settings without manipulating or altering them. These designs provide a snapshot or overview of the status quo, allowing researchers to identify patterns, trends, or relationships between variables. They rely on descriptive data analytic procedures and to not involve hypothesis testing. This type of design may be suitable for measuring variables and exploring potential associations between them. However, it's important to note that such designs do not establish relationships between variables. Descriptive research, often known as "observational studies," positions the researcher purely as an observer. Descriptive research is particularly useful for generating hypotheses, exploring topics that are not well understood, or providing a foundation for further investigation. Below is a description of descriptive research designs in educational research:

Purpose. The primary goal of descriptive research designs is to provide a detailed description of variables or phenomena within educational settings. Researchers seek to answer questions such as "What is happening?" or "What are the characteristics of this phenomenon?" without attempting to establish causal relationships.

Nature of the Study. Descriptive research designs are observational and non-experimental in nature. Researchers observe and record behaviors, attitudes, or characteristics of individuals or groups within educational settings without intervening or manipulating variables. Descriptive studies may involve surveys, interviews, observations, or archival data analysis to collect information.

Variables. Descriptive research may focus on various types of variables, including demographic variables (e.g., age, gender, ethnicity), academic variables (e.g., grades, test scores, enrollment rates), behavioral variables (e.g., classroom behavior, study habits), or attitudinal variables (e.g., attitudes towards school, motivation).

Data Collection. Data in descriptive research designs are collected through various methods, depending on the research questions and objectives. Researchers may administer surveys or questionnaires to collect self-report data, observe behaviors directly in educational settings, or analyze existing datasets or archival records.

Data Analysis. Descriptive data analysis involves summarizing and organizing the collected data to identify patterns, trends, or relationships between variables. Researchers may use descriptive statistics, such as measures of central tendency (e.g., mean, median, mode) and measures of variability (e.g., standard deviation, range), to describe the characteristics of variables.

Advantages. Descriptive research designs offer several advantages, including the ability to provide a detailed overview of educational phenomena, generate hypotheses for further investigation, and inform educational practice and policy. Descriptive studies are relatively straightforward to conduct and can be useful for exploring topics that are not well understood or documented.

Limitations. Descriptive research designs have limitations, including the inability to establish relationships between variables. Because descriptive studies do not manipulate variables or control for confounding factors, researchers cannot determine cause-and-effect relationships. Additionally, descriptive research may be limited by the quality of data collected, sampling biases, or the representativeness of the sample.

Overall, descriptive research designs play a valuable role in educational research by providing insights into the characteristics, behaviors, and attitudes of individuals or groups within educational settings.

These designs serve as the foundation for further investigation and contribute to the broader understanding of educational phenomena.

Meta-Analysis

Meta-analysis in educational research is a quantitative research method used to synthesize findings from multiple studies on a specific topic. It involves systematically collecting and analyzing data from individual studies to provide a comprehensive summary of the existing research literature. Meta-analysis allows researchers to quantitatively assess the magnitude and consistency of effects across studies, identify sources of variability, and draw more robust conclusions than any single study alone. Below is a description of meta-analysis in educational research:

Purpose. The primary goal of meta-analysis is to integrate findings from multiple studies to produce a more reliable and generalizable estimate of the true effect size or relationship between variables. Meta-analysis helps researchers identify patterns, trends, or inconsistencies across studies, clarify conflicting findings, and address research questions that cannot be adequately addressed by individual studies alone.

Nature of the Study. Meta-analysis is a systematic and rigorous research method that follows a predefined protocol to identify, select, and analyze relevant studies. Researchers conduct a comprehensive literature review to identify all studies relevant to the research question and apply inclusion and exclusion criteria to select eligible studies for inclusion in the meta-analysis.

Data Collection. Meta-analysis involves extracting relevant data from each included study, such as sample sizes, effect sizes, measures of variability, and study characteristics. Researchers may also collect additional information on study design, methodology, and participant characteristics to assess study quality and potential sources of bias.

Data Analysis. Meta-analysis uses statistical techniques to combine and analyze data from individual studies quantitatively. Effect sizes from each study are weighted based on sample size and variance and then aggregated to produce an overall effect size estimate. Common effect size measures used in meta-analysis include Cohen's d for continuous outcomes and odds ratios or risk ratios for categorical outcomes. Heterogeneity across studies is assessed using statistical tests such as the Q-statistic and I^2 statistic, which indicate the degree of variability or inconsistency between study findings.

Results. The results of a meta-analysis typically include a summary of effect sizes, confidence intervals, and forest plots representing the findings from individual studies. Researchers may also conduct subgroup analyses or moderator analyses to explore sources of variability and assess the robustness of the overall effect size estimate.

Interpretation. The findings of a meta-analysis are interpreted in light of the strengths and limitations of the included studies, potential biases, and sources of heterogeneity. Meta-analysts discuss the implications of their findings for theory, practice, and future research, highlighting areas of consensus, controversy, or uncertainty within the literature.

Meta-analysis offers several advantages in educational research, including increased statistical power, enhanced precision of effect size estimates, and the ability to synthesize findings across diverse studies and populations. However, meta-analysis also has limitations, such as the potential for publication bias, variability in study quality, and challenges in synthesizing heterogeneous studies.

Introduction to Educational Research

The research designs described so far differ based on sampling or data analytic procedures. Based on the timing of the data collection(s), research designs can be classified as longitudinal or cross-sectional.

Longitudinal Design

Longitudinal research designs in educational research involve the collection of data from the same individuals or groups over an extended period of time to examine changes or trends in variables of interest. These designs allow researchers to track the development of individuals or cohorts over time and investigate the long-term effects of interventions or experiences. Below is a description of longitudinal research designs in educational research:

Purpose. The primary goal of longitudinal research designs is to study changes or stability in variables of interest over time. Researchers aim to identify patterns, trends, or developmental trajectories that may occur within individuals or groups as they progress through different stages of life or educational experiences.

Nature of the Study. Longitudinal studies involve the repeated measurement of variables at multiple time points, typically spaced out over months or years. Researchers collect data from the same participants or cohorts at each time point, allowing them to examine how variables evolve or remain stable over time.

Types of Longitudinal Designs:

- **Trend Studies**: Trend studies involve the repeated measurement of variables in different cohorts over time. Researchers examine changes or trends in variables across generations or age groups to identify broad patterns or shifts in behavior, attitudes, or outcomes.

- **Panel Studies**: Panel studies involve the repeated measurement of variables in the same group of individuals over time. Researchers follow a cohort of participants longitudinally, collecting data at regular intervals to track changes or stability in variables within the same group.

- **Cohort Studies**: Cohort studies focus on specific birth cohorts or groups of individuals who share a common characteristic or experience. Researchers examine how variables evolve within these cohorts as they age or experience different life events, such as changes in educational attainment or career trajectories.

Data Collection. Longitudinal studies require careful planning and coordination to ensure data collection occurs at regular intervals over an extended period of time. Researchers may use a variety of methods to collect data, including surveys, interviews, observations, or standardized assessments, depending on the nature of the variables being studied.

Data Analysis. Longitudinal data are typically analyzed using statistical techniques that account for the nested structure of the data and the repeated measurements within individuals or groups over time. Techniques such as growth curve modeling, hierarchical linear modeling (HLM), or structural equation modeling (SEM) are commonly used to examine longitudinal relationships and trajectories.

Advantages. Longitudinal research designs offer several advantages, including the ability to study developmental processes, track changes or stability in variables over time, and examine the long-term effects of interventions or experiences. Longitudinal data also allow researchers to investigate the timing and sequencing of events and explore causal relationships between variables.

Challenges. Longitudinal research designs also present challenges, such as participant attrition, logistical constraints, and the need for long-term commitment and resources. Researchers must carefully plan and manage data collection to minimize attrition and maintain the validity and reliability of findings over time.

Example of Longitudinal Study in Educational Research

Research Question: How does parental involvement in early childhood predict academic achievement in later years of schooling?

Longitudinal Design:

1. **Participants**: The participants are 200 children enrolled in a longitudinal study at the age of 5. The children are from diverse socioeconomic backgrounds and attend various preschools in the same region.

2. **Data Collection Time Points**:
   - Time 1 (Age 5): Parents complete surveys assessing their level of involvement in their child's education, including activities such as reading to their child, helping with homework, and involvement in school events.
   - Time 2 (Age 10): Academic achievement data are collected from school records, including standardized test scores, grades, and teacher ratings of academic performance.
   - Time 3 (Age 15): Follow-up academic achievement data are collected from school records to assess academic outcomes in adolescence.

3. **Data Analysis**: Researchers use longitudinal data analysis techniques, such as growth curve modeling or hierarchical linear modeling, to examine the relationship between parental involvement at age 5 and academic achievement at ages 10 and 15 while controlling for relevant covariates, such as socioeconomic status and parental education.

4. **Results**: The longitudinal analysis reveals that higher levels of parental involvement in early childhood are associated with higher academic achievement in later years of schooling. Specifically, children whose parents were more involved in their education at age 5 tend to have higher standardized test scores, better grades, and more positive teacher ratings of academic performance at ages 10 and 15, even after controlling for socioeconomic factors.

In this longitudinal study, researchers track the same cohort of children over multiple time points to examine how parental involvement in early childhood predicts academic outcomes in later years of schooling. By collecting data at multiple time points and controlling for potential confounding variables, the study provides valuable insights into the long-term effects of parental involvement on children's academic achievement.

Cross-Sectional Design

Cross-sectional research designs in educational research involve collecting data from a single point in time to examine relationships between variables across different groups or populations. Unlike longitudinal designs that track the same individuals over time, cross-sectional designs provide a snapshot of data at a specific moment, allowing researchers to compare groups or assess differences in variables of interest. Below is a description of cross-sectional designs in educational research:

Purpose: The primary goal of cross-sectional research designs is to examine relationships between variables at a single point in time. Researchers aim to identify patterns, trends, or differences in variables across different groups or populations, providing insights into the current state of educational phenomena.

Nature of the Study: Cross-sectional studies involve the simultaneous collection of data from multiple groups or populations at a specific moment in time. Researchers sample participants from different age groups, grade levels, or demographic categories to capture variability in the variables of interest within the population.

Sampling: Cross-sectional studies use a cross-sectional sample, where participants are selected from different groups or populations based on predetermined criteria. Researchers may use random sampling, stratified sampling, or convenience sampling methods to ensure representativeness and generalizability of findings.

Data Collection: Data in cross-sectional studies are collected through surveys, questionnaires, interviews, observations, or standardized assessments administered at a single time point. Researchers measure the variables of interest and collect demographic information to characterize the sample.

Data Analysis: Statistical techniques such as analysis of variance (ANOVA), chi-square tests, or regression analysis are commonly used to analyze cross-sectional data. These techniques allow researchers to examine differences or associations between variables across different groups or populations.

Advantages: Cross-sectional research designs offer several advantages, including efficiency, cost-effectiveness, and the ability to capture variability in variables across diverse groups or populations at a specific moment in time. Cross-sectional studies are useful for generating hypotheses, exploring associations, or identifying trends in educational phenomena.

Limitations: Despite their advantages, cross-sectional research designs have limitations. They cannot establish causality or infer temporal relationships between variables, as data are collected at a single point in time. Cross-sectional studies are also vulnerable to cohort effects, where differences between groups may be influenced by generational or historical factors rather than the variables of interest.

Example of Cross-Sectional Study in Educational Research

Research Question: Do different age groups exhibit differences in technology use and digital literacy skills?

Cross-sectional Design:

1. **Participants:** The participants are 500 individuals from diverse age groups, including children (ages 8-12), adolescents (ages 13-18), young adults (ages 19-25), adults (ages 26-40), and older adults (ages 41 and above). Participants are sampled from schools, colleges, workplaces, and community centers to ensure representation across different age cohorts.

2. **Data Collection:** Data are collected through surveys and assessments administered at a single point in time. Participants complete self-report measures assessing their use of technology devices (e.g., smartphones, tablets, computers) and digital literacy skills (e.g., internet browsing, email usage, social media engagement).

3. **Variables:** The independent variable is participants' age group, categorized into different cohorts based on age ranges. The dependent variables include measures of technology use and digital literacy skills, such as frequency of device usage, proficiency in using digital tools, and

Example of Cross-Sectional Study in Educational Research
attitudes towards technology. 4. **Data Analysis:** Researchers use statistical analysis techniques, such as analysis of variance (ANOVA) or chi-square tests, to examine differences in technology use and digital literacy skills across different age groups. Post-hoc analyses may be conducted to identify specific group differences if the overall analysis indicates significant differences between age cohorts. 5. **Results:** The cross-sectional analysis reveals significant differences in technology use and digital literacy skills across different age groups. For example, younger age groups may report higher levels of smartphone usage and social media engagement, while older age groups may demonstrate greater proficiency in email communication and internet browsing. These findings provide insights into age-related trends in technology adoption and digital literacy skills. In this cross-sectional study, researchers collect data from participants representing different age cohorts at a single point in time to examine differences in technology use and digital literacy skills. By sampling individuals from diverse age groups, the study provides insights into age-related variations in technology-related behaviors and competencies within the population.

Each quantitative research design has its strengths and limitations, and researchers should select the most appropriate design based on their research questions, hypotheses, and practical constraints.

Single Subject Designs

Single-subject design, also known as single-case design, is a research method commonly used in educational research to study the effects of interventions or treatments on individual subjects. It is particularly useful when investigating interventions for students with special needs or when examining the effectiveness of teaching strategies. Below is a brief overview of single-subject design research designs:

Focus on Individual Subjects. Unlike traditional group-based research designs where data is collected from multiple subjects, single-subject design focuses on one participant at a time. This allows researchers to closely monitor the progress of each participant and to tailor interventions to individual needs.

Repeated Measures. Single-subject design typically involves measuring the dependent variable (e.g., academic performance, behavior) multiple times before, during, and after the intervention period. This repeated measurement helps to establish a baseline level of behavior and track changes over time.

Baseline Phase. The research begins with a baseline phase during which data is collected on the dependent variable in the absence of any intervention. This baseline data serves as a point of comparison for evaluating the effects of the intervention.

Intervention Phase. After establishing a baseline, the intervention phase begins, during which the researcher introduces the intervention or treatment designed to produce a change in the dependent variable. The intervention may involve implementing a teaching strategy, providing additional support, or modifying the learning environment.

Monitoring and Data Collection. Throughout the intervention phase, the researcher continues to collect data on the dependent variable at regular intervals. This allows them to assess the effectiveness of the intervention and make any necessary adjustments.

Withdrawal or Reversal Phase. In some single-subject designs, a withdrawal or reversal phase may be included after the intervention phase. During this phase, the intervention is removed or reversed to determine if the changes in the dependent variable are indeed attributable to the intervention rather than other factors.

Visual Analysis. Data collected in single-subject designs are often graphed to visually depict changes in the dependent variable over time. Visual analysis of the data can help researchers identify trends, patterns, and the effectiveness of the intervention.

Single-subject design offers several advantages, including the ability to directly assess the effects of interventions on individual students, the flexibility to customize interventions based on individual needs, and the potential for identifying causal relationships between interventions and outcomes. However, it also has limitations, such as difficulties in generalizing findings to broader populations and the potential for confounding variables to influence results.

Summary

The chapter discusses the significance of quantitative research designs in educational research, emphasizing their role in systematically gathering, analyzing, and interpreting numerical data to understand educational phenomena. The chapter provides detailed explanations of experimental designs, such as pretest-posttest control group design, posttest-only control group design, Solomon four-group design, factorial design, and randomized controlled trials (RCTs), highlighting their advantages and disadvantages in educational research. Additionally, it delves into quasi-experimental designs, including non-equivalent control group design, time-series design, interrupted time-series design, regression discontinuity design, and matched groups design, outlining their applications and limitations. Furthermore, the chapter explores causal-comparative research designs, also known as ex post facto designs, which examine relationships between variables based on pre-existing differences or conditions. It also discusses correlational research, which focuses on identifying relationships between variables without manipulation. Further, the chapter presents descriptive designs, which provide snapshots of educational phenomena without establishing relationships, and meta-analyses, which synthesize findings from multiple studies to provide comprehensive summaries, enhancing the robustness of conclusions. Longitudinal studies track individuals or groups over time to examine developmental changes, while cross-sectional studies compare different groups at a single time point. Each design offers unique insights and has its strengths and limitations, catering to different research questions and objectives in educational research. Overall, the chapter serves as a comprehensive guide to quantitative research designs in educational research, offering insights into their methodologies, applications, and implications for advancing knowledge in the field.

Suggestions for Students

Key Questions

1. What are the primary purposes of quantitative research designs in educational research, and how do they contribute to understanding educational phenomena?
2. Can you differentiate between experimental, quasi-experimental, and causal-comparative research designs, including their methodologies and applications in educational research?
3. Describe two common experimental designs discussed in the chapter, highlighting their advantages, disadvantages, and suitability for investigating causal relationships in educational research.
4. What are the ethical considerations associated with conducting experimental research in educational settings, and how can researchers address these concerns while ensuring participant well-being?
5. Discuss the practical constraints and challenges researchers may encounter when implementing experimental or quasi-experimental designs in educational research, and propose strategies for overcoming these obstacles.
6. What is the primary purpose of correlational research designs in educational research, and how do they differ from experimental designs?
7. Explain the concept of predictive validity in correlational studies and provide an example from educational research.
8. What are some advantages and disadvantages of using descriptive research designs in educational research?
9. Describe the difference between trend studies, panel studies, and cohort studies in longitudinal research designs, providing examples of each.
10. Discuss the limitations of cross-sectional research designs and how they impact the interpretation of study findings in educational research.

Suggestions for Instructors

Suggested Learning Activities

Experimental Design Simulation. Divide the students into groups and assign each group a specific experimental design discussed in the chapter (e.g., pretest-posttest control group design, factorial design). Provide them with a hypothetical educational scenario and ask them to design an experiment using their assigned design to investigate a research question related to the scenario. Have each group present their experimental design to the class, explaining the rationale behind their choices and how they plan to address potential confounding variables.

Case Study Analysis. Provide students with real-world case studies of educational research projects that employed experimental or quasi-experimental designs. Ask students to analyze the case studies, identifying the research design used, the research question investigated, the methodology employed, and the findings. Encourage students to discuss the strengths and limitations of the research design used in each case study and suggest potential improvements or alternative approaches.

Ethical Dilemma Discussion. Present students with hypothetical ethical dilemmas related to conducting experimental research in educational settings (e.g., issues with informed consent, potential harm to participants). Divide the class into small groups and ask them to discuss the ethical considerations involved in each scenario and propose solutions or strategies to address the dilemmas. Facilitate a class discussion where groups share their insights and solutions, encouraging critical reflection on the ethical responsibilities of researchers in educational research.

Data Analysis Exercise. Provide students with a dataset containing quantitative research data collected from an educational study (e.g., pretest and posttest scores of students in an experimental

Suggestions for Instructors

and control group). Ask students to perform statistical analyses, such as t-tests or ANCOVA, to compare the outcomes between the experimental and control groups. Guide students through the process of interpreting the results, drawing conclusions, and discussing the implications of their findings for educational practice.

Research Proposal Development. Have students work individually or in small groups to develop a research proposal for a quantitative study in educational research. Ask students to choose a research question of interest, select an appropriate research design (e.g., experimental, quasi-experimental), and outline the methodology, including sampling procedures, data collection methods, and statistical analyses. Provide feedback on the research proposals, encouraging students to refine their ideas and consider the feasibility, validity, and ethical implications of their proposed studies.

Case Study Analysis. Provide students with a set of educational research case studies employing different correlational designs. Ask them to identify the variables involved, the purpose of the study, and potential implications of the findings.

Data Interpretation Exercise. Present students with a dataset containing variables relevant to educational research (e.g., academic performance, parental involvement, socioeconomic status). Have them conduct correlational analyses using statistical software and interpret the results.

Research Proposal Development. Divide students into groups and assign each group a specific educational research question. Have them design a correlational study to investigate the question, including selecting variables, outlining data collection methods, and discussing potential limitations.

Journal Article Review. Assign students to read and critique a peer-reviewed journal article that utilizes a correlational research design in educational research. Encourage them to analyze the strengths, weaknesses, and implications of the study's findings.

Interactive Discussion. Facilitate a classroom discussion on the ethical considerations of conducting correlational research in educational settings. Present students with hypothetical scenarios and encourage them to debate the potential risks and benefits of various research practices.

References

Babbie, E. R. (2015). The practice of social research. Cengage Learning.

Barlow, D. H., & Hersen, M. (1984). Single case experimental designs: Strategies for studying behavior change. Pergamon Press.

Borenstein, M., Hedges, L. V., Higgins, J. P. T., & Rothstein, H. R. (2009). Introduction to meta-analysis. John Wiley & Sons.

Campbell, D. T., & Stanley, J. C. (1963). Experimental and quasi-experimental designs for research. Houghton Mifflin.

Cohen, L., Manion, L., & Morrison, K. (2017). Research methods in education. Routledge.

Cook, T. D., & Campbell, D. T. (1979). Quasi-experimentation: Design & analysis issues for field settings. Houghton Mifflin.

Cooper, H. M., Hedges, L. V., & Valentine, J. C. (Eds.). (2019). The handbook of research synthesis and meta-analysis (3rd ed.). Russell Sage Foundation.

Creswell, J. W., & Creswell, J. D. (2017). Research design: Qualitative, quantitative, and mixed methods approaches. Sage Publications.

Fraenkel, J. R., Wallen, N. E., & Hyun, H. H. (2014). How to design and evaluate research in education. McGraw-Hill Education.

Gall, M. D., Gall, J. P., & Borg, W. R. (2007). Educational research: An introduction. Pearson.

Gay, L. R., Mills, G. E., & Airasian, P. (2018). Educational research: Competencies for analysis and applications. Pearson.

Horner, R. H., Carr, E. G., Halle, J., McGee, G., Odom, S., & Wolery, M. (2005). The use of single-subject research to identify evidence-based practice in special education. Exceptional Children, 71(2), 165-179.

Johnson, B., & Christensen, L. (2019). Educational research: Quantitative, qualitative, and mixed approaches. Sage Publications.

Kennedy, C. H. (2005). Single-case designs for educational research. Allyn & Bacon.

Kratochwill, T. R., Hitchcock, J. H., Horner, R. H., Levin, J. R., Odom, S. L., Rindskopf, D. M., & Shadish, W. R. (2010). Single-case intervention research design standards. Remedial and Special Education, 31(3), 205-214.

Lipsey, M. W., & Wilson, D. B. (2001). Practical meta-analysis. Sage Publications.

Little, T. D. (2013). Longitudinal structural equation modeling. Guilford Press.

McMillan, J. H., & Schumacher, S. (2018). Research in education: Evidence-based inquiry. Pearson.

Menard, S. (2002). Longitudinal research. Sage Publications.

Muthén, B., & Curran, P. J. (1997). General longitudinal modeling of individual differences in experimental designs: A latent variable framework for analysis and power estimation. Psychological Methods, 2(4), 371-402.

Nesselroade, J. R., & Baltes, P. B. (1979). Longitudinal research in the study of behavior and development. Academic Press.

Pallant, J. (2016). SPSS survival manual. McGraw-Hill Education.

Rogosa, D. (1988). Myths about longitudinal research. In T. D. Cook, C. S. Cooper, D. S. Cordray, H. Hartmann, L. V. Hedges, R. J. Light, T. A. Louis, & F. Mosteller (Eds.), Meta-analysis for explanation: A casebook (pp. 217-237). Russell Sage Foundation.

Rosenthal, R. (1991). Meta-analytic procedures for social research. Sage Publications.

Scruggs, T. E., Mastropieri, M. A., & Casto, G. (1987). The quantitative synthesis of single-subject research: Methodology and validation. Remedial and Special Education, 8(2), 24-33.

Shadish, W. R., Cook, T. D., & Campbell, D. T. (2002). Experimental and quasi-experimental designs for generalized causal inference. Houghton Mifflin.

Sutton, A. J., Abrams, K. R., Jones, D. R., Sheldon, T. A., & Song, F. (2000). Methods for meta-analysis in medical research. John Wiley & Sons.

Trochim, W. M., & Donnelly, J. P. (2008). The research methods knowledge base. Atomic Dog Publishing.

Chapter 10. Quantitative Data Analysis

This chapter will address the following learning objectives:
• Define quantitative research in education.
• Explain data cleaning and management procedures.
• Compare and contrast univariate, bivariate, and multivariate procedures.
• Select appropriate data visualizations procedure based on objectives and the nature of the data.
• Define descriptive statistics.
• Distinguish parametric and non-parametric data analytic procedure.
• Differentiate between parameters and statistics.
• Explain the concept of confidence interval.
• Define inferential procedures.
• Describe the steps of hypothesis testing.
• Distinguish between Type I and Type II errors.
• Select appropriate quantitative data analytic procedures based on the research questions and the nature of the data.
• Compare the frequentist and Bayesian assumptions and inferential processes.

Quantitative data analysis serves as a fundamental approach in educational research, providing systematic means to explore various phenomena within educational settings. Researchers utilize numerical data to examine relationships, patterns, and trends, employing statistical techniques and computational tools to derive meaningful insights and test hypotheses.

The utilization of quantitative methods in educational research offers several advantages. Firstly, it enables the investigation of large datasets, facilitating the exploration of broad patterns and trends across diverse populations. Moreover, quantitative analysis allows researchers to establish relationships and generalize findings to broader populations, enhancing the external validity of research outcomes. Additionally, the precision of quantitative data facilitates study replication, promoting the validation and verification of research findings over time.

In the realm of educational research, quantitative data analysis encompasses a diverse array of topics and methodologies. Researchers may explore academic achievement, student attitudes, teaching effectiveness, school climate, and educational policies, among other areas of interest. They employ various quantitative techniques such as descriptive statistics, inferential statistics, regression analysis, factor analysis, or structural equation modeling, depending on their research questions and objectives. Nevertheless, it's essential to acknowledge the assumptions and limitations associated with quantitative data analysis procedures. These include assumptions about data distribution, sample representativeness, and the potential for confounding variables. Additionally, the interpretation of quantitative findings requires careful consideration of context, potential biases, and alternative explanations.

Quantitative data analysis procedures offer a systematic framework for extracting insights and making informed decisions based on numerical data. By employing rigorous methodologies and statistical techniques, researchers and practitioners can uncover patterns, relationships, and trends that inform understanding and drive actionable insights in various domains.

Quantitative data analytic procedures are systematic methodologies employed to extract meaningful insights from numerical data in research and decision-making contexts. These procedures encompass a diverse range of techniques and tools aimed at organizing, summarizing, interpreting, and drawing conclusions from quantitative data sets. In education, social sciences, economics, healthcare, and market research, quantitative data analysis plays a pivotal role in uncovering patterns, trends, and relationships, thereby informing evidence-based decisions and enhancing understanding. The procedures involved in quantitative data analysis typically follow a structured process, starting with data collection and preparation, followed by exploration, analysis, and interpretation. Researchers utilize statistical methods and computational tools to examine relationships between variables, test hypotheses, make predictions, and draw inferences from the data.

Key quantitative data analysis procedures include descriptive statistics, which involve summarizing and describing the basic features of the data, such as measures of central tendency (e.g., mean, median, mode) and measures of variability (e.g., range, variance, standard deviation). Inferential statistics are then employed to make inferences and draw conclusions about populations based on sample data, using techniques such as hypothesis testing, confidence intervals, and regression analysis. Moreover, advanced quantitative analysis techniques, including multivariate analyses such as factor analysis, cluster analysis, and structural equation modeling, allow researchers to explore complex relationships between multiple variables and uncover underlying structures within the data. These procedures enable researchers to identify significant predictors, causal pathways, and moderating or mediating effects, thereby enhancing the depth and complexity of analysis.

Quantitative data analysis procedures are not only limited to academic research contexts but also find application in various fields such as data analytics, practitioner research, program and policy evaluations, performance monitoring, and quality improvement initiatives. Organizations leverage quantitative analysis to make data-driven decisions, optimize processes, identify opportunities, mitigate risks, and evaluate the effectiveness of interventions.

Data Cleaning and Management

Data cleaning and data management procedures are essential preliminary steps in the data analysis process, ensuring that datasets are accurate, complete, and ready for analysis. These procedures involve identifying and correcting errors, inconsistencies, and missing values in the data, as well as organizing, documenting, and preparing the data for analysis. Data management procedures focus on organizing and documenting the dataset to facilitate efficient analysis and interpretation. This includes creating a data dictionary or codebook that provides descriptions of variables, their labels, and permissible values. Additionally, data management involves structuring the dataset in a logical and consistent manner, ensuring that variables are appropriately labeled and organized for easy reference. Furthermore, data management procedures may involve merging data files, selecting subsets of cases, creating derived variables or aggregating data to generate new variables of interest, or standardization or transformation of variable formats. This could include calculating summary statistics, creating categorical variables from continuous variables, or aggregating data across multiple time periods or levels of analysis.

Introduction to Educational Research

Data cleaning procedures typically begin with a thorough inspection of the dataset to identify any anomalies or discrepancies. Common tasks include checking for missing values, outliers, duplicates, and inconsistencies in variable names or formats. Once identified, these issues can be addressed through various methods, such as imputation for missing values, removal or correction of duplicates and outliers.

Imputation of Missing Values

Data imputation procedures are used to estimate or substitute missing values in a dataset, enabling the inclusion of incomplete observations in the analysis. Missing data can occur for various reasons, including non-response, data entry errors, or system failures. Data imputation techniques aim to address missingness while preserving the integrity and validity of the dataset. One commonly used data imputation method is mean imputation, where missing values are replaced with the mean of the observed values for that variable. This approach is simple and easy to implement but may lead to biased estimates, especially if the data have significant variability.

Another approach is regression imputation, where missing values are predicted based on the relationships between variables in the dataset. Regression models are fitted using the observed data, and the missing values are then estimated using the fitted model. This method can produce more accurate imputations, particularly when there are strong relationships between variables. Multiple imputation is a more sophisticated technique that generates multiple imputed datasets, each containing different plausible values for the missing data. This approach accounts for uncertainty in the imputed values and produces more reliable estimates of parameters and variances in the analysis. Other data imputation methods include hot deck imputation, cold deck imputation, and k-nearest neighbors imputation, each with its own strengths and limitations depending on the characteristics of the dataset. It is important to note that data imputation procedures should be carefully considered and justified, taking into account the assumptions and limitations of the chosen method. Additionally, sensitivity analyses can be conducted to assess the robustness of the results to different imputation strategies.

Duplicate Removal

Duplicate removal procedures are used to identify and eliminate duplicate observations or records from a dataset. Duplicates can arise from various sources, such as data entry errors, system glitches, or merging multiple datasets. Removing duplicates is essential for ensuring data integrity and avoiding biases in analysis results. The first step in duplicate removal is to identify potential duplicates within the dataset. This can be achieved by comparing observations across one or more variables that uniquely identify each record. Commonly used identifiers include unique IDs, combinations of variables, or a combination of identifiers that are expected to be unique. Once potential duplicates are identified, various procedures can be used to remove them:

Exact Match Removal. This method involves identifying observations that are exact duplicates of one another across all variables. These duplicates are then removed, leaving only one instance of each unique record in the dataset.

Partial Match Removal. In cases where exact duplicates are not present, partial match removal procedures can be used to identify observations that are similar or nearly identical across selected variables. Thresholds or similarity measures can be defined to determine when observations are considered duplicates and should be removed.

Hierarchical Removal. Hierarchical removal involves prioritizing certain variables over others when identifying duplicates. For example, if two records have identical values for a primary identifier variable, they are considered duplicates and one is removed. If no primary identifier is available, secondary variables can be used to identify potential duplicates.

Time-Based Removal. In datasets containing temporal information, duplicates may be identified based on timestamps or other time-related variables. Observations that occur within a specified time window of each other can be flagged as duplicates and removed accordingly.

Manual Review. In some cases, manual review may be necessary to identify and remove duplicates that cannot be identified through automated procedures. This may involve visual inspection of records or comparison with external sources to verify uniqueness.

It's important to document the duplicate removal process and the criteria used for identifying and removing duplicates to ensure transparency and reproducibility of the analysis and to save copies of the original and modified data files at each stage of the process.

Outlier Removal

Outlier removal procedures are used to identify and handle observations in a dataset that deviate significantly from the rest of the data. Outliers can distort statistical analyses and model estimates, leading to biased results and inaccurate conclusions. Therefore, it's essential to identify and address outliers appropriately to ensure the validity and reliability of data analysis. Several outlier detection and removal procedures can be employed:

Visual Inspection. Visual inspection involves plotting the data using scatter plots, histograms, box plots, or other graphical representations to identify observations that appear to be unusually distant from the bulk of the data. Visual inspection can provide an initial indication of potential outliers.

z-Score Method. The z-score method involves calculating the standardized score (z-score) for each observation based on its deviation from the mean or median of the variable. Observations with z-scores exceeding a specified threshold (e.g., ±3) are considered outliers and can be removed from the dataset.

Modified z-Score Method. The modified z-score method is a variation of the z-score method that is robust to the presence of skewness and outliers in the data. It uses the median and median absolute deviation (MAD) instead of the mean and standard deviation to calculate the z-score.

Interquartile Range (IQR) Method. The IQR method involves calculating the interquartile range (the difference between the third quartile and the first quartile) of the variable. Observations lying outside a specified range (e.g., 1.5 times the IQR above the third quartile or below the first quartile) are considered outliers and can be removed.

Machine Learning-Based Methods. Machine learning algorithms, such as clustering, isolation forests, and support vector machines, can be used to detect outliers in multidimensional datasets. These methods can identify observations that are unusual in terms of their relationships with other variables in the dataset.

It's important to note that outlier removal should be done judiciously, considering the context and objectives of the analysis. Outliers may represent genuine data points of interest or indicate underlying phenomena that require further investigation. Additionally, the choice of outlier removal method may depend on the distributional characteristics of the data and the specific requirements of the analysis.

Throughout the data cleaning and data management process, it is crucial to maintain transparency and documentation to ensure reproducibility and facilitate collaboration. This includes documenting all data cleaning and transformation steps, as well as providing clear descriptions of variable definitions and coding schemes in the data dictionary. Overall, data cleaning and data management procedures are critical for ensuring the integrity, reliability, and usability of datasets in the analysis process.

Univariate, Bivariate, and Multivariate Data Analytic Procedures

Depending on the number of variables involved, quantitative data analytic procedures may be described as univariate, bivariate, or multivariate. Univariate analyses focus on analyzing a single variable at a time. It aims to understand the distribution, central tendency, and variability of a variable. Common techniques used in univariate analysis include measures of central tendency (e.g., mean, median, mode), measures of dispersion (e.g., variance, standard deviation), graphical representations (e.g., histograms, box plots), one-sample tests, or confidence intervals. Univariate analysis provides a foundational understanding of individual variables before exploring relationships between variables.

Bivariate analyses examine the relationship between two variables simultaneously. It assesses how changes in one variable correspond to changes in another variable. Common techniques used in bivariate analysis include correlation analysis, simple linear regression, and contingency table analysis (e.g., chi-square test). Bivariate analyses are essential for exploring associations, predicting outcomes, and identifying potential cause-and-effect relationships between two variables.

Multivariate analyses involve the simultaneous examination of three or more variables. Common techniques used in multivariate analyses include multiple regression analysis, cluster analysis, factor analysis, principal component analysis, path analysis, or structural equation modeling. Multivariate analyses allow researchers to understand the joint influence of multiple variables on an outcome, identify underlying dimensions or structures within data, and classify observations into meaningful groups. Univariate, bivariate, and multivariate analyses play complementary roles in statistical analysis, providing researchers with a comprehensive toolkit for exploring and understanding data across different levels of complexity.

Descriptive Data Analytic Procedures

Descriptive data analysis procedures involve summarizing and describing the basic features of a dataset. These procedures aim to provide a clear and concise understanding of the data's characteristics without making inferences or drawing conclusions beyond what is observed. Descriptive statistics play a crucial role in exploring and understanding the distribution, central tendency, and variability of variables within a dataset. They can be used independently, but most often represent a preliminary step for more complex procedures such as inferential analyses.

Data Visualization

Descriptive data analysis typically begins with organizing and presenting the data in a meaningful format, such as tables, charts, or graphs. This initial step helps researchers and analysts gain a visual understanding of the data's structure and patterns. Descriptive analysis using charts involves visually summarizing and presenting data to gain insights into its distribution, trends, and relationships. Various types of charts can be used depending on the nature of the data and the research objectives. Below are some commonly used types of charts for descriptive analysis:

Histograms. Histograms are used to visualize the distribution of a continuous variable. They display the frequencies or relative frequencies of observations within predefined intervals or bins. Histograms provide insights into the shape, central tendency, and variability of the data. The histogram plot below represents the GRE scores of a sample of graduate students.

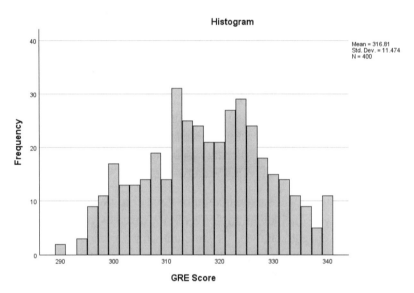

Box Plots. Box plots, also known as box-and-whisker plots, are used to visualize the distribution of a continuous variable and to identify outliers. They display the median, quartiles, and range of the data, providing insights into its central tendency, variability, and symmetry. The following box plot represents the GRE scores of the same sample of graduate students.

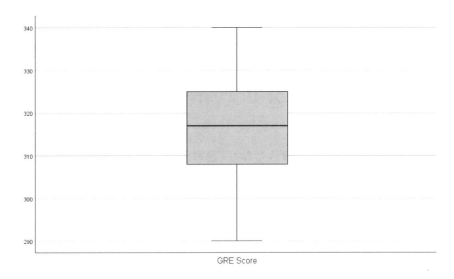

Stem-and-Leaf Plots. A stem-and-leaf plot, commonly known as a stemplot, is a graphical tool used to display the distribution of a dataset. Stemplots are particularly useful for visualizing small to moderately sized datasets, providing insights into the shape, central tendency, and variability of the data. In a stemplot, each data point is split into two parts: the stem and the leaf. The stem consists of the leading digits (or digits to the left of the decimal point) of the data values, while the leaf represents the trailing digits (or digits to the right of the decimal point). Below is a stemplot representing the GRE scores of the same sample of graduate students.

```
GRE Score
Stem-and-Leaf Plot

  Frequency    Stem &  Leaf

      5.00      29 .  00344
     28.00      29 .  5555666667777888888899999999
     35.00      30 .  00000000011111111222223333344444444
     39.00      30 .  555555555666666777777778888888888999999
     64.00      31 .  0000000011111111111122222222222222222222333333333334444444444444
     54.00      31 .  555555555556666666666666677777777777788888888899999999
     68.00      32 .  00000000000011111111111111222222222222223333333333344444444444444444444
     51.00      32 .  55555555555556666666666667777777777777888888999999999
     31.00      33 .  0000001111111122222233334444444
     17.00      33 .  55556666678888999
      8.00      34 .  00000000

 Stem width:    10
 Each leaf:        1 case(s)
```

Bar Charts. Bar charts are used to compare the frequencies or proportions of categorical variables. They consist of rectangular bars, where the height or length of each bar represents the frequency or proportion of observations within each category. Bar charts are effective for visualizing comparisons across categories that may not add up to 100%, such as responses on "check all that apply" survey questions. The bar chart below illustrates the distribution of U.S. undergraduate students at degree granting postsecondary institutions who participated exclusively in distance educations courses during the Fall 2021 semester.

Introduction to Educational Research

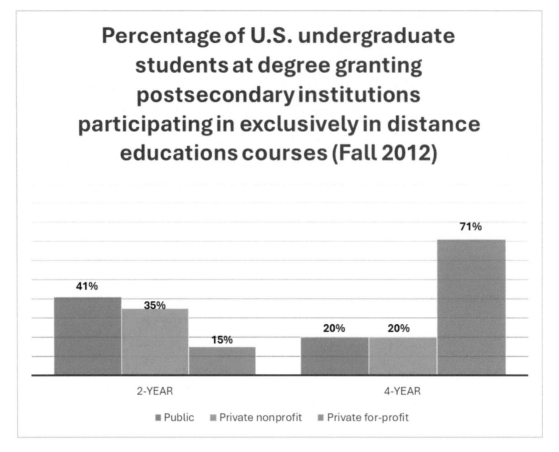

Data Source: U.S. Department of Education, National Center for Education Statistics, Integrated Postsecondary Education Data System (IPEDS), Spring 2022, Fall Enrollment component. See *Digest of Education Statistics 2022*, table 311.15.

Time Plots. Time plots, also known as a time series plot, is a graphical representation of data collected over time. It is commonly used to visualize trends, patterns, and seasonal variations in time-dependent data, such as stock prices, temperature fluctuations, or sales figures. In a time plot, time is typically represented on the x-axis, while the variable of interest is plotted on the y-axis. Each data point is connected by a line to show the progression of the variable over time. Time plots can also include additional elements such as trend lines, confidence intervals, or annotations to provide further insights into the data. The figure below is a time plot representing historical and projected undergraduate enrollment in the U. S. by gender (U.S. Department of Education, National Center for Educations Statistics, Integrated Postsecondary Educations Data System, 2023)

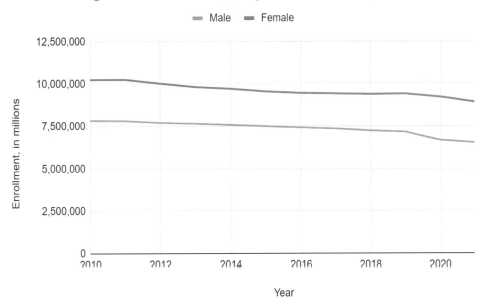

Data source: U.S. Department of Education, National Center for Education Statistics, Integrated Postsecondary Education Data System (IPEDS), Spring 2011 through Spring 2022, Fall Enrollment component. Enrollment in Degree-Granting Institutions Projection Model, through 2031, *Digest of Education Statistics 2022*, table 303.70.

Pie Charts. Pie charts represent the composition of a whole by dividing it into segments or slices, with each slice representing a proportion or percentage of the total. Pie charts are useful for visualizing the relative distribution of categorical variables but are less effective for comparing values across categories or displaying large numbers of categories. The example below illustrates the use of pie charts to represent the 2010, 2019, and 2021 undergraduate enrollment in degree-granting postsecondary institutions in the U.S. by race/ethnicity and non-resident status. The pies help visualize and quicky identify changes in the diversity of the undergraduate student population across time.

Introduction to Educational Research

Undergraduate enrollment in degree-granting postsecondary institutions, by race/ethnicity and nonresident status: Fall 2010, 2019, and 2021

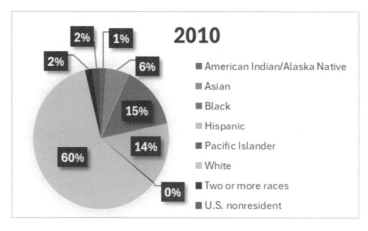

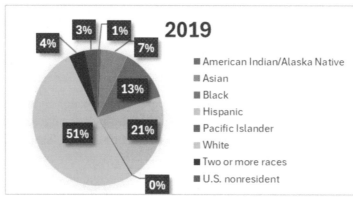

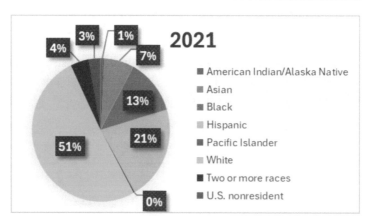

Data source: U.S. Department of Education, National Center for Education Statistics, Integrated Postsecondary Education Data System (IPEDS), Spring 2011, Spring 2020, and Spring 2022, Fall Enrollment component, *Digest of Education Statistics 2022*, table 306.10.

Line Charts: Line charts are used to visualize trends or patterns in data over time or across ordered categories. They consist of data points connected by straight lines, with the x-axis representing time or an ordered variable and the y-axis representing the variable of interest. Line charts are effective for identifying trends, fluctuations, or patterns in the data. Additionally, line charts may be used when the line(s) represent(s) values of the same individuals or groups across multiple measures. The line chart below represents the 2023 average evidence-based writing (ERW) and Math scores by gender.

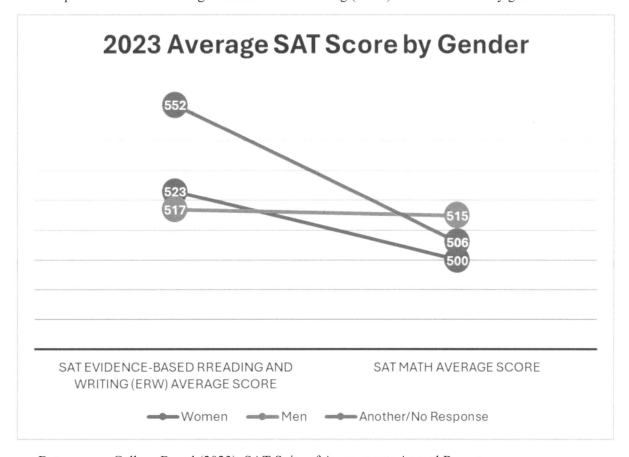

Data source: College Board (2023). SAT Suite of Assessments Annual Report

Scatter Plots: Scatter plots are used to visualize the relationship between two continuous variables. Each data point represents an observation, with its position on the plot determined by the values of the two variables. Scatter plots are useful for identifying patterns, trends, or correlations between variables. The first scatterplot below illustrates the relationship between school closure due to the COVID-19 pandemic and student average performance on the Programme for International Student Assessment (PISA) mathematics test. In this scatterplot data are aggregated by country. The second scatterplot illustrates the relationship between public and private schools' socio-economic status and students' performance on the 2022 PISA mathematics test. This this scatterplot data points represent each individual school participating in the study (OECD, 2023).

Introduction to Educational Research

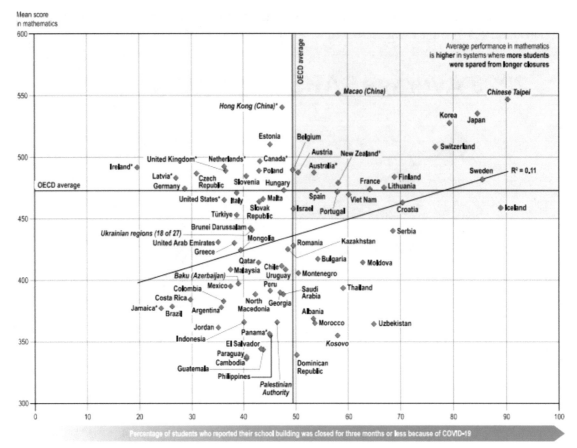

Source: OECD, PISA 2022 Database, Annex B1, Chapter 2; and Volume I, Annex B1.

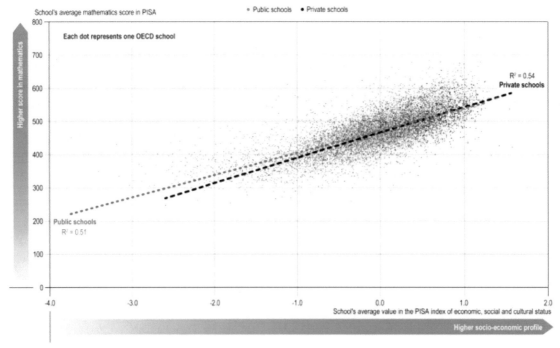

Note: The regression lines need to be interpreted with caution because only within-school student-level weights have been applied.
Source: OECD, PISA 2022 Database.

Introduction to Educational Research

Geographical plots. Geographical plots, also known as geo-plots or maps, are visual representations that display data points or statistical information on a map, typically using different colors, symbols, or shading to represent variations in the data across geographic regions. They are powerful tools for visualizing spatial patterns, relationships, and trends in data, making them particularly useful in examining variations across geographical areas. The geographical plot below uses a color gradient to depict the U.S. 2021 public high school graduation rates by state. In electronic versions, geographical plots can be interactive and indicate exact values as users hover over the regions of interest.

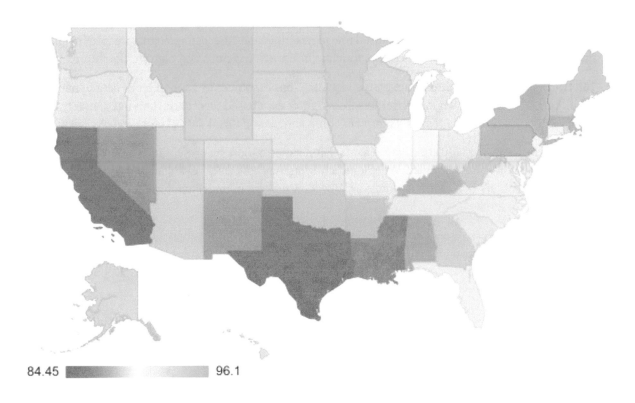

84.45 ▬▬▬▬▬ 96.1

In summary, graphs play a crucial role in descriptive statistical analysis by visually representing the data, aiding in the interpretation of key features, patterns, and trends. They help visualize data distribution, identify outliers, and identify relationships or trends. Data visualizations play several critical roles in various aspects of data analysis and communication:

Exploratory Data Analysis (EDA). Visualizations are instrumental in exploring datasets to understand their structure, patterns, and relationships. Techniques like scatter plots, histograms, and box plots help analysts uncover insights and identify trends or anomalies in the data.

Communication of Insights. Visualizations provide a means to effectively communicate complex data and findings to diverse audiences. By presenting information in a visually appealing and intuitive format, visualizations enhance understanding and engagement, whether in reports, presentations, or dashboards.

Pattern Recognition. Visualizations facilitate the identification of patterns and trends that might not be apparent from raw data alone. Through graphical representations, analysts can discern correlations, clusters, or trends, aiding in hypothesis generation and decision-making.

Detection of Outliers and Anomalies. Graphical representations such as scatter plots and box plots are valuable for detecting outliers and anomalies in the data. These visualizations enable analysts to identify data points that deviate significantly from the norm, prompting further investigation.

Comparison and Benchmarking. Visualizations allow for easy comparison of different datasets, groups, or time periods. Techniques like bar charts, line graphs, and heatmaps enable analysts to compare values, distributions, and trends across categories, facilitating benchmarking and performance evaluation.

Prediction and Forecasting. Visualizations support predictive modeling and forecasting by visualizing historical trends and patterns. Time series plots and forecasting charts provide insights into future trends, enabling organizations to make informed decisions and plan for the future.

Interactive Data Exploration. Interactive visualizations empower users to explore data dynamically, enabling them to drill down into specific subsets, filter data based on criteria, and interactively manipulate variables. This fosters a more engaging and personalized data exploration experience.

Decision Support. Visualizations serve as decision support tools by presenting data-driven insights in a clear and compelling manner. Whether identifying market trends, evaluating performance metrics, or assessing risks, visualizations aid decision-makers in understanding complex information and taking appropriate action.

Storytelling and Persuasion. Visualizations are powerful storytelling tools that help convey narratives and persuade audiences. By weaving together data, analysis, and visualizations into a coherent narrative, storytellers can effectively communicate messages, influence opinions, and drive action.

Accessibility and Inclusivity. Thoughtfully designed visualizations prioritize accessibility and inclusivity, ensuring that they are understandable and usable by diverse audiences, including those with visual or cognitive impairments. Techniques such as colorblind-friendly palettes, clear labeling, and alternative text descriptions enhance accessibility.

In conclusion, data visualizations play a multifaceted role in data analysis, enabling exploration, communication, pattern recognition, decision support, and storytelling. They serve as powerful tools for understanding data, deriving insights, and driving informed decision-making across various domains.

Descriptive Statistics

In addition to exploring data distributions through visualizations, descriptive procedures include the calculation of summary statistics. Common descriptive statistics used in this process include measures of central tendency, such as the mean, median, and mode, which provide insight into the typical or central value of a variable. Measures of variability, such as the range, variance, and standard deviation, quantify the spread or dispersion of data points around the central value. Additionally, descriptive data analysis encompasses the calculation and interpretation of other summary statistics, such as percentiles, quartiles, and interquartile range, which provide information about the relative position of data points within the dataset, and measures of association, such as correlation coefficients, which can be used to quantify the strength and direction of relationships between variables. The table below defines the descriptive statistics most frequently used to summarize and describe data distributions.

Introduction to Educational Research

Definitions Descriptive Statistics

Mean. The mean, also known as the arithmetic average, is computed by summing all values in a dataset and dividing by the total number of observations.

Standard Deviation: The standard deviation measures the dispersion or spread of a set of values from its mean. It indicates how much individual values differ from the mean.

Variance. The variance is a statistical measure that quantifies the dispersion or spread of a set of data points around their mean or average. Mathematically, it is the average of the squared differences between each data point and the mean of the dataset.

Median: The median is the middle value in a dataset when it is arranged in ascending order. If there is an even number of observations, the median is the average of the two middle values.

Mode: The mode is the value that appears most frequently in a dataset.

Minimum: The minimum is the smallest value in a dataset.

Maximum: The maximum is the largest value in a dataset.

Range: The range is the difference between the maximum and minimum values in a dataset. It measures the spread of the data.

Quartiles: Quartiles divide a dataset into four equal parts. The first quartile (Q1) is the value below which 25% of the data falls, the second quartile (Q2) is the median, and the third quartile (Q3) is the value below which 75% of the data falls.

Interquartile Range (IQR): The interquartile range is the difference between the third quartile (Q3) and the first quartile (Q1). It measures the spread of the middle 50% of the data.

Five Number Summary: The five-number summary consists of the minimum, first quartile (Q1), median, third quartile (Q3), and maximum values of a dataset. It provides a concise summary of the distribution of the data.

Percentiles: Percentiles divide a dataset into hundredths. The pth percentile is the value below which p% of the data falls.

Skewness: Skewness measures the asymmetry of the distribution of values in a dataset. Positive skewness indicates a longer right tail, while negative skewness indicates a longer left tail.

Kurtosis: Kurtosis measures the peakedness or flatness of the distribution of values in a dataset. It compares the tails of the distribution to the tails of a normal distribution.

Overall, descriptive data analysis procedures serve as a foundational step in exploratory data analysis, providing researchers and analysts with a comprehensive overview of the dataset's key.

Descriptive statistics provide a powerful framework for summarizing and understanding datasets, allowing analysts to gain valuable insights into the characteristics and patterns of the data. Through measures such as measures of central tendency, variability, and distribution, descriptive statistics offer a comprehensive overview of the dataset's key features. In conclusion, descriptive statistics serve several essential purposes:

Data Summarization. Descriptive statistics condense large datasets into manageable summaries, providing a concise representation of the data's central tendency, variability, and distribution.

Pattern Identification. Descriptive statistics enable analysts to identify patterns, trends, and anomalies within the data, helping to uncover underlying relationships and structures.

Data Exploration. Descriptive statistics facilitate exploratory data analysis, allowing analysts to visually inspect the data and generate hypotheses for further investigation.

Decision Support. Descriptive statistics aid decision-making by providing stakeholders with clear, quantifiable insights into the characteristics of the data, guiding strategic planning and resource allocation.

Communication. Descriptive statistics serve as a common language for communicating data-driven insights to diverse audiences, facilitating understanding and collaboration across interdisciplinary teams.

Overall, descriptive statistics play a fundamental role in the data analysis process, serving as a foundation for more advanced statistical techniques and informing evidence-based decision-making in various domains, from scientific research to business analytics. By providing a systematic framework for summarizing and interpreting data, descriptive statistics empower analysts to extract meaningful insights and derive actionable recommendations from complex datasets.

Data Distributions

Data distributions refer to the patterns and arrangements of values within a dataset. They provide information about how frequently different values occur and how they are spread across the range of possible values. A data distribution describes the shape, central tendency, variability, and any other notable characteristics of the data. Common types of data distributions include:

Normal Distribution. Also known as the Gaussian distribution, it is symmetric and bell-shaped, with the mean, median, and mode located at the center. Many natural phenomena and measurements in various fields follow approximately normal distributions. Below is a histogram representing a variable with a normal distribution.

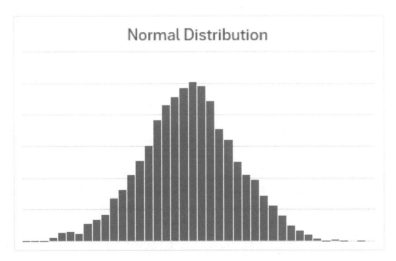

Skewed Distribution. Skewed distributions are asymmetric, with a longer tail on one side. Positive skewness indicates a tail extending to the right, while negative skewness indicates a tail extending to the left. Skewed distributions can occur when extreme values (outliers) are present in the data.

Introduction to Educational Research

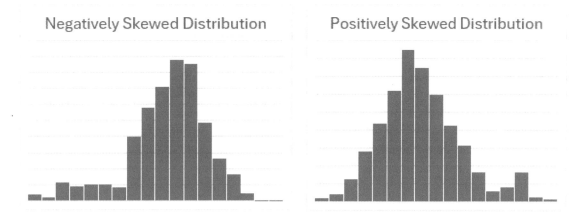

Uniform Distribution. In a uniform distribution, all values within a given range have equal probability of occurrence. It appears as a flat, rectangular shape, with no apparent peaks, as illustrated in the image below.

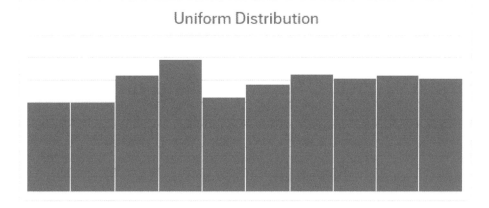

Bimodal Distribution. Bimodal distributions have two distinct peaks or modes, indicating the presence of two separate groups or subpopulations within the dataset, as illustrated in the image below.

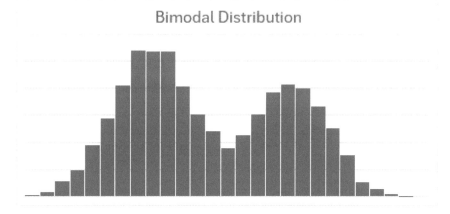

Multimodal Distribution. Similar to bimodal distributions, multimodal distributions have multiple peaks, suggesting the presence of multiple subgroups or underlying processes contributing to the data.

Introduction to Educational Research

Exponential Distribution. Exponential distributions are characterized by a rapid decrease in frequency as values increase. They often describe phenomena where events occur randomly over time, such as waiting times or decay processes.

Examining data distributions is essential for selecting appropriate statistical methods, interpreting results, and making informed decisions in data analysis. Visualizations such as histograms, box plots, and density plots are commonly used to visualize and analyze data distributions, providing insights into their shape, central tendency, and variability.Understanding data distributions is fundamental in data analysis as it provides insights into the characteristics, patterns, and behaviors of the dataset. Below are some important reasons for examining data distributions:

Identifying Central Tendency. The shape of the distribution helps identify the central tendency of the data, such as the mean, median, and mode. For example, in a symmetric distribution, the mean, median, and mode may coincide, while in skewed distributions, they may differ, indicating the presence of outliers or unusual patterns.

Assessing Variability. Data distributions reveal the variability or spread of the data around the central tendency. Measures such as standard deviation, variance, and interquartile range quantify the dispersion of the data points. Wide distributions indicate higher variability, whereas narrow distributions suggest less variability.

Detecting Outliers and Anomalies. Visual inspection of data distributions helps detect outliers, anomalies, or unusual patterns that deviate significantly from the main body of the data. Outliers may indicate data entry errors, measurement variability, or meaningful insights requiring further investigation.

Choosing Statistical Tests. The shape and characteristics of data distributions inform the selection of appropriate statistical tests for data analysis. Parametric tests, such as t-tests and ANOVA, assume specific distributional properties (e.g., normality), while non-parametric tests, such as Mann-Whitney U test and Kruskal-Wallis test, are distribution-free and applicable to a broader range of data distributions.

Modeling and Inference. Data distributions guide the selection and fitting of statistical models to the data. For example, linear regression assumes normally distributed errors, while generalized linear models accommodate non-normal distributions through appropriate link functions and error distributions.

Decision Making and Inference. Understanding data distributions facilitates data-driven decision-making and inference. By analyzing the distributional properties, stakeholders can draw conclusions, make predictions, and formulate strategies based on the observed patterns and trends in the data.

Communicating Insights. Visual representations of data distributions, such as histograms, box plots, and density plots, facilitate effective communication of insights to diverse audiences. Clear and informative visualizations help stakeholders interpret the data, understand key findings, and derive actionable insights.

In summary, data distributions play a crucial role in data analysis by providing essential information about the central tendency, variability, outliers, and patterns within the dataset. By understanding and analyzing data distributions, analysts can make informed decisions, select appropriate statistical methods, and communicate insights effectively to stakeholders.

Inferential Data Analytic Procedures

Inferential data analytic procedures involve making inferences or predictions about a population based on sample data. Specifically, these procedures estimate population parameters based on sample statistics. These procedures aim to draw conclusions that generalize beyond the observed sample to the larger population from which the sample was drawn through hypothesis testing. Hypothesis testing is a statistical method used to evaluate the validity of a hypothesis about a population parameter. It involves formulating a null hypothesis (H0) and an alternative hypothesis (H1), collecting sample data, and using statistical tests to assess whether there is enough evidence to reject the null hypothesis in favor of the alternative hypothesis.

Parameters versus Statistics

Inferential procedures involve making inferences or predictions about a population based on sample data. Specifically, these procedures estimate population parameters based on sample statistics. In educational research, parameters and statistics play crucial roles in summarizing, analyzing, and interpreting data They are numerical characteristics of populations that researchers seek to estimate or describe. In educational research, parameters may include population means, variances, proportions, correlations, and regression coefficients. Parameters provide insights into the true underlying characteristics of the population being studied. Estimation of parameters often involves inferential statistical methods such as confidence intervals and hypothesis testing.

In contrast, statistics are numerical measures calculated from sample data that serve as estimates or approximations of population parameters. In educational research, statistics include sample means, standard deviations, proportions, correlation coefficients, and regression coefficients. Statistics summarize the characteristics of the sample and are used to make inferences about the population. Descriptive statistics are used to summarize and describe the main features of the data, while inferential statistics are used to make predictions and draw conclusions about populations based on sample data. Parameters and statistics in educational research provide researchers with essential tools for summarizing data, testing hypotheses, and drawing conclusions about populations. By understanding and applying statistical concepts effectively, researchers can derive meaningful insights and make informed decisions to improve educational practices and policies.

Confidence Intervals

Confidence intervals (CIs) are a statistical tool used to estimate the range within which a population parameter, such as a mean or proportion, is likely to lie. They provide a measure of the uncertainty associated with estimating the true value of a parameter based on a sample from the population. A confidence interval is defined as a range of values derived from sample data that is believed to include the true population parameter with a certain level of confidence. For instance, if a 95% confidence interval for the population mean is [10, 20], it implies that if we were to draw many samples and compute a confidence interval for each sample, we would expect 95% of those intervals to contain the true population mean. The formula for calculating a confidence interval depends on the type of parameter being estimated and the distribution of the data. The level of confidence, often denoted by $1-\alpha$, represents the probability that the interval will contain the true population parameter. Commonly used levels of confidence include 90%, 95%, and 99%. Confidence intervals are widely used in various fields such as education, psychology, medicine, economics, and social sciences. They provide a way to quantify the uncertainty associated with sample estimates and make inferences about population parameters.

Parametric versus Non-Parametric Procedures

Parametric and non-parametric inferential procedures are two broad categories of statistical methods used to analyze data and make inferences about population parameters. The distinction between these approaches lies in their assumptions about the underlying distribution of the data.

Parametric Inferential Procedures. Parametric procedures assume that the data follow a specific probability distribution, typically the normal distribution. This assumption is crucial for accurate estimation and hypothesis testing. Common parametric tests include t-tests, analysis of variance (ANOVA), regression analysis, and chi-square tests for independence. Advantages of parametric tests are that they are often more powerful (i.e., have higher statistical power) when the data meet the distributional assumptions. Further, they provide more precise estimates of population parameters when the assumptions are met. However, parametric tests are sensitive to violations of distributional assumptions. When data do not meet these assumptions, the results may be biased or unreliable and they may not be suitable for analyzing non-normally distributed or ordinal data.

Non-parametric Inferential Procedures. Non-parametric procedures make fewer assumptions about the distribution of the data. Instead of relying on specific probability distributions, they focus on ranking or ordering the data values. Non-parametric tests include Wilcoxon signed-rank test, Mann-Whitney U test, Kruskal-Wallis test, and Spearman's rank correlation coefficient. Advantages on non-parametric tests are that they are robust to violations of distributional assumptions, making them suitable for analyzing non-normally distributed data and can be used with ordinal or non-continuous data. Some disadvantages are that non-parametric tests may have lower statistical power compared to parametric tests when the distributional assumptions are met and may provide less precise estimates of population parameters, particularly with smaller sample sizes.

Key Differences. Parametric procedures rely on specific distributional assumptions, while non-parametric procedures are distribution-free or have fewer assumptions. Parametric tests are typically used for continuous, normally distributed data, whereas non-parametric tests can analyze a broader range of data types, including ordinal and non-normally distributed data. Non-parametric tests are generally more robust to violations of assumptions, making them suitable for analyzing data with unknown or non-standard distributions. Parametric tests may have higher statistical power under ideal conditions, but non-parametric tests may be more appropriate when data do not meet parametric assumptions. In summary, the choice between parametric and non-parametric inferential procedures depends on the nature of the data, the assumptions underlying the analysis, and the specific research question. Researchers should carefully consider these factors when selecting the appropriate statistical method for their study.

Hypothesis Testing

Hypothesis testing is a fundamental procedure in educational research used to assess the significance of relationships or differences between variables of interest. Below is a step-by-step description of the hypothesis testing process in educational research:

Introduction to Educational Research

1. **Formulate the Research Hypotheses**: The first step is to clearly define the research question and formulate the null hypothesis ($H0$) and alternative hypothesis ($H1$). The null hypothesis typically states that there is no effect or relationship, while the alternative hypothesis proposes a specific effect or relationship between variables.

2. **Select a Statistical Test**: Choose an appropriate statistical test based on the research design, nature of the variables, and assumptions of the data. Common tests in educational research include t-tests, ANOVA, chi-square tests, correlation analysis, and regression analysis, among others.

3. **Collect Data**: Collect data from participants or sources relevant to the research question. Ensure that the data collection process adheres to ethical guidelines and is designed to minimize bias and errors.

4. **Preprocess Data**: Clean and preprocess the collected data to address missing values, outliers, and other data quality issues. Data preprocessing steps may include data cleaning, transformation, and normalization to ensure the reliability and validity of the analysis.

5. **Conduct the Statistical Test**: Perform the selected statistical test to evaluate the hypotheses. Calculate the test statistic (e.g., t-value, F-value, chi-square statistic) based on the collected data and the chosen test method.

6. **Determine the Significance Level**: Set the significance level (α), which represents the probability of rejecting the null hypothesis when it is true. Common significance levels include 0.05 (5%) and 0.01 (1%), indicating the threshold for accepting or rejecting the null hypothesis.

7. **Calculate the p-value**: Calculate the p-value associated with the test statistic. The p-value represents the probability of observing the test results, or more extreme results, under the assumption that the null hypothesis is true.

8. **Make a Decision**: Compare the p-value to the significance level (α) to make a decision regarding the null hypothesis. If the p-value is less than or equal to the significance level ($p \leq \alpha$), reject the null hypothesis in favor of the alternative hypothesis. If the p-value is greater than the significance level ($p > \alpha$), fail to reject the null hypothesis.

9. **Interpret the Results**: Interpret the findings of the hypothesis test in the context of the research question and objectives. Discuss the implications of the results, including the practical significance of any observed effects or relationships.

10. **Report the Findings**: Communicate the results of the hypothesis test in a clear and concise manner, following the conventions of academic writing and reporting. Provide relevant statistics, such as test statistics, p-values, effect sizes, and confidence intervals, to support the conclusions drawn from the analysis.

By following these steps, researchers can effectively apply hypothesis testing techniques to investigate research questions and draw valid conclusions based on empirical evidence.

Type I and Type II Errors. In hypothesis testing, Type I and Type II errors represent the two possible mistakes that researchers can make when interpreting the results of a statistical test. Type I error occurs when a true null hypothesis is incorrectly rejected. In other words, it is the error of concluding that there is a significant effect or difference when there is no true effect or difference in the population. The probability of committing a Type I error is denoted by the significance level (α), which is typically set at

0.05 or 0.01. The significance level represents the threshold for rejecting the null hypothesis. If the p-value of the statistical test is less than or equal to the significance level, the null hypothesis is rejected, leading to a Type I error.

Type II error occurs when a false null hypothesis is incorrectly retained or accepted. It is the error of failing to reject the null hypothesis when there is a true effect or difference in the population. The probability of committing a Type II error is denoted by β. Type II error is influenced by factors such as sample size, effect size, and the chosen significance level. Increasing sample size, effect size, or significance level reduces the likelihood of committing a Type II error.

In summary, Type I error involves incorrectly rejecting a true null hypothesis (false positive), whereas Type II error involves incorrectly retaining a false null hypothesis (false negative). Researchers aim to minimize both Type I and Type II errors in hypothesis testing. However, there is often a trade-off between the two types of errors. Adjusting the significance level (α) affects the likelihood of Type I and Type II errors inversely: decreasing α reduces the risk of Type I error but increases the risk of Type II error, and vice versa. Understanding Type I and Type II errors is critical in hypothesis testing, as it helps researchers interpret the results of statistical tests accurately and make informed decisions based on the evidence provided by the data.

Inferential Procedures for Comparing Groups

Depending on the nature and distribution of the data and the objectives of the study, researchers may choose either parametric or non-parametric procedures for comparing groups. Some of the most frequently used parametric procedures for comparing groups are t-test and analysis of variance (ANOVA), whereas non-parametric procedures for comparing groups are Mann-Whitney U Test, the Kruskal-Wallis Test, Wilcoxon signed-rank test, and the Friedman test.

t-Test: The t-test is used to compare the mean of one group to a known value such as a population mean, the means of two independent groups, or the means of two paired samples (consisting of the same individuals or matched individuals). Depending on the research design, researchers may use a one sample t-test, an independent samples t-test, or a paired samples t-test. The t-test involves the calculation of the t test statistics and is commonly used when the data are approximately normally distributed, and the variances are equal or can be assumed to be equal (equal variances assumed) or unequal (equal variances not assumed). If the probability of the test statistics p is lower than the significance level α, mean differences are considered statistically significant.

Introduction to Educational Research

Example of t-Test in Educational Research

In the following example, a researcher wants to investigate whether there is a significant difference in exam scores between students who attended a traditional lecture-based course and students who participated in an interactive online course. Below are the steps that the researcher takes:

1. **Hypothesis formulation**:
   - Null Hypothesis (H0): There is no significant difference in exam scores between students in the traditional lecture-based course and the interactive online course.
   - Alternative Hypothesis (H1): There is a significant difference in exam scores between students in the traditional lecture-based course and the interactive online course.

2. **Data collection**:
   - The researcher collects exam scores from two groups of students: one group who attended the traditional lecture-based course (Group A) and another group who participated in the interactive online course (Group B).
   - Each group ideally should have similar characteristics and backgrounds to minimize confounding variables.

3. **Data analysis**:
   - The researcher performs an independent samples t-test to compare the mean exam scores of Group A and Group B.
   - Let's assume the null hypothesis is true. The t-test will determine the probability of observing the obtained difference in means (or more extreme) under the assumption that the null hypothesis is true.

4. **Interpretation**:
   - If the p-value obtained from the t-test is less than the chosen significance level (usually 0.05), the researcher rejects the null hypothesis.
   - If the p-value is greater than 0.05, the researcher fails to reject the null hypothesis, indicating that there is not enough evidence to suggest a significant difference in exam scores between the two groups.

5. **Conclusion**:
   - If the null hypothesis is rejected, the researcher concludes that there is a significant difference in exam scores between the traditional lecture-based course and the interactive online course.
   - If the null hypothesis is not rejected, the researcher concludes that there is no significant difference in exam scores between the two courses.

It's important to note that other factors such as sample size, randomization, and controlling for confounding variables should also be considered to ensure the validity and reliability of the results.

Analysis of Variance (ANOVA). ANOVA is a statistical method used to compare the means of three or more groups to determine if there are statistically significant differences among them. It assesses whether the variability between group means is greater than the variability within groups. ANOVA calculates an F-statistic, which compares the variance between groups to the variance within groups. If the F-statistic exceeds a critical value, indicating that the between-group variance is significantly larger than the within-group variance, the ANOVA test concludes that there are significant differences among the group means. ANOVA is commonly used in experimental and causal-comparative studies to analyze categorical independent variables with continuous dependent variables. Depending on the research design, researchers should use specific types of ANOVA such as:

- **One-Way ANOVA**: Compares the means of three or more independent groups on a single dependent variable.

Introduction to Educational Research

- **Two-Way ANOVA**: Examines the effects of two independent variables (factors) on a single dependent variable.
- **Repeated Measures ANOVA**: Analyzes the effects of within-subject factors (repeated measurements) on a dependent variable.
- **Analysis of Covariance (ANCOVA):** Assesses group differences on a continuous outcome variable while controlling for the influence of one or more covariates.
- **Mixed ANOVA**: Combines features of both one-way ANOVA and repeated measures ANOVA, allowing for the analysis of between-subjects and within-subject factors simultaneously.
- **Multivariate Analysis of Variance (MANOVA):** Simultaneously analyzes the differences in means of multiple dependent variables between two or more groups.
- **Multivariate Analysis of Covariance (MANCOVA):** Simultaneously analyzes multiple dependent variables while controlling for the influence of one or more covariates.

When finding a significant result in ANOVA, researchers conduct post hoc analyses. These analyses aim to identify which specific groups differ significantly from each other when there are more than two groups involved. Since ANOVA only tells us that there are differences between groups, but not which groups are different, post hoc tests provide this additional information. Common types of post hoc analyses include:

- **Tukey's Honestly Significant Difference (HSD)**. Tukey's HSD test compares all possible pairs of group means and identifies which pairs are significantly different from each other. It controls for familywise error rate, ensuring that the overall Type I error rate remains at the desired level.
- **Bonferroni Correction**. The Bonferroni correction adjusts the significance level for multiple comparisons to maintain an overall Type I error rate. It divides the desired significance level (usually $\alpha = 0.05$) by the number of comparisons being made.
- **Sidak Correction**. Similar to the Bonferroni correction, the Sidak correction adjusts the significance level for multiple comparisons. It is slightly more powerful than the Bonferroni correction but can be less conservative in some situations.
- **Dunnett's Test**. Dunnett's test is used when comparing multiple treatment groups to a control group. It controls for Type I error rate while allowing for comparisons between treatment groups and a control group.

Scheffé's Test. Scheffé's test is a conservative post hoc test that can be used for unequal sample sizes and unequal variances. It provides simultaneous confidence intervals for all possible pairwise comparisons.

Example of ANOVA in Educational Research

In the following example, a researcher wants to compare the effectiveness of three different teaching methods (traditional lecture-based, flipped classroom, and problem-based learning) on student performance in mathematics. Below are the steps that the researcher should take in this scenario:
1. **Hypothesis formulation**:
   - Null Hypothesis (H0): There is no significant difference in student performance among the three teaching methods.
   - Alternative Hypothesis (H1): There is a significant difference in student performance among the three teaching methods.
2. **Data collection**:
   - The researcher collects performance data (such as exam scores or grades) from students who have been taught using each of the three teaching methods.
   - The data should ideally be collected from similar groups of students to minimize confounding variables.
3. **Data analysis**:

Example of ANOVA in Educational Research
<ul><li>The researcher performs a one-way ANOVA test to analyze whether there are statistically significant differences in the mean performance scores among the three teaching methods.</li><li>ANOVA compares the variance within each group to the variance between groups. If the variance between groups is significantly larger than the variance within groups, it suggests that there are significant differences among the groups.</li></ul>4. **Interpretation**:<ul><li>If the p-value obtained from the ANOVA test is less than the chosen significance level (usually 0.05), the researcher rejects the null hypothesis.</li><li>If the p-value is greater than 0.05, the researcher fails to reject the null hypothesis, indicating that there is not enough evidence to suggest significant differences among the teaching methods.</li></ul>5. **Post-hoc analysis** (if necessary):<ul><li>If the ANOVA test indicates significant differences among the groups, the researcher may conduct post-hoc tests (such as Tukey's HSD test) to determine which specific pairs of teaching methods have significant differences in student performance.</li></ul>6. **Conclusion**:<ul><li>If the null hypothesis is rejected, the researcher concludes that there are significant differences in student performance among the teaching methods.</li><li>If the null hypothesis is not rejected, the researcher concludes that there are no significant differences in student performance among the teaching methods.</li></ul>As with any statistical analysis, it's important to ensure that the assumptions of ANOVA are met, including the normality of data distribution and homogeneity of variances among groups. Additionally, controlling for potential confounding variables and ensuring random assignment of students to teaching methods can improve the validity of the results.

Mann-Whitney U Test. The Mann-Whitney U test, also known as the Wilcoxon rank-sum test, is a non-parametric statistical test used to compare two independent groups on a continuous or ordinal outcome variable. It assesses whether there is a statistically significant difference between the medians of the two groups. The test ranks all the observations from both groups combined, calculates the sum of ranks for each group, and then compares these sums to determine if there is a significant difference between the groups. The Mann-Whitney U test is particularly useful when the assumptions of parametric tests like the t-test are violated, such as when the data are not normally distributed or the sample sizes are small.

Kruskal-Wallis Test: The Kruskal-Wallis test is a non-parametric statistical test used to compare the median ranks of two or more independent groups on a continuous or ordinal outcome variable. It extends the Mann-Whitney U test to more than two groups. The test ranks all the observations from all groups combined, calculates the sum of ranks for each group, and then compares these sums to determine if there is a significant difference between the groups. The Kruskal-Wallis test is particularly useful when the assumptions of parametric tests like ANOVA are violated, such as when the data are not normally distributed or the sample sizes are small.

Wilcoxon Signed-Rank Test. The Wilcoxon signed-rank test is a non-parametric statistical test used to compare two related groups or conditions on a continuous or ordinal outcome variable. It is particularly useful when the assumptions of parametric tests like the paired t-test are violated, such as when the data are not normally distributed or the sample size is small. The test ranks the absolute differences between paired observations, assigns positive or negative ranks based on the direction of the differences, and then calculates the sum of ranks for each group. The Wilcoxon signed-rank test compares these sums to determine if there is a significant difference between the groups.

Friedman Test. The Friedman test is a non-parametric statistical test used to compare the median ranks of two or more related groups on a continuous or ordinal outcome variable. It is often referred to as the non-parametric alternative to repeated measures ANOVA. The test ranks the observations within each group, calculates the mean rank for each observation across all groups, and then compares these mean ranks to determine if there is a significant difference between the groups. The Friedman test is particularly useful when the assumptions of parametric tests like repeated measures ANOVA are violated, such as when the data are not normally distributed or the sample sizes are small.

Inferential Procedures for Examining Relationships

Depending on the nature and distribution of the data and the objectives of the study, researchers may choose either parametric or non-parametric procedures to test the significance of relationships among variables. Parametric procedures include the Pearson correlation coefficient, simple and multiple linear regression analysis, path analysis, factor analysis, principal component analysis, structural equations modeling, cluster analysis, or latent class analysis. Non-parametric procedures include Spearman's rank correlation coefficient, Kendall's tau correlation coefficient, or the chi-square test.

Pearson Correlation: The Pearson correlation coefficient, often denoted as r, is a measure of the strength and direction of the linear relationship between two continuous variables. The Pearson correlation coefficient measures the degree of linear association between two variables. It ranges from -1 to 1, where: $r=1$ indicates a perfect positive linear relationship, $r=-1$ indicates a perfect negative linear relationship, $r=0$ indicates no linear relationship. The sign of r indicates the direction of the relationship. Positive r values indicate a positive association (as one variable increases, the other tends to increase). Negative r values indicate a negative association (as one variable increases, the other tends to decrease). The magnitude of r represents the strength of the linear relationship, with larger absolute values indicating stronger associations. The Pearson correlation coefficient assumes that the relationship between variables is linear. It also assumes that the variables are approximately normally distributed and have homoscedasticity (constant variance). The Pearson correlation coefficient is widely used in various fields, including psychology, education, sociology, economics, and natural sciences, to quantify relationships between continuous variables. The Pearson correlation coefficient provides a simple and intuitive measure of the linear relationship between two continuous variables. It is widely used due to its simplicity and ease of interpretation, although it is sensitive to outliers and non-linear relationships.

Regression Analysis: Regression analysis is a statistical method used to examine the relationship between one or more independent variables (predictors) and a dependent variable (outcome). It aims to model the relationship between the variables and make predictions based on the observed data. Linear regression is one of the most common types of regression analysis. In simple linear regression, there is one independent variable and one dependent variable, and the relationship between them is modeled using a straight line. In multiple linear regression, there are two or more independent variables, and the relationship between them and the dependent variable is modeled using a linear equation. Besides linear regression, there are various types of regression analysis, including:

- Logistic regression: Used when the dependent variable is binary (e.g., yes/no, success/failure) and aims to predict the probability of an event occurring.

Introduction to Educational Research

- Polynomial regression: Models the relationship between the independent and dependent variables using polynomial functions.

- Ridge regression and Lasso regression: Used for regularization in cases of multicollinearity or overfitting.

- Time series regression: Used to analyze time-series data, where the dependent variable changes over time.

Regression analysis is a complex procedure and implies the completion of multiple steps:

- Model specification: Decide on the type of regression model to use and select the independent variables.

- Model estimation: Estimate the parameters of the regression model using statistical techniques.

- Model evaluation: Assess the goodness-of-fit of the model and test for the significance of the regression coefficients.

- Interpretation: Interpret the results of the regression analysis, including the coefficients and their significance, and make predictions based on the model.

Before conducting the regression analysis, researchers must verify that the assumptions of regression analysis were met, including linearity, independence of errors, homoscedasticity (constant variance), and normality of residuals. Violations of these assumptions may affect the validity of the results. After completing the data analysis, researchers must interpret the results. Interpreting the results of regression analysis involves understanding the relationships between the independent variables (predictors) and the dependent variable (outcome), as well as assessing the overall fit and significance of the model. The first step is examining the overall fit of the regression model. Common metrics for assessing model fit include R-squared (or adjusted R-squared), which measures the proportion of variance in the dependent variable explained by the independent variables. R-squared values range from 0 to 1 where values closer to 1 indicate better fit. Next, researchers must examine regression coefficients (beta coefficients or slopes) associated with each independent variable in the model. These coefficients represent the change in the dependent variable for a one-unit change in the corresponding independent variable, holding other variables constant. Researchers must check the sign (+/-) of each coefficient to determine the direction of the relationship. A positive coefficient indicates a positive relationship (as the independent variable increases, the dependent variable also increases), while a negative coefficient indicates a negative relationship (as the independent variable increases, the dependent variable decreases). The p-values associated with each coefficient indicate whether they are statistically significant. Typically, coefficients with p-values less than a predetermined significance level (e.g., 0.05) are considered statistically significant. Significant coefficients indicate that the corresponding independent variables have a statistically significant effect on the dependent variable. Further, researchers must examine the magnitude and direction of the coefficients in the context of the research question. For example, if the coefficient for a predictor variable is 0.5, it means that a one-unit increase in that predictor is associated with a 0.5-unit increase in the dependent variable, all else being equal.

It is important to also evaluate the practical significance of the coefficients by considering the context of the study and the magnitude of the effects. A statistically significant effect may not necessarily be practically meaningful if it is very small. By following these steps, researchers can effectively interpret the results of regression analysis and draw meaningful conclusions about the relationships between variables in their study.

Example of Regression Analysis in Educational Research

In the following example, a researcher wants to explore the relationship between students' study hours and their exam scores in a particular subject, while considering other relevant variables such as previous academic performance (e.g., GPA), attendance, and socioeconomic status. Below are the steps that the researcher should follow:

1. **Data collection**:
   - The researcher collects data on several variables from a sample of students, including:
     - Exam scores (the dependent variable)
     - Study hours per week
     - Previous academic performance (e.g., GPA)
     - Attendance rate
     - Socioeconomic status (e.g., parental income, education level)
   - The data should ideally be collected through surveys, academic records, and other relevant sources.

2. **Data analysis**:
   - The researcher performs multiple regression analysis, with the exam scores as the dependent variable and study hours, previous academic performance, attendance, and socioeconomic status as independent variables.
   - The regression analysis estimates the relationship between the dependent variable (exam scores) and each independent variable.

3. **Interpretation**:
   - The regression analysis results provide coefficients for each independent variable, indicating the strength and direction of their relationship with the dependent variable.
   - For example, a positive coefficient for study hours suggests that increasing study hours is associated with higher exam scores, while a negative coefficient for socioeconomic status suggests that higher socioeconomic status is associated with lower exam scores.
   - The statistical significance of each coefficient (p-value) indicates whether the relationship is likely to be significant or due to random chance.

4. **Model evaluation**:
   - The researcher evaluates the overall fit of the regression model using metrics such as R-squared (the proportion of variance in the dependent variable explained by the independent variables) and adjusted R-squared.
   - Additionally, the researcher may assess the assumptions of regression analysis, such as linearity, independence of errors, homoscedasticity, and normality of residuals.

5. **Conclusion**:
   - Based on the regression analysis results, the researcher can draw conclusions about the relationship between study hours and exam scores, while estimating the impact of other factors.
   - The researcher may also identify which independent variables have the most significant impact on exam scores and provide recommendations for educational interventions or policies based on the findings.

Regression analysis allows researchers to examine the complex relationships between multiple variables in educational research and identify factors that influence student outcomes.

Path Analysis. Path analysis is a multivariate statistical method used to assess and quantify the relationships between variables in a hypothesized causal model. It extends multiple regression analysis by allowing for the simultaneous estimation of direct and indirect effects among variables. Assumptions of path analysis include linearity, normality, and independence of errors. Further, path analysis assumes that the specified model accurately represents the underlying causal structure of the variables, which may not always be the case. Path analysis begins with the formulation of a theoretical model that specifies the relationships between variables based on prior knowledge or theory. The model is represented graphically as a path diagram, where variables are represented by nodes and hypothesized relationships between variables are represented by arrows (paths). Path analysis estimates the parameters of the model using techniques such as ordinary least squares (OLS) regression or maximum likelihood estimation. The coefficients obtained from the estimation represent the strength and direction of the relationships between variables in the model. Path analysis assesses the goodness-of-fit of the model to the data using fit indices such as the chi-square statistic, Comparative Fit Index (CFI), Root Mean Square Error of Approximation (RMSEA), and others. Model modification indices may be used to identify areas of the model that could be improved. Interpretation of path analysis results involves examining the estimated path coefficients to understand the direct and indirect effects between variables. Path coefficients represent standardized regression coefficients and indicate the strength and direction of the relationships between variables. Direct effects are represented by the coefficients of the paths connecting variables directly, while indirect effects are the product of coefficients along multiple paths connecting variables indirectly. Significance testing of path coefficients helps determine whether the relationships between variables are statistically significant.

Cluster Analysis. Cluster analysis is a multivariate statistical technique used to group similar objects or observations into clusters based on their characteristics or attributes. The main objective of cluster analysis is to partition a dataset into groups (clusters) so that observations within each cluster are more similar to each other than to observations in other clusters. Clusters are formed based on the distance or similarity between observations, with the goal of maximizing within-cluster similarity and minimizing between-cluster similarity. There are several types of clustering algorithms:

- Hierarchical clustering: Builds a hierarchy of clusters by iteratively merging or splitting clusters based on the distance between observations.

- Partitioning clustering: Divides the dataset into a predetermined number of clusters, with each observation assigned to the cluster that minimizes a chosen criterion (e.g., within-cluster variance).

- Density-based clustering: Identifies clusters as regions of high density separated by regions of low density, without assuming a specific number of clusters.

Euclidean distance, Manhattan distance, and Mahalanobis distance are commonly used distance measures to quantify the dissimilarity or similarity between observations. Other distance measures, such as correlation distance and cosine distance, may be used depending on the characteristics of the data. The quality of the clustering solution can be assessed using internal validity measures (e.g., silhouette coefficient, Dunn index) or external validity measures (e.g., Adjusted Rand Index) that compare the clustering solution to known class labels. Cluster analysis is widely used in social sciences and various fields, including market research, customer segmentation, image analysis, text mining, biological classification, and social network analysis. It provides valuable insights into the structure of data, helps identify patterns or groups within datasets, and aids in decision-making and knowledge discovery in various domains.

Factor Analysis and Principal Component Analysis. Factor analysis and principal component analysis (PCA) are both multivariate techniques used to reduce the dimensionality of data and identify underlying patterns or structures. Factor analysis is a statistical method used to identify latent factors underlying observed variables. It assumes that observed variables are influenced by one or more underlying factors that cannot be directly measured. Factor analysis aims to uncover these latent factors and understand how they contribute to the observed correlations between variables. The technique estimates factor loadings, which represent the correlations between observed variables and latent factors. Factor analysis can be exploratory or confirmatory, depending on whether the researcher aims to explore the structure of the data or test a specific theoretical model. PCA is a dimensionality reduction technique that transforms observed variables into a smaller set of uncorrelated variables called principal components. Principal components are linear combinations of the original variables that capture the maximum variance in the data. PCA aims to summarize the information contained in the original variables while minimizing information loss. The first principal component explains the most variance in the data, followed by subsequent components in descending order of explained variance. PCA is widely used for data exploration, visualization, and preprocessing in various fields such as machine learning, signal processing, and social sciences. Both factor analysis and principal component analysis are powerful tools for exploring the structure of data, identifying underlying patterns, and reducing the dimensionality of complex datasets. The choice between them depends on the research goals, the nature of the data, and the underlying assumptions about the relationships between variables.

Structural Equations Modeling (SEM). SEM is a multivariate statistical technique used to analyze complex relationships among variables by simultaneously estimating a series of regression-like equations. SEM begins with model specification, which involves the formulation of a theoretical model that represents the hypothesized relationships among observed variables and latent constructs. The model is specified using path diagrams, which visually depict the relationships between variables with arrows representing causal pathways. SEM includes both a measurement model and a structural model. The measurement model specifies the relationships between latent constructs (factors) and their observed indicators (manifest variables). Factor loadings represent the correlations between latent constructs and observed variables, while error terms capture the unique variance in the observed variables not accounted for by the latent constructs. The structural model specifies the relationships between latent constructs and predicts the relationships between them. Paths in the structural model represent hypothesized causal relationships between latent constructs and are estimated using regression-like equations. Direct and indirect effects between latent constructs can be estimated, allowing for the testing of complex theoretical models. SEM estimates the parameters of the model using techniques such as maximum likelihood estimation or weighted least squares. The fit of the model to the data is assessed using fit indices such as the chi-square statistic, Comparative Fit Index (CFI), Root Mean Square Error of Approximation (RMSEA), and others. Model fit indices are used to assess the goodness-of-fit of the model to the data. Modification indices may be used to identify areas of the model that could be improved. SEM is a powerful statistical technique widely used in social sciences, psychology, education, and other fields to test complex theoretical models, evaluate hypotheses, and explore relationships among variables.

Latent Class Analysis (LCA). LCA is a multivariate statistical technique used to identify unobserved (latent) subgroups, or classes, within a population based on patterns of observed variables. The main objective of latent class analysis is to identify homogeneous subgroups within a heterogeneous population based on observed categorical or continuous variables. LCA assumes that the observed variables are manifestations of an underlying categorical latent variable (class membership), and individuals within each class have similar response patterns on the observed variables. In latent class analysis, a series of latent class models with different numbers of classes (e.g., one-class model, two-class model, etc.) are specified and compared to determine the best-fitting model. The probability of observing specific response patterns on the observed variables is modeled for each latent class. The parameters of the latent class model, including class probabilities and item-response probabilities, are estimated using maximum likelihood estimation or Bayesian estimation techniques. The model estimation process involves iteratively assigning individuals to latent classes based on their response patterns and updating the model parameters until convergence is achieved. Model fit indices, such as the Bayesian Information Criterion

(BIC), Akaike Information Criterion (AIC), and likelihood ratio tests, are used to evaluate the fit of alternative latent class models. The best-fitting model is selected based on criteria such as parsimony, interpretability, and substantive theory. Latent class analysis is widely used in various fields, including psychology, education, sociology, epidemiology, marketing research, and public health. Common applications include identifying consumer segments, profiling individuals based on behavior or attitudes, and examining heterogeneity in response patterns to interventions or treatments. Latent class analysis provides a valuable tool for identifying and characterizing unobserved subgroups within populations, allowing researchers to better understand heterogeneity and tailor interventions or policies to specific subgroups.

Spearman Rank Correlation. The Spearman rank correlation coefficient, often denoted as ρ (rho), is a non-parametric measure of the strength and direction of the monotonic relationship between two variables. Spearman's rank correlation does not assume that the relationship between variables is linear or that the variables are normally distributed. It only requires that the variables are measured on an ordinal or interval scale. Unlike the Pearson correlation coefficient, which measures the linear relationship between variables, Spearman's rank correlation assesses the degree to which the relationship between variables can be described by a monotonic function. Spearman's rank correlation coefficient is calculated based on the ranks of observations in the variables rather than their actual values. It ranges from -1 to 1, where: $\rho=1$ indicates a perfect monotonic positive relationship, $\rho=-1$ indicates a perfect monotonic negative relationship, and $\rho=0$ indicates no monotonic relationship. Spearman's correlation coefficient is less sensitive to outliers and non-linear relationships than the Pearson correlation coefficient. To compute Spearman's rank correlation coefficient, the ranks of observations in both variables are determined. The differences between the ranks in each pair of observations are then squared, and Spearman's correlation coefficient is calculated as the Pearson correlation coefficient between the ranks of the two variables. The sign of Spearman's correlation coefficient indicates the direction of the monotonic relationship. Positive ρ values indicate a monotonic increasing relationship. Negative ρ values indicate a monotonic decreasing relationship. The magnitude of ρ represents the strength of the monotonic relationship, with larger absolute values indicating stronger associations. Spearman's rank correlation coefficient is commonly used in various fields, including psychology, education, sociology, economics, and biology, when the assumptions of parametric correlation measures like Pearson's correlation coefficient are not met. Spearman's rank correlation coefficient provides a robust measure of association for ordinal and interval variables, particularly when the assumptions of parametric correlation measures cannot be met. It is widely used in situations where the relationship between variables may be non-linear or non-normally distributed.

Kendall's tau. Kendall's tau correlation coefficient, often denoted as τ (tau), is a non-parametric measure of association between two ordinal variables. It quantifies the degree of concordance or agreement between the rankings of observations in the two variables, regardless of the actual values of the variables. Kendall's tau coefficient measures the similarity in ranking between two variables. It ranges from -1 to 1, where: $\tau = 1$ indicates perfect agreement or perfect positive correlation, $\tau = -1$ indicates perfect disagreement or perfect negative correlation, and $\tau = 0$ indicates no association between the rankings. Kendall's tau considers all possible pairs of observations and compares their rankings in both variables. Kendall's tau correlation coefficient provides a robust measure of association for ordinal data and is particularly useful when variables are ranked rather than measured on a continuous scale. It is widely used in situations where Pearson correlation may not be appropriate due to violations of assumptions or the nature of the data.

Chi-Square Test: The chi-square test is a non-parametric statistical test used to determine whether there is a significant association between two categorical variables. The chi-square ($\chi 2$) test statistic measures the discrepancy between observed and expected frequencies of the categorical variables. It is calculated as the sum of the squared differences between observed (O) and expected (E) frequencies, divided by the expected frequencies. The larger the value of the chi-square statistic, the greater the discrepancy between observed and expected frequencies. The null hypothesis ($H0$) in the chi-square test states that there is no association between the two categorical variables. The chi-square test assumes that any differences between observed and expected frequencies are due to random chance. The chi-square test provides a p-value that indicates the probability of observing the observed frequencies (or more extreme) under the null hypothesis. If the p-value is less than a chosen significance level (e.g., 0.05), the null hypothesis is rejected, and it is concluded that there is a significant association between the categorical variables. The chi-square test is commonly used in various fields, including psychology, education, sociology, biology, and market research, to analyze contingency tables and test hypotheses about relationships between categorical variables. It is a fundamental tool for analyzing categorical data and determining whether there is evidence of association between variables. It is widely used due to its simplicity and versatility, making it applicable to a wide range of research questions and study designs.

Frequentist versus Bayesian Inference

The inferential procedures described in the previous section are frequentist methods. Frequentist inference is a statistical approach to inference and decision-making that focuses on properties of observed data and sampling distributions. In frequentist inference, probability is interpreted as the long-run relative frequency of an event occurring in repeated trials. Bayesian analysis is a different statistical approach to inference and decision-making that applies Bayes' theorem to update beliefs or probabilities about hypotheses, parameters, or unknown quantities based on observed evidence or data. In Bayesian analysis, probability is interpreted as a measure of uncertainty or belief, and prior knowledge or beliefs about the parameters of interest are represented using prior probability distributions. These priors are combined with observed data using Bayes' theorem to obtain posterior probability distributions, which represent updated beliefs about the parameters after observing the data. Bayesian analysis provides a principled framework for incorporating prior information, quantifying uncertainty, and making probabilistic inferences.

Bayesian analysis and frequentist analysis are two distinct approaches to statistical inference, each with its own set of principles, assumptions, and techniques. In Bayesian analysis, probability is interpreted as a measure of uncertainty or belief. Prior knowledge or beliefs about the parameters of interest are represented using prior probability distributions, which are updated based on observed data using Bayes' theorem. In frequentist analysis, probability is interpreted as the long-run relative frequency of an event occurring in repeated trials. Parameters are treated as fixed, unknown values, and inference is based on properties of the sampling distribution of estimators.

Bayesian analysis allows for the explicit incorporation of prior information or beliefs into the analysis through the specification of prior probability distributions. These priors represent existing knowledge about the parameters of interest. In contrast, frequentist analysis does not incorporate prior information directly. Inferences are based solely on the observed data, and prior information is not explicitly accounted for. Bayesian parameter estimation involves deriving the posterior probability distribution of the parameters given the observed data. This posterior distribution represents updated beliefs about the parameters after observing the data. In frequentist analysis, parameter estimation typically involves using point estimates (e.g., maximum likelihood estimates) or confidence intervals based on properties of the sampling distribution of estimators.

Bayesian analysis approaches hypothesis testing in terms of comparing the posterior probabilities of competing hypotheses. Bayes factors or posterior probabilities are used to quantify the evidence in favor of one hypothesis over another. Frequentist analysis conducts hypothesis testing using p-values, which indicate the probability of observing the data, or more extreme data, under the null hypothesis. Hypotheses are typically tested based on the sampling distribution of test statistics.

Bayesian analysis provides probability distributions for parameters and hypotheses, allowing for direct quantification of uncertainty and intuitive interpretation of results in terms of probabilities. Frequentist analysis provides point estimates or confidence intervals, which convey information about the precision of estimates but do not directly quantify uncertainty in terms of probabilities.

Bayesian analysis often involves more computationally intensive methods, such as Markov chain Monte Carlo (MCMC) simulation, especially for complex models or high-dimensional parameter spaces. Frequentist analysis typically relies on simpler computational techniques, such as optimization algorithms, and may be computationally less demanding.

Overall, Bayesian analysis and frequentist analysis offer different perspectives on statistical inference, with Bayesian analysis providing a more probabilistic framework that explicitly incorporates prior information, while frequentist analysis focuses on properties of observed data and sampling distributions. The choice between the two approaches depends on the research question, the availability of prior information, and the underlying assumptions of the analysis.

Bayesian inference involves the following steps:

Specify the prior: Begin by specifying an initial belief or prior probability distribution for the hypothesis based on existing knowledge or information.

Observe the evidence: Collect new evidence or data relevant to the hypothesis.

Update the posterior: Apply Bayes' theorem to update the prior probability distribution based on the observed evidence, resulting in the posterior probability distribution.

Make inference: Use the posterior probability distribution to make inferences, such as estimating parameters, making predictions, or selecting the most likely hypothesis.

One advantage of Bayesian inference is that it allows researchers to incorporate existing knowledge or beliefs into the analysis through the specification of prior probabilities, and can accommodate complex models, hierarchical structures, and uncertainty in parameters or hypotheses. Unlike frequentist methods, Bayesian inference provides probability distributions for parameters or hypotheses, allowing for more nuanced interpretations of uncertainty. Bayesian inference is used in various fields, including social sciences, statistics, machine learning, economics, biology, and physics, for tasks such as parameter estimation, hypothesis testing, model comparison, and decision-making. Bayesian inference provides a powerful framework for updating beliefs and making probabilistic inferences in the presence of uncertainty. By combining prior knowledge with observed evidence, Bayesian methods offer a flexible and intuitive approach to statistical inference.

In conclusion, quantitative data analysis plays a vital role in advancing knowledge and understanding within the field of educational research. By employing systematic and rigorous methods, researchers can uncover empirical evidence, identify trends, and inform evidence-based practices to enhance teaching, learning, and educational outcomes. Nonetheless, it is essential to recognize the complementary nature of qualitative research and to adopt a holistic approach that integrates quantitative and qualitative methodologies for a comprehensive understanding of educational phenomena.

Summary

The chapter delves into the importance and key aspects of quantitative methods within educational research. Quantitative data analysis in this field covers a wide range of topics and methodologies, such as academic achievement, student attitudes, teaching effectiveness, school climate, and educational policies. These methods allow researchers to examine extensive datasets, identifying broad patterns and trends across diverse populations. Furthermore, they facilitate the establishment of relationships and the generalization of findings to broader populations, thereby enhancing the external validity of research outcomes. The precision of quantitative data also supports study replication, fostering the validation and verification of research findings over time. Moreover, the chapter underscores the significance of data cleaning and management procedures as essential preliminary steps to data analysis. It then delves into descriptive data analytic procedures, including data visualization and descriptive statistics, emphasizing the importance of examining data distributions. Furthermore, the chapter explains inferential data analytic procedures, elucidating the differences between statistics and parameters, as well as between parametric and non-parametric inferential procedures. It describes the hypothesis testing process and presents various parametric and non-parametric procedures for comparing groups and exploring relationships among variables. Finally, the chapter distinguishes between frequentist and Bayesian inferential procedures, outlining disparities in statistical assumptions and the inferential process. It underscores the crucial role of quantitative analyses in advancing knowledge and understanding within educational research. Through systematic and rigorous methods, researchers can uncover empirical evidence, discern trends, and inform evidence-based practices to enhance teaching, learning, and educational outcomes.

Suggestions for Students

Key Questions

1. Can you explain the main characteristics of quantitative research in education, and how do these characteristics contribute to a deeper understanding of educational phenomena?
2. Describe the process of data cleaning and explain its importance.
3. Describe two types of data visualization and explain when they are most appropriately used.
4. What are some advantages and disadvantages of using non-parametric data analysis procedures?
5. What is the distinction between parameters and statistics? Provide examples.
6. What are the steps of hypothesis testing? Explain the concepts of Type I and Type II error and provide examples.
7. Can you describe the t-test procedure? Explain when it can be used and provide some examples.
8. What is regression analysis and when can it be used?
9. What is analysis of variance (ANOVA) and when can this procedure be used?
10. What are the main distinctions between frequentist and Bayesian inferential procedures?

Suggestions for Instructors

Suggested Learning Activities

Quantitative Study Analysis. Provide students with a selection of quantitative studies related to educational settings or phenomena. Ask them to critically analyze each study, identifying the research questions, methodologies used, data collection techniques, and key findings. Encourage students to discuss the strengths and limitations of each quantitative study and how they contribute to our understanding of education.

Data Visualization Practice. Have students create data visualizations using publicly available data and present or share their data visualization with the group or online. Provide them with guidance on selecting the correct type of graphs depending on the nature of the data and the purpose of their analysis. Encourage students to reflect on the process of summarizing data and discuss strategies for improving their data analytic and presentations skills.

Research Proposal Development. Divide students into small groups and task each group with developing a research proposal for a quantitative study in education. Provide them with a list of potential research topics or allow them to choose their own. Guide students through the process of formulating research questions, selecting appropriate methodologies, designing data collection instruments, and considering ethical considerations. Have each group present their research proposal to the class and engage in peer feedback and discussion.

Critique a causal-comparative study. Provide students with a published quantitative study in educational research using parametric or non-parametric inferential procedures for comparing groups. Ask students to outline the strengths and limitations of the study by analyzing the sampling, instrumentations, choice of data analysis procedures, reporting and interpretation of the results.

Critique a correlational study. Provide students with a published quantitative study in educational research using parametric or non-parametric inferential procedures for comparing groups. Ask students to outline the strengths and limitations of the study by analyzing the sampling, instrumentations, choice of data analysis procedures, reporting and interpretation of the results.

Debate: Frequentist versus Bayesian Inference. Divide students in two groups. Each group will research, summarize, present information, and construct an argument supporting the use of the assigned inferential procedure. The two groups will then discuss the advantages and disadvantages of each approach and propose strategies for selecting the appropriate approach depending on research questions and the nature of the data.

References

Abdi, H., & Williams, L. J. (2010). Principal Component Analysis. *Wiley Interdisciplinary Reviews: Computational Statistics*, 2(4), 433–459.

Agresti, A. (2018). *Categorical Data Analysis* (3rd ed.). Wiley.

Agresti, A., & Franklin, C. (2018). *Statistics: The Art and Science of Learning from Data* (4th ed.). Pearson.

Bollen, K. A. (1989). *Structural Equations with Latent Variables*. Wiley.

Byrne, B. M. (2013). *Structural Equation Modeling with AMOS: Basic Concepts, Applications, and Programming* (2nd ed.). Routledge.

Cairo, A. (2016). *The Truthful Art: Data, Charts, and Maps for Communication*. New Riders.

Cleveland, W. S. (1993). Visualizing Data. Hobart Press.

Cohen, L., Manion, L., & Morrison, K. (2018). Research methods in education. Routledge.

College Board (2023). SAT Suite of Assessments Annual Report.

Collins, L. M., & Lanza, S. T. (2010). *Latent Class and Latent Transition Analysis: With Applications in the Social, Behavioral, and Health Sciences*. Wiley.

Conover, W. J. (1999). *Practical Nonparametric Statistics* (3rd ed.). Wiley.

Creswell, J. W. (2014). Research design: Qualitative, quantitative, and mixed methods approaches. Sage publications.

Creswell, J. W., & Creswell, J. D. (2017). *Research Design: Qualitative, Quantitative, and Mixed Methods Approaches* (5th ed.). SAGE Publications.

Diez, D. M., Barr, C. D., & Çetinkaya-Rundel, M. (2017). OpenIntro statistics (3rd ed.). OpenIntro, Inc.

Everitt, B. S., & Hothorn, T. (2011). *An introduction to applied multivariate analysis with R* (1st ed.). Springer Science & Business Media.

Everitt, B. S., & Skrondal, A. (2010). *The Cambridge Dictionary of Statistics* (4th ed.). Cambridge University Press.

Everitt, B. S., Landau, S., Leese, M., & Stahl, D. (2011). *Cluster Analysis* (5th ed.). Wiley.

Fabrigar, L. R., Wegener, D. T., MacCallum, R. C., & Strahan, E. J. (1999). Evaluating the Use of Exploratory Factor Analysis in Psychological Research. *Psychological Methods*, 4(3), 272–299.

Few, S. (2012). *Show Me the Numbers: Designing Tables and Graphs to Enlighten*. Analytics Press.

Field, A. (2013). *Discovering statistics using IBM SPSS statistics* (4th ed.). SAGE Publications.

Fraenkel, J. R., Wallen, N. E., & Hyun, H. H. (2021). *How to Design and Evaluate Research in Education* (10th ed.). McGraw-Hill Education.

Friedman, M. (1937). The Use of Ranks to Avoid the Assumption of Normality Implicit in the Analysis of Variance. *Journal of the American Statistical Association*, 32(200), 675–701.

Gall, M. D., Gall, J. P., & Borg, W. R. (2007). *Educational Research: An Introduction* (8th ed.). Pearson.

Gay, L. R., Mills, G. E., & Airasian, P. (2019). Educational research: Competencies for analysis and applications. Pearson.

Gelman, A., & Hill, J. (2006). Data analysis using regression and multilevel/hierarchical models. Cambridge University Press.

Gibbons, J. D., & Chakraborti, S. (2011). *Nonparametric Statistical Inference* (5th ed.). Chapman and Hall/CRC.

Gnanadesikan, R., and John R. Kettenring. "Minimax Confidence Intervals." The Annals of Mathematical Statistics 41, no. 1 (1970): 106-11. doi:10.1214/aoms/1177697172.

Gorsuch, R. L. (1983). *Factor Analysis* (2nd ed.). Lawrence Erlbaum Associates.

Graham, J. W. (2009). Missing data analysis: Making it work in the real world. Annual Review of Psychology, 60, 549-576.

Grolemund, G., & Wickham, H. (2017). R for data science: Import, tidy, transform, visualize, and model data. O'Reilly Media, Inc.

Hair, J. F., Black, W. C., Babin, B. J., & Anderson, R. E. (2019). *Multivariate Data Analysis* (8th ed.). Cengage Learning.

Healy, K. (2019). *Data Visualization: A Practical Introduction*. Princeton University Press.

Heiman, G. W. (2011). *Basic Statistics for the Behavioral Sciences* (6th ed.). Cengage Learning.

Hodges, J. L., and E. L. Lehmann. "The Efficiency of Some Nonparametric Competitors of the t-Test." Annals of Mathematical Statistics 34, no. 2 (1963): 324-28. doi:10.1214/aoms/1177704172.

Howell, D. C. (2012). *Statistical Methods for Psychology* (8th ed.). Cengage Learning.

Hoyle, R. H. (2012). *Handbook of Structural Equation Modeling* (1st ed.). Guilford Press.

Jain, A. K., Murty, M. N., & Flynn, P. J. (1999). Data Clustering: A Review. *ACM Computing Surveys (CSUR)*, 31(3), 264–323.

Janssen, D., & Grossmann, A. (2019). SQL quickStart guide: The simplified beginner's guide to managing, analyzing, and manipulating data with SQL. ClydeBank Media LLC.

Johnson, B., & Christensen, L. (2019). Educational research: Quantitative, qualitative, and mixed approaches. Sage publications.

Jolliffe, I. T. (2002). *Principal Component Analysis* (2nd ed.). Springer.

Kendall, M. G. (1938). A New Measure of Rank Correlation. *Biometrika*, 30(1/2), 81–93.

Kenney, John F., and E. S. Keeping. "Chapter 3: Measures of Location and Spread." In Mathematics of Statistics, Pt. 1, 3rd ed., 39-68. Princeton, NJ: Van Nostrand, 1962.

Kimerling, A. J., & Muehrcke, P. C. (2012). Map use: Reading, analysis, interpretation (Vol. 7). Esri Press.

King, G. "Mode." In Encyclopedia of Research Design, edited by Neil J. Salkind, 807-09. Thousand Oaks, CA: SAGE Publications, Inc., 2010. doi:10.4135/9781412961288.n297.

Kirk, R. E. (1996). Practical significance: A concept whose time has come. *Educational and Psychological Measurement,* 56(5), 746-759.

Kline, R. B. (2015). *Principles and Practice of Structural Equation Modeling* (4th ed.). Guilford Press.

Kruskal, W. H., & Wallis, W. A. (1952). Use of Ranks in One-Criterion Variance Analysis. *Journal of the American Statistical Association*, 47(260), 583–621.

Leedy, P. D., & Ormrod, J. E. (2018). *Practical Research: Planning and Design* (12th ed.). Pearson.

Little, R. J. A., & Rubin, D. B. (2019). Statistical analysis with missing data (3rd ed.). Wiley.

Longley, P. A., Goodchild, M. F., Maguire, D. J., & Rhind, D. W. (2015). Geographic information science & systems. John Wiley & Sons.

Mann, H. B., & Whitney, D. R. (1947). On a Test of Whether one of Two Random Variables is Stochastically Larger than the Other. *The Annals of Mathematical Statistics*, 18(1), 50–60.

Maxwell, S. E., Delaney, H. D., & Kelley, K. (2018). *Designing Experiments and Analyzing Data: A Model Comparison Perspective* (3rd ed.). Routledge.

McCutcheon, A. L. (1987). *Latent Class Analysis*. Sage Publications.

McElreath, R. (2015). *Statistical Rethinking: A Bayesian Course with Examples in R and Stan*. CRC Press.

McKinney, W. (2018). Python for data analysis: Data wrangling with pandas, numpy, and ipython. O'Reilly Media, Inc.

Milligan, G. W., & Hirtle, S. C. (2003). Clustering and Classification Methods. In J. M. Schinka & W. F. Velicer (Eds.), *Handbook of Psychology, Research Methods in Psychology* (Vol. 2, pp. 109–143). Wiley.

Montgomery, D. C., Peck, E. A., & Vining, G. G. (2012). *Introduction to Linear Regression Analysis* (5th ed.). Wiley.

Moore, D. S., McCabe, G. P., & Craig, B. A. (2014). Introduction to the practice of statistics. W. H. Freeman.

Mosteller, Frederick, and John W. Tukey, eds. Data Analysis and Regression: A Second Course in Statistics. Reading, MA: Addison-Wesley, 1977.

Newbold, P., Carlson, W. L., & Thorne, B. M. (2012). *Statistics for Business and Economics* (8th ed.). Prentice Hall.

OECD (2023), PISA 2022 Results (Volume II): Learning During – and from – Disruption, PISA, OECD Publishing, Paris, https://doi.org/10.1787/a97db61c-en.

Pearson, K. (1895). Contributions to the Mathematical Theory of Evolution. II. Skew Variation in Homogeneous Material. *Philosophical Transactions of the Royal Society A: Mathematical, Physical and Engineering Sciences*, 186, 343–414.

Pearson, K. (1900). On the Criterion that a Given System of Deviations from the Probable in the Case of a Correlated System of Variables is Such that it Can be Reasonably Supposed to have Arisen from Random Sampling. *Philosophical Magazine Series 5*, 50(302), 157–175.

Pearson, Karl. "Contributions to the Mathematical Theory of Evolution. II. Skew Variation in Homogeneous Material." Philosophical Transactions of the Royal Society of London. Series A, Containing Papers of a Mathematical or Physical Character 186 (1895): 343-414. doi:10.1098/rsta.1895.0010.

Peterson, G. N. (2019). Geographic information systems in action. Wiley.

Rubin, D. B. (1987). Multiple imputation for nonresponse in surveys. Wiley.

Schumacker, R. E., & Lomax, R. G. (2016). *A Beginner's Guide to Structural Equation Modeling* (4th ed.). Routledge.

Sherman-Morris, K., & Pickle, L. W. (2018). Introduction to geographic information systems. McGraw-Hill Education.

Siegel, S., & Castellan, N. J. (1988). *Nonparametric Statistics for the Behavioral Sciences* (2nd ed.). McGraw-Hill.

Slocum, T. A., McMaster, R. B., Kessler, F. C., & Howard, H. H. (2009). Thematic cartography and geovisualization (3rd ed.). Pearson Education.

Ward, H. H. (2009). Thematic cartography and geovisualization (3rd ed.). Pearson Education.

Spatz, C. (2005). The essentials of statistics: A tool for social research. Cengage Learning.

Spearman, C. (1904). "The Proof and Measurement of Association between Two Things". The American Journal of Psychology. 15 (1): 72–101.

Sterne, J. A. C., White, I. R., Carlin, J. B., Spratt, M., Royston, P., Kenward, M. G., ... & Carpenter, J. R. (2009). Multiple imputation for missing data in epidemiological and clinical research: Potential and pitfalls. BMJ, 338, b2393.

Stevens, S. S. "On the Theory of Scales of Measurement." Science 103, no. 2684 (1946): 677-80. doi:10.1126/science.103.2684.677.

Tabachnick, B. G., & Fidell, L. S. (2019). *Using Multivariate Statistics* (7th ed.). Pearson.

Triola, M. F. (2017). Elementary statistics (13th ed.). Pearson.

Trochim, W. M. K., & Donnelly, J. P. (2008). *The Research Methods Knowledge Base* (3rd ed.). Atomic Dog Publishing.

Tufte, E. R. (2001). *The Visual Display of Quantitative Information*. Graphics Press.

Tukey, J. W. Exploratory Data Analysis. Reading, MA: Addison-Wesley, 1977.

U.S. Department of Education, National Center for Education Statistics, Integrated Postsecondary Education Data System (IPEDS), Spring 2011 through Spring 2022, Fall Enrollment component. Enrollment in Degree-Granting Institutions Projection Model, through 2031. *Digest of Education Statistics 2022*

van Buuren, S., & Groothuis-Oudshoorn, K. (2011). MICE: Multivariate imputation by chained equations in R. Journal of Statistical Software, 45(3), 1-67.

Vermunt, J. K., & Magidson, J. (2005). *Technical Guide for Latent GOLD 4.0: Basic, Advanced, and Syntax*. Statistical Innovations Inc.

Weisberg, S. (2005). Applied Linear Regression. John Wiley & Sons.

Wickham, H., & Grolemund, G. (2016). R for data science: Import, tidy, transform, visualize, and model data. O'Reilly Media, Inc.

Wilcox, R. R. (2017). *Introduction to Robust Estimation and Hypothesis Testing* (4th ed.). Academic Press.

Wilcoxon, F. (1945). Individual Comparisons by Ranking Methods. *Biometrics Bulletin*, 1(6), 80–83.

Wilcoxon, F. (1945). Individual Comparisons by Ranking Methods. *Biometrics Bulletin*, 1(6), 80–83.

Wilks, D. S. (2011). Statistical Methods in the Atmospheric Sciences. Academic Press.

Chapter 11. Qualitative Research

This chapter will address the following learning objectives:

- Define qualitative research in education.

- Explain key characteristics of qualitative research in education, including in-depth exploration, subjectivity, naturalistic settings, flexible design, rich data collection methods, and holistic understanding.

- Compare and contrast common qualitative research designs used in educational research.

- Analyze the advantages and disadvantages of qualitative research in education, considering factors such as depth of exploration, contextual understanding, generalizability, subjectivity, and ethical considerations.

- Discuss the foundational principles and key components of phenomenological research in educational contexts, including bracketing, in-depth interviews, phenomenological reduction, thematic analysis, and rich descriptions.

- Analyze the advantages and disadvantages of phenomenological research in educational settings, including its ability to provide deep insights into lived experiences, its potential for bias and subjectivity, and its implications for educational practice and policy.

- Examine the strengths and limitations of grounded theory in educational research, including its flexibility and adaptability, challenges related to time-intensive data analysis and potential bias, and considerations for ensuring the validity and reliability of findings.

- Describe narrative inquiry as a qualitative research approach in education, including its focus on storytelling, narrative analysis techniques, such as emplotment and reflexivity, and its contributions to understanding human experiences, identities, and relationships within educational contexts.

Qualitative research in education is a vital approach to understanding the complexities of teaching, learning, and educational environments. Unlike quantitative methods that focus on numerical data and statistical analysis, qualitative research delves into the rich narratives, perspectives, and meanings embedded within educational contexts. Through qualitative inquiry, researchers aim to uncover the nuanced experiences, beliefs, and practices of students, teachers, administrators, and other stakeholders.

This approach embraces various methodologies such as ethnography, case studies, phenomenology, grounded theory, and narrative inquiry, allowing researchers to explore diverse aspects of education, including classroom dynamics, school culture, curriculum development, and educational policy. By engaging in qualitative research, scholars can illuminate the lived realities of individuals within educational settings, providing insights that may inform educational practice, policymaking, and theory-building.

Qualitative research in education often involves techniques such as interviews, observations, document analysis, and participant observation, enabling researchers to immerse themselves in the context under study and capture the complexity of human interactions and experiences. Moreover, qualitative research in education acknowledges the subjective nature of knowledge construction, recognizing that multiple perspectives contribute to a comprehensive understanding of educational phenomena.

Characteristics of Qualitative Research

Qualitative research in education possesses several distinctive characteristics that differentiate it from quantitative approaches. Below are some key characteristics of qualitative research:

In-depth Exploration. Qualitative research in education emphasizes the exploration of complex educational phenomena in depth. Researchers seek to understand the intricacies of educational experiences, processes, and contexts through detailed examination of individual perspectives, social interactions, and cultural dynamics (Merriam & Tisdell, 2015).

Subjectivity and Interpretivism. Qualitative research acknowledges the subjective nature of knowledge construction and emphasizes interpretivism. Researchers recognize that multiple realities exist and that meaning is socially constructed. They aim to understand how individuals interpret and make sense of their educational experiences within specific cultural, social, and historical contexts (Denzin & Lincoln, 2018).

Naturalistic Setting. Qualitative research in education often takes place in naturalistic settings, such as classrooms, schools, or communities, where the phenomena of interest naturally occur. Researchers immerse themselves in these settings to observe, interact with participants, and capture authentic data in context (Wolcott, 2008).

Flexible and Emergent Design. Qualitative research designs in education are flexible and emergent, allowing researchers to adapt their methods and approaches based on ongoing data collection and analysis. They may refine research questions, sampling strategies, or data collection techniques in response to emerging insights and findings (Creswell, 2013).

Rich Data Collection Methods. Qualitative research in education employs diverse and rich data collection methods, including interviews, observations, document analysis, and participant observation. These methods enable researchers to gather in-depth, contextually rich data that capture the complexity of educational phenomena from multiple perspectives (Patton, 2014).

Holistic Understanding. Qualitative research in education aims to achieve a holistic understanding of educational phenomena by considering the interplay of various factors, including individual experiences, social interactions, institutional structures, and cultural contexts. Researchers seek to uncover patterns, themes, and relationships that contribute to a comprehensive understanding of the phenomenon under study (Stake, 2010).

These characteristics highlight the unique strengths and perspectives that qualitative research brings to the study of education, enriching our understanding of the complexities inherent in teaching, learning, and educational environments.

Qualitative Research Designs

Qualitative research methods in education encompass a range of methodologies tailored to explore the multifaceted dimensions of educational phenomena. Here are descriptions of some common qualitative research designs along with references for further exploration:

Ethnography

Ethnography involves deep immersion into a particular cultural or educational setting to understand the beliefs, practices, and social dynamics within that context. Researchers often spend extensive time in the field, engaging in participant observation, interviews, and document analysis to capture the insider perspectives of the participants. Ethnographic studies in education shed light on cultural norms, power dynamics, and everyday experiences within schools and classrooms (Wolcott, 2008).

Ethnographers aim to provide rich descriptions and interpretations of the everyday practices, beliefs, and norms that shape educational processes. In educational research, ethnography involves the systematic study of educational settings, such as classrooms, schools, or educational institutions, through prolonged engagement and observation. Ethnographers immerse themselves in the field, often spending extended periods of time to gain a deep understanding of the context, participants, and cultural dynamics at play. Key components of ethnography in educational research include:

Participant Observation. Ethnographers actively participate in the daily activities of the educational setting they study, observing interactions, routines, and practices. This immersion allows researchers to gain insider perspectives and understand the context from the viewpoint of the participants.

Interviews. Ethnographic research often includes interviews with various stakeholders, including teachers, students, administrators, and parents. These interviews provide additional insights into individual experiences, beliefs, and perspectives within the educational context.

Document Analysis. Ethnographers analyze documents such as school policies, curriculum materials, student work, and administrative records to understand the formal structures and discourses that influence educational practices.

Reflexivity. Ethnographers engage in reflexivity, acknowledging their own positionality, biases, and perspectives throughout the research process. They reflect on how their background and experiences may influence their interpretations of the data and strive to maintain awareness of their role in shaping the research findings.

Thick Description. Ethnographic research aims to provide "thick descriptions" that capture the depth and complexity of the social phenomena under study. Researchers describe not only what they observe but also the meanings, interpretations, and cultural contexts surrounding those observations.

Example. One notable example of ethnography in educational research is the study conducted by Annette Lareau (2003), titled "Unequal Childhoods: Class, Race, and Family Life." In this ethnographic research, Lareau examined the impact of social class and race on children's educational experiences by studying the daily lives of families from different socioeconomic backgrounds. Lareau conducted her research by immersing herself in the lives of families from diverse socioeconomic backgrounds over a period of several years. She observed and interacted with families, accompanied children to school and extracurricular activities, and conducted in-depth interviews with parents, children, and teachers. Through her ethnographic study, Lareau identified distinct parenting styles and child-rearing practices associated with different social classes. She found that middle-class families tended to engage in what she termed "concerted cultivation," involving organized activities, structured schedules, and extensive parent-child communication aimed at developing children's skills and talents. In contrast, working-class and poor families tended to adopt a "natural growth" approach, allowing children more independence and freedom in unstructured activities and relying less on organized enrichment activities. Lareau's ethnographic research revealed how these differing parenting strategies influenced children's educational experiences and outcomes. She found that children from middle-class families were more likely to navigate educational institutions successfully, while children from working-class and poor families faced greater challenges and barriers in accessing educational opportunities. "Unequal Childhoods" not only provided valuable insights into the role of social class and race in shaping children's educational experiences but also demonstrated the power of ethnographic research to uncover the complexities of educational inequality. Lareau's study has had a significant impact on our understanding of the social determinants of educational achievement and has informed discussions and policies aimed at addressing educational disparities.

Ethnographic research in education offers several advantages and disadvantages, each of which impacts the depth and breadth of insights gained from the research.

Advantages:

1. **Rich, Contextual Understanding.** Ethnographic research allows researchers to gain a deep understanding of the cultural, social, and institutional contexts of educational settings. By immersing themselves in the field, researchers can capture the nuances and complexities of everyday practices, beliefs, and interactions.

2. **Insider Perspectives.** Ethnographers have the opportunity to develop close relationships with participants and gain insider perspectives on educational phenomena. This enables researchers to access tacit knowledge, understand implicit meanings, and appreciate the viewpoints of those directly involved in the educational context.

3. **Flexibility and Adaptability.** Ethnographic research methods are flexible and adaptable, allowing researchers to adjust their approach based on emerging insights and changing circumstances in the field. This flexibility enables researchers to explore unexpected phenomena and pursue new lines of inquiry as they arise.

4. **Holistic Analysis.** Ethnographic research facilitates a holistic analysis of educational phenomena by considering multiple factors, including individual experiences, social interactions, cultural norms, and institutional structures. This comprehensive approach enhances the richness and depth of understanding of the phenomenon under study.

5. **Potential for Empowerment.** Ethnographic research has the potential to empower participants by amplifying their voices, experiences, and perspectives. By highlighting the lived realities of individuals within educational settings, ethnographic research can inform advocacy efforts, policy-making, and social change initiatives aimed at addressing educational inequalities.

Disadvantages:

1. **Time-Intensive.** Ethnographic research is often time-intensive, requiring prolonged periods of fieldwork to develop rapport with participants, collect data, and gain insights into the context

under study. The extensive time commitment may limit the feasibility of conducting ethnographic research within certain timeframes or budget constraints.

2. **Subjectivity and Bias.** Ethnographic research is inherently subjective, as researchers interpret and make meaning of their observations and interactions in the field. This subjectivity may introduce bias into the research process, influencing the selection of data, the interpretation of findings, and the representation of participants' experiences.

3. **Limited Generalizability.** Ethnographic findings are often context-specific and may have limited generalizability to other educational settings or populations. The rich, detailed descriptions provided by ethnographic research may not always be easily transferable or applicable to broader contexts, limiting the extent to which findings can be extrapolated.

4. **Ethical Considerations.** Ethnographic research raises ethical considerations related to privacy, confidentiality, and informed consent, particularly when studying sensitive topics or vulnerable populations within educational settings. Researchers must navigate ethical dilemmas to ensure the well-being and rights of participants are respected throughout the research process.

5. **Potential for Observer Effects.** The presence of researchers in the field may influence participants' behavior and interactions, leading to observer effects that can affect the authenticity and validity of the data collected. Researchers must be mindful of their impact on the research context and strive to minimize any unintended influence on participants.

Overall, while ethnographic research in education offers valuable insights into the complexities of educational phenomena, researchers must carefully consider the advantages and disadvantages of this approach to ensure rigor, ethical integrity, and relevance to the research objectives.

Case Study

Case studies involve in-depth examination of a particular individual, group, program, or phenomenon within its real-life context. Researchers gather rich data through multiple sources such as interviews, observations, documents, and artifacts to provide detailed descriptions and analyses of the case under study. Case studies in education offer valuable insights into specific educational issues, processes, and interventions (Yin, 2018).

Case study qualitative research in education focuses on gaining a comprehensive understanding of a specific case or cases within the educational context. A case can be an individual student, teacher, school, classroom, educational program, policy initiative, or any other unit of analysis relevant to the research question. Researchers conduct detailed investigations of the case, collecting and analyzing data from multiple sources to illuminate various aspects of the phenomenon under study. Key components of case study qualitative research in education include:

Selection of Cases. Researchers carefully select cases that are relevant to their research questions and objectives. Cases may be chosen for their uniqueness, representativeness, or significance in relation to the research topic. Multiple cases may be studied to provide comparative insights or to explore diverse manifestations of the phenomenon.

Data Collection Methods. Case study researchers employ a variety of data collection methods to gather rich, contextually embedded data. These methods may include interviews, observations, document analysis, and artifact collection. Researchers often use a combination of qualitative techniques to triangulate data and enhance the validity and reliability of their findings.

Detailed Description and Analysis. Case study research emphasizes detailed description and analysis of the case under study. Researchers provide rich, thick descriptions of the case, including its historical context, relevant background information, and key features. They analyze the data using qualitative analytic techniques such as thematic analysis, narrative analysis, or content analysis to identify patterns, themes, and relationships within the data.

Contextualization. Case study researchers contextualize their findings within the broader educational context, considering the influence of social, cultural, historical, and institutional factors on the case under study. By situating the case within its larger context, researchers can better understand the complexities and dynamics at play and draw meaningful conclusions from their analysis.

Theory Building or Testing. Case study research may contribute to theory building by generating new insights, hypotheses, or conceptual frameworks related to the research topic. Alternatively, researchers may use case studies to test existing theories or concepts within the specific context of education, thereby enriching theoretical understanding and advancing knowledge in the field.

Example of Qualitative Case Study in Educational Research

One exemplary qualitative case study in education is the research conducted by Pamela L. Grossman and colleagues titled "Teaching with Cases: A Situative View" (1991). In this study, the researchers employed a qualitative case study approach to investigate how teachers engage with and utilize case-based teaching methods in their classrooms. Below is an overview of the study:

Research Objective: The objective of the study was to understand the process of teaching with cases and how teachers make sense of and adapt case-based teaching methods in their instructional practice.

Methodology: The researchers conducted a qualitative case study involving multiple cases of teachers using case-based teaching methods in different educational settings. They collected data through observations of classroom instruction, interviews with teachers, and analysis of instructional materials such as cases and lesson plans.

Cases Studied: The researchers selected several cases of teachers using case-based teaching methods across various subject areas and grade levels. Each case represented a unique instructional context, including differences in teacher experience, student demographics, curriculum content, and instructional goals.

Data Collection: Data collection methods included:

- Observations of classroom instruction: Researchers observed teachers' implementation of case-based teaching methods in their classrooms, noting instructional strategies, student engagement, and interactions.

- Interviews with teachers: Researchers conducted semi-structured interviews with teachers to explore their beliefs, experiences, and decision-making processes related to teaching with cases.

- Analysis of instructional materials: Researchers analyzed instructional materials such as cases, lesson plans, and student work to understand how cases were integrated into the curriculum and adapted to meet instructional goals.

Data Analysis: Data analysis involved qualitative coding and thematic analysis to identify patterns,

Introduction to Educational Research

Example of Qualitative Case Study in Educational Research

themes, and insights across cases. Researchers examined the data for recurring patterns of instructional practice, teacher decision-making, and student learning experiences.

Findings: The study identified several key findings regarding the process of teaching with cases:

- Teachers' adaptation of cases: Teachers adapted cases to suit their instructional goals, student needs, and classroom context, demonstrating flexibility and creativity in their use of case-based teaching methods.

- Teacher decision-making: Teachers made deliberate decisions about how to use cases in their instruction, including selecting appropriate cases, framing discussions, and facilitating student engagement.

- Student learning experiences: Students engaged actively with cases, drawing on prior knowledge, collaborating with peers, and applying critical thinking skills to analyze complex problems and scenarios.

Implications: The study's findings have implications for teacher professional development, curriculum design, and educational policy related to the use of case-based teaching methods in education. The research highlights the importance of supporting teachers in effectively integrating cases into their instructional practice and leveraging the potential of case-based learning to promote deep learning and critical thinking skills among students.

Case studies are powerful research designs allowing researchers to gather rich data about the selected cases. Nevertheless, researchers must consider both the advantages and disadvantages of this method.

Advantages:

1. **In-depth Exploration.** Case studies allow researchers to delve deeply into specific educational phenomena, providing rich and detailed insights into complex issues that may not be fully captured by quantitative methods alone (Stake, 1995).

2. **Contextual Understanding.** Qualitative case studies enable researchers to examine the context in which educational phenomena occur, including social, cultural, and institutional factors. This contextual understanding enhances the validity and applicability of the findings to real-world educational settings (Yin, 2018).

3. **Holistic Perspective.** Case studies facilitate a holistic perspective on educational issues by considering multiple dimensions and perspectives within a single case. Researchers can explore interactions between individuals, institutions, and broader socio-cultural contexts, leading to a more nuanced understanding of the phenomenon under study (Merriam, 2009).

4. **Theory Development.** Qualitative case studies contribute to theory development in education by generating new insights, hypotheses, or conceptual frameworks. Through in-depth analysis of specific cases, researchers can refine existing theories or propose new theoretical perspectives that enhance understanding of educational phenomena (Baxter & Jack, 2008).

5. **Flexibility.** Case study research offers flexibility in data collection and analysis methods, allowing researchers to adapt their approach to the unique characteristics of each case. This

flexibility enables researchers to explore unexpected findings, incorporate diverse sources of data, and address emergent research questions (Creswell, 2013).

Disadvantages:

1. **Limited Generalizability.** One of the main limitations of qualitative case studies is their limited generalizability to broader populations or contexts. Findings from a single case may not be representative of other educational settings, and researchers must exercise caution when drawing conclusions beyond the specific case under study (Yin, 2018).

2. **Subjectivity and Bias.** Qualitative case studies are susceptible to researcher subjectivity and bias, as researchers interpret and analyze data based on their own perspectives and experiences. This subjectivity may influence the selection of data, the interpretation of findings, and the representation of the case under study (Merriam, 2009).

3. **Time-Intensive.** Conducting qualitative case studies can be time-intensive, requiring prolonged periods of data collection, analysis, and interpretation. Researchers must invest significant time and resources in building relationships with participants, collecting rich data, and conducting rigorous analysis, which may limit the feasibility of studying multiple cases within a single research project (Stake, 1995).

4. **Ethical Considerations.** Qualitative case studies raise ethical considerations related to confidentiality, privacy, and informed consent, particularly when studying sensitive topics or vulnerable populations within educational settings. Researchers must navigate ethical dilemmas to ensure the well-being and rights of participants are respected throughout the research process (Baxter & Jack, 2008).

5. **Validity and Reliability.** Ensuring the validity and reliability of qualitative case study research can be challenging, as there are fewer established criteria and procedures compared to quantitative research methods. Researchers must employ strategies such as triangulation, member checking, and peer debriefing to enhance the trustworthiness of their findings and interpretations (Creswell, 2013).

Phenomenology

Phenomenological research aims to explore the lived experiences and perceptions of individuals regarding a particular phenomenon. Researchers seek to understand the essence of these experiences through in-depth interviews, reflective journaling, or focus groups. Phenomenological studies in education illuminate the subjective meanings, interpretations, and emotions associated with educational events and practices (Creswell & Poth, 2017).

Phenomenology in educational research involves the systematic study of the subjective experiences and perceptions of individuals within educational contexts. Drawing on the philosophical tradition of phenomenology, researchers aim to elucidate the essential structures of lived experiences, uncovering the underlying meanings, patterns, and themes that characterize them. Key components of phenomenological research in education include:

Bracketing. Phenomenological researchers engage in a process of bracketing or epoché, setting aside their preconceptions, assumptions, and biases to approach the phenomenon under study with openness and curiosity. By suspending judgment and attending to the phenomena as they appear in consciousness, researchers strive to grasp the essence of the lived experience (Moustakas, 1994).

In-depth Interviews. Phenomenological research typically involves in-depth, semi-structured interviews with individuals who have direct experience with the phenomenon of interest, such as students, teachers, or administrators. These interviews allow researchers to explore participants' subjective experiences, perceptions, emotions, and interpretations in rich detail (Creswell & Poth, 2017).

Phenomenological Reduction. Researchers employ phenomenological reduction or eidetic variation to identify the essential features and structures of the lived experience. Through a process of iterative analysis, researchers uncover commonalities and variations in participants' accounts, discerning the underlying meanings and patterns that characterize the phenomenon (Giorgi, 2009).

Thematic Analysis. Phenomenological research often involves thematic analysis, whereby researchers identify and analyze themes or patterns that emerge from participants' descriptions of their experiences. Researchers strive to capture the essence of the phenomenon by identifying recurring themes, significant moments, and core aspects of the lived experience (Moustakas, 1994).

Rich Descriptions. Phenomenological research prioritizes the provision of rich, detailed descriptions of participants' experiences, capturing the nuances, complexities, and subtleties of their lived realities. Researchers strive to convey the depth and richness of the phenomenon under study, enabling readers to gain a profound understanding of the lived experience (Creswell & Poth, 2017).

Example of Phenomenological Study in Educational Research

One example of a phenomenological study in educational research is a study conducted by Smith and Osborn (2007) titled "Understanding the Lived Experience of Being a Novice English Language Teacher." In this study, the researchers aimed to explore the subjective experiences and perceptions of novice English language teachers as they navigated their roles and responsibilities in the classroom. **Methodology:** The researchers conducted in-depth, semi-structured interviews with a group of novice English language teachers to capture their lived experiences. The interviews focused on topics such as the challenges, joys, frustrations, and moments of growth experienced by the teachers in their first year of teaching. Participants were encouraged to reflect on their thoughts, feelings, and interactions in the classroom, providing rich descriptions of their experiences.

Data Analysis: Using phenomenological analysis techniques, the researchers analyzed the interview data to uncover the essential themes and patterns that characterized the lived experience of being a novice English language teacher. They engaged in a process of bracketing or epoché to set aside their preconceptions and biases and approached the data with openness and curiosity. Through iterative analysis, the researchers identified commonalities and variations in participants' accounts, discerning the underlying meanings and structures of the lived experience.

Findings: The phenomenological analysis revealed several key themes that captured the essence of the novice English language teachers' experiences. These included feelings of uncertainty and self-doubt, moments of connection and rapport with students, challenges in classroom management and lesson planning, and the development of confidence and competence over time. The study highlighted the complex and multifaceted nature of the novice teacher experience, shedding light on the joys and struggles inherent in the journey of becoming an effective educator.

Implications: The findings of the study have implications for teacher preparation programs, professional development initiatives, and educational policy aimed at supporting novice teachers in

Example of Phenomenological Study in Educational Research
their transition to the classroom. By gaining a deeper understanding of the lived experiences of novice English language teachers, educators and policymakers can better tailor support mechanisms and resources to address the specific needs and challenges faced by early-career educators.

When conducting phenomenological studies, researchers should consider the advantages and disadvantages of this method:

Advantages:

1. **In-depth Exploration of Lived Experiences,** Phenomenological studies offer a deep exploration of the lived experiences and perspectives of individuals within educational settings. By focusing on the subjective meaning-making processes of participants, researchers can uncover rich insights into the nuances and complexities of educational phenomena (Creswell & Poth, 2017).

2. **Humanizes Educational Research.** Phenomenological research humanizes educational research by foregrounding the voices, experiences, and perspectives of individuals. By centering the lived experiences of participants, researchers can gain a deeper appreciation for the human dimensions of teaching, learning, and educational practice (van Manen, 2016).

3. **Reveals Underlying Meaning Structures.** Phenomenological studies reveal the underlying meaning structures that shape individuals' experiences and perceptions within educational contexts. By identifying common themes, patterns, and essences across participants' accounts, researchers can uncover the deeper meanings and understandings that inform educational phenomena (Giorgi, 2009).

4. **Generates Rich Descriptions.** Phenomenological research generates rich, detailed descriptions of participants' lived experiences, providing a nuanced portrayal of the phenomenon under study. Researchers strive to capture the depth, complexity, and richness of participants' narratives, enabling readers to gain a profound understanding of the phenomenon (Moustakas, 1994).

5. **Enhances Empathy and Understanding.** Phenomenological studies promote empathy and understanding by encouraging researchers to adopt a phenomenological attitude of openness, curiosity, and empathic engagement with participants' experiences. By immersing themselves in participants' worlds, researchers can develop a deeper understanding of the human dimensions of education (Smith & Osborn, 2007).

Disadvantages:

1. **Subjectivity and Bias.** Phenomenological studies are susceptible to researcher subjectivity and bias, as researchers interpret and analyze participants' experiences based on their own perspectives and assumptions. This subjectivity may influence the selection of data, the interpretation of findings, and the representation of participants' experiences (Creswell & Poth, 2017).

2. **Limited Generalizability.** Phenomenological findings may have limited generalizability to broader populations or contexts due to their focus on the subjective experiences of a specific group of participants. The unique nature of participants' experiences may not be representative of other educational settings or populations, limiting the applicability of the findings (van Manen, 2016).

3. **Difficulty in Bracketing.** Phenomenological research requires researchers to engage in bracketing or epoché, setting aside their preconceptions, assumptions, and biases to approach the phenomenon under study with openness and curiosity. However, achieving complete bracketing can be challenging, and researchers may struggle to fully suspend their own perspectives and interpretations (Giorgi, 2009).

4. **Time-Intensive Data Analysis.** Phenomenological data analysis can be time-intensive, requiring researchers to engage in iterative processes of coding, categorizing, and synthesizing participants' narratives. The depth and richness of phenomenological data may necessitate prolonged periods of analysis, which may pose challenges in terms of time and resource constraints (Moustakas, 1994).

5. **Ethical Considerations.** Phenomenological studies raise ethical considerations related to confidentiality, privacy, and informed consent, particularly when exploring sensitive topics or personal experiences within educational settings. Researchers must navigate ethical dilemmas to ensure the well-being and rights of participants are respected throughout the research process (Smith & Osborn, 2007).

Grounded Theory

Grounded theory in educational research involves the systematic collection and analysis of data to develop theories or conceptual frameworks that are grounded in the empirical realities of educational contexts.

Developed by sociologists Barney Glaser and Anselm Strauss, grounded theory is characterized by its inductive, iterative, and emergent approach to theory building (Glaser & Strauss, 1967). Researchers use an iterative process of data collection, coding, and analysis to develop theoretical insights that emerge from the data itself. Grounded theory studies in education contribute to the development of explanatory models or frameworks to understand complex educational phenomena (Charmaz, 2014). Key components of grounded theory in educational research include:

Data Collection: Grounded theory researchers collect data through various methods, such as interviews, observations, and document analysis. Data collection is typically open-ended and iterative, allowing researchers to gather rich and diverse sources of information relevant to the research question (Glaser & Strauss, 1967).

Constant Comparison: Grounded theory involves a process of constant comparison, whereby researchers systematically compare data to identify patterns, themes, and relationships. Through this iterative process, researchers develop categories and concepts that emerge from the data itself rather than imposing preconceived theoretical frameworks (Charmaz, 2014).

Theoretical Sampling: Grounded theory employs theoretical sampling, whereby researchers purposefully select participants and collect data that will help refine and develop emerging theoretical concepts. Sampling decisions are guided by theoretical insights gleaned from ongoing data analysis, allowing researchers to delve deeper into key themes and concepts (Glaser & Strauss, 1967).

Coding and Analysis: Grounded theory researchers use coding and analysis techniques to systematically organize and analyze data. Initial coding involves breaking down raw data into discrete units, while focused coding involves identifying and refining core categories and concepts. Through axial coding and theoretical coding, researchers develop a coherent theoretical framework that explains the relationships between categories and concepts (Charmaz, 2014).

Theory Building: Grounded theory aims to generate substantive theories or conceptual frameworks that explain and interpret empirical phenomena within educational contexts. These theories are grounded in the data collected from the field and offer insights into the underlying processes, mechanisms, and structures that shape educational phenomena (Glaser & Strauss, 1967).

Example of Grounded Theory Study in Educational Research
Title: "Understanding Student Motivation in Online Learning Environments: A Grounded Theory Approach" **Research Question:** How do students experience and perceive motivation in online learning environments? **Methodology:** Researchers conducted semi-structured interviews with a diverse group of undergraduate and graduate students enrolled in online courses at a university. The interviews explored students' experiences, perceptions, and motivations related to their online learning experiences. Sampling was guided by theoretical sampling, with participants selected to represent a range of demographic characteristics and academic disciplines. **Data Collection:** Interviews were audio-recorded and transcribed verbatim. Researchers used open-ended questions to encourage participants to share their thoughts, feelings, and experiences related to motivation in online learning. Data collection continued until saturation was reached, meaning no new themes or insights emerged from the interviews. **Data Analysis:** Using grounded theory methodology, researchers conducted iterative cycles of coding and analysis to identify patterns, themes, and relationships in the data. Initial open coding involved breaking down the data into discrete units and assigning descriptive codes to relevant segments. Through constant comparison, researchers refined codes and identified higher-order categories and themes. **Theory Development:** From the analysis of the data, researchers developed a substantive theory of student motivation in online learning environments. The theory identified several key factors influencing student motivation, including the perceived relevance of course content, instructor support and feedback, peer interaction and collaboration, self-regulation strategies, and the flexibility and convenience of online learning. The theory elucidated the dynamic interplay between these factors and their impact on students' motivation and engagement in online courses. **Findings and Implications:** The grounded theory study yielded insights into the multifaceted nature of student motivation in online learning environments. The findings highlighted the importance of designing online courses that promote student autonomy, foster social interaction and collaboration, and provide meaningful feedback and support. The theory generated from the study has implications for online course design, pedagogy, and student support services, informing efforts to enhance student motivation and engagement in online learning.

When using grounded theory, researchers should examine the advantages and disadvantages of this method:

Introduction to Educational Research

Advantages:

Generates Rich, Contextual Understanding. Grounded theory allows researchers to develop theories that are grounded in the empirical data collected from educational settings. This approach generates rich, contextual understanding of the phenomena under study, providing insights into the complex dynamics and processes at play (Charmaz, 2014).

Flexible and Iterative Process. Grounded theory methodology is flexible and iterative, allowing researchers to adapt their approach to the evolving data and research questions. Researchers can engage in constant comparison, theoretical sampling, and iterative coding to refine and develop emerging concepts and theories (Glaser & Strauss, 1967).

Theory Building. Grounded theory facilitates theory building in educational research by providing a systematic framework for generating new theoretical insights and conceptual frameworks. Researchers can develop substantive theories that explain and interpret empirical phenomena within educational contexts, contributing to the advancement of knowledge in the field (Strauss & Corbin, 1998).

Allows for Participant Voice. Grounded theory prioritizes the voices and perspectives of participants, allowing them to shape the development of theories and concepts through their lived experiences. This participatory approach ensures that the resulting theories are grounded in the realities of those directly involved in educational settings (Charmaz, 2014).

Applicable Across Educational Settings. Grounded theory methodology can be applied across diverse educational settings, including K-12 schools, higher education institutions, and informal learning environments. Researchers can use grounded theory to explore a wide range of educational phenomena, from teaching and learning processes to educational policy and practice (Glaser & Strauss, 1967).

Disadvantages:

Time-Intensive. Grounded theory research can be time-intensive, requiring prolonged periods of data collection, analysis, and theory development. The iterative nature of grounded theory methodology may extend the duration of the research process, particularly when engaging in constant comparison and theoretical sampling (Charmaz, 2014).

Complex Data Analysis. Grounded theory data analysis can be complex and challenging, particularly for novice researchers. Researchers must navigate the process of coding, constant comparison, and theory development, which requires a solid understanding of qualitative research methods and theoretical frameworks (Strauss & Corbin, 1998).

Potential for Bias. Grounded theory research is susceptible to researcher bias, as researchers interpret and analyze data based on their own perspectives and assumptions. Researchers must be vigilant in conducting reflexive practices to minimize the influence of bias and ensure the credibility and trustworthiness of their findings (Charmaz, 2014).

Limited Generalizability. Grounded theory findings may have limited generalizability to broader populations or contexts, as theories are developed from data collected within specific educational settings. Researchers must carefully consider the transferability of their findings and theories to other contexts and populations (Glaser & Strauss, 1967).

Ethical Considerations. Grounded theory research raises ethical considerations related to confidentiality, privacy, and informed consent, particularly when studying sensitive topics or vulnerable populations within educational settings. Researchers must navigate ethical dilemmas to ensure the well-being and rights of participants are respected throughout the research process (Strauss & Corbin, 1998).

Narrative Inquiry

Narrative inquiry focuses on the collection and analysis of stories or narratives shared by individuals about their educational experiences. Researchers explore how stories are constructed, interpreted, and conveyed to make sense of personal and collective identities, relationships, and learning journeys. Narrative inquiry in education highlights the power of storytelling as a means of understanding human experiences and meaning-making processes (Clandinin & Connelly, 2000)

Narratives may take various forms, including personal anecdotes, life histories, autobiographical accounts, or fictional stories. Through narrative inquiry, researchers seek to uncover the meanings, themes, and patterns embedded within these narratives, shedding light on the complexities of human experience in education. Key components of narrative inquiry in educational research include:

Storytelling as Data. Narrative inquiry treats stories or narratives as primary sources of data. Researchers collect narratives through various methods, such as interviews, focus groups, written reflections, or ethnographic observations. Participants are invited to share their stories, experiences, and perspectives related to their educational journeys, allowing researchers to capture the richness and diversity of lived experiences within educational settings.

Narrative Analysis. Narrative inquiry involves systematic analysis of the collected narratives to identify common themes, plot structures, character dynamics, and rhetorical devices. Researchers examine narrative elements such as plot development, characterization, setting, dialogue, and symbolism to uncover underlying meanings and patterns. Analysis may involve coding, categorizing, and interpreting narrative data to generate insights into the phenomena under study.

Emplotment and Retelling. Narrative inquiry often involves the process of emplotment, whereby researchers construct overarching narratives or storylines that weave together individual narratives into coherent wholes. Researchers may engage in retelling or re-narrating participants' stories to highlight key themes, amplify marginalized voices, or challenge dominant narratives. Through emplotment and retelling, researchers aim to convey the complexity and diversity of educational experiences while respecting participants' voices and perspectives.

Reflexivity and Interpretation. Narrative inquiry emphasizes reflexivity and interpretation, encouraging researchers to reflect critically on their own role in the research process and the ways in which their interpretations shape the analysis. Researchers acknowledge their subjectivity, biases, and positionalities as they engage with participants' narratives, striving to maintain ethical integrity and rigor in their interpretations.

Knowledge Production and Representation. Narrative inquiry contributes to knowledge production in educational research by generating rich, nuanced accounts of human experience in education. Researchers represent findings through narrative forms, such as written narratives, audiovisual recordings, or multimedia presentations, that capture the depth, complexity, and diversity of

Introduction to Educational Research

participants' stories. These representations serve as vehicles for sharing insights, fostering dialogue, and informing educational practice and policy.

Narrative inquiry is used in educational research to explore a wide range of topics, including student identity formation, teacher professional development, educational leadership, curriculum design, school culture, and educational policy. Researchers employ narrative inquiry in diverse educational settings, such as K-12 schools, higher education institutions, adult education programs, and informal learning environments.

Example. The study titled "Voices of Resilience: A Narrative Inquiry into the Experiences of High School Dropouts Who Successfully Re-Engaged in Education" conducted by Johnson and Smith (2019) delved into the narratives of high school dropouts who later re-engaged in education and successfully obtained their high school diplomas or equivalent credentials. Through in-depth interviews and narrative analysis, the researchers explored the stories, challenges, and triumphs of these resilient individuals. The study aimed to uncover the factors that contributed to their educational re-engagement and success, offering valuable insights into the experiences of individuals who overcame barriers to achieve academic success.

Narrative inquiry offers a powerful approach for understanding the lived experiences of students, teachers, administrators, parents, and other stakeholders within educational contexts, contributing to a deeper understanding of the complexities of education and informing efforts to promote equity, inclusion, and social justice in education. When using this method, researcher must considers the advantages as well as the limitations of this method:

Advantages:

Rich, Contextual Understanding. Narrative inquiry allows researchers to explore the lived experiences and perspectives of individuals within educational contexts, providing rich, detailed insights into their stories, meanings, and interpretations (Clandinin & Connelly, 2000).

Empowerment of Participants. Narrative inquiry empowers participants to share their stories and perspectives in their own words, giving voice to marginalized or underrepresented individuals within educational settings (Connelly & Clandinin, 2006).

Flexible and Accessible. Narrative inquiry is a flexible and accessible research methodology that can be adapted to various educational contexts and populations, including students, teachers, administrators, and other stakeholders (Riessman, 2008).

Engagement and Reflexivity. Narrative inquiry promotes engagement and reflexivity among researchers, encouraging them to actively listen to participants' stories, reflect on their own biases and assumptions, and co-construct meaning collaboratively with participants (Riessman, 2008).

Holistic Understanding. Narrative inquiry allows researchers to gain a holistic understanding of educational phenomena by considering the interconnectedness of individual stories within broader social, cultural, and historical contexts (Clandinin & Connelly, 2000).

Disadvantages:

Subjectivity and Bias. Narrative inquiry is susceptible to researcher subjectivity and bias, as researchers interpret and analyze participants' stories based on their own perspectives and experiences (Riessman, 2008).

Validity and Reliability. Ensuring the validity and reliability of narrative inquiry findings can be challenging, as there are fewer established criteria and procedures compared to quantitative research methods (Clandinin & Connelly, 2000).

Ethical Considerations. Narrative inquiry raises ethical considerations related to confidentiality, privacy, and informed consent, particularly when studying sensitive topics or vulnerable populations within educational settings (Riessman, 2008).

Time-Intensive Data Analysis. Analyzing narrative data can be time-intensive and laborious, as researchers must engage in detailed coding, thematic analysis, and interpretation to uncover underlying patterns and themes (Connelly & Clandinin, 2006).

Limited Generalizability. Narrative inquiry findings may have limited generalizability to broader populations or contexts, as they are based on the unique stories and perspectives of individuals within specific educational settings (Clandinin & Connelly, 2000).

Qualitative research designs offer valuable approaches for exploring the complexities of human experiences, behaviors, and social phenomena within educational contexts. Through methodologies such as phenomenology, ethnography, grounded theory, and narrative inquiry, researchers can delve deeply into the lived realities of individuals and communities, generating rich, contextual understandings that complement quantitative research approaches. These qualitative designs allow researchers to explore the subjective meanings, perspectives, and interpretations that individuals ascribe to their educational experiences, shedding light on the nuances and complexities of teaching, learning, and educational practices. By privileging participant voices and perspectives, qualitative research designs empower individuals to share their stories, challenge dominant narratives, and contribute to the co-construction of knowledge. While qualitative research designs offer numerous advantages, including flexibility, depth, and richness of data, they also pose challenges related to subjectivity, validity, and generalizability. Researchers must navigate these challenges with rigor and reflexivity, employing strategies such as triangulation, member checking, and reflexivity to enhance the trustworthiness and credibility of their findings.

In conclusion, qualitative research designs play a vital role in educational research by providing holistic, nuanced understandings of educational phenomena. By complementing quantitative approaches and privileging participant voices, qualitative research designs contribute to the advancement of knowledge and the promotion of equity, inclusion, and social justice within educational contexts.

Summary

The chapter outlines the significance of qualitative methods in exploring the complexities of teaching, learning, and educational environments. Unlike quantitative approaches that rely on numerical data, qualitative research delves into rich narratives, perspectives, and meanings within educational contexts. Various methodologies, such as ethnography, case studies, phenomenology, grounded theory, and narrative inquiry, offer diverse lenses to explore educational phenomena.

Key characteristics of qualitative research in education include its emphasis on in-depth exploration, subjectivity, naturalistic settings, flexible design, rich data collection methods, and holistic understanding. Researchers aim to achieve a comprehensive understanding of educational phenomena by considering individual experiences, social interactions, institutional structures, and cultural contexts. Ethnography involves deep immersion into a cultural or educational setting to understand beliefs, practices, and social dynamics. Case studies focus on detailed examination of specific cases within real-life contexts.

Suggestions for Students

Key Questions

1. What distinguishes qualitative research from quantitative research in education, and why is it important to have both approaches in educational research?
2. Can you explain the main characteristics of qualitative research in education, and how do these characteristics contribute to a deeper understanding of educational phenomena?
3. Describe two common qualitative research designs used in educational research and outline their methodologies, data collection techniques, and analytical approaches.
4. What are some advantages and disadvantages of using qualitative research methods in education, and how might researchers address the limitations associated with qualitative approaches?
5. How can qualitative research in education inform educational practice, policymaking, and theory-building, and what are some examples of how qualitative research has been applied in the field of education?
6. What are the key components of phenomenological research in educational contexts, and how do they contribute to understanding lived experiences?
7. Can you explain the process of grounded theory methodology in educational research, including its iterative approach to theory building and data collection techniques?
8. What are the advantages and disadvantages of using phenomenological research in educational settings, and how might researchers address potential biases in their studies?
9. How does narrative inquiry contribute to understanding human experiences in education, and what techniques are commonly used in narrative analysis?
10. In what ways can grounded theory methodology be applied to explore complex educational phenomena, and what are some challenges researchers might encounter during the data analysis process?

Suggestions for Instructors

Suggested Learning Activities

Case Study Analysis: Provide students with a selection of case studies related to educational settings or phenomena. Ask them to critically analyze each case, identifying the research questions, methodologies used, data collection techniques, and key findings. Encourage students to discuss the strengths and limitations of each case study and how they contribute to our understanding of education.

Field Observation: Organize a field trip to an educational setting, such as a school or classroom. Ask students to observe and take notes on the interactions, practices, and dynamics they observe. Afterward, facilitate a group discussion where students can share their observations, reflect on the experience, and connect it to the concepts of qualitative research discussed in the chapter.

Interview Practice: Have students conduct mock interviews with their peers or teachers on educational topics of interest. Provide them with guidance on developing interview questions, conducting interviews, and analyzing qualitative data. After the interviews, encourage students to reflect on the interview process, consider the challenges they encountered, and discuss strategies for improving their interviewing skills.

Ethnographic Inquiry: Assign students to conduct mini ethnographies of specific educational contexts, such as a school club, extracurricular activity, or community learning center. Provide them with guidance on conducting participant observation, collecting field notes, and analyzing ethnographic data. Instruct students to write up their findings in a short ethnographic report, highlighting key themes, patterns, and insights from their fieldwork.

Research Proposal Development: Divide students into small groups and task each group with developing a research proposal for a qualitative study in education. Provide them with a list of potential research topics or allow them to choose their own. Guide students through the process of formulating research questions, selecting appropriate methodologies, designing data collection instruments, and considering ethical considerations. Have each group present their research proposal to the class and engage in peer feedback and discussion.

Conduct a mini-phenomenological study: Divide students into small groups and ask them to select an educational phenomenon of interest (e.g., student engagement in online learning). Have each group conduct mini in-depth interviews with their peers to explore their lived experiences and perceptions related to the chosen phenomenon. Afterward, facilitate a discussion where groups share their findings and reflect on the process of conducting phenomenological research.

Analyze a grounded theory study: Provide students with a published grounded theory study in educational research and ask them to critically analyze its methodology, data collection techniques, and theoretical framework. Encourage students to identify key themes, patterns, and relationships in the data and consider the implications of the study's findings for educational practice and policy.

Suggestions for Instructors

Storytelling workshop: Organize a storytelling workshop where students have the opportunity to share personal narratives or stories related to their educational experiences. Provide prompts or themes to guide their storytelling, such as memorable learning moments, challenges overcome, or influential teachers. Afterward, facilitate a reflective discussion where students explore common themes and connections across their stories.

Coding and thematic analysis exercise: Present students with a set of qualitative data (e.g., interview transcripts, journal entries) related to an educational topic of interest. Divide students into pairs or small groups and ask them to independently code the data using grounded theory methodology. Afterward, have groups compare their codes, discuss any discrepancies, and collaboratively identify emerging themes and patterns in the data.

Reflective journaling: Assign students to keep a reflective journal throughout the course, where they document their thoughts, insights, and questions related to qualitative research methods in education. Prompt students to engage in critical reflection on their understanding of phenomenology, grounded theory, and narrative inquiry, as well as their own experiences with qualitative research methodologies. Encourage students to draw connections between course concepts and real-world applications in educational research.

References

Baxter, P., & Jack, S. (2008). Qualitative case study methodology: Study design and implementation for novice researchers. *The Qualitative Report, 13*(4), 544-559.

Charmaz, K. (2014). Constructing grounded theory. Sage Publications.

Clandinin, D. J., & Connelly, F. M. (2000). Narrative inquiry: Experience and story in qualitative research. Jossey-Bass.

Connelly, F. M., & Clandinin, D. J. (2006). Narrative inquiry. In J. L. Green, G. Camilli, & P. B. Elmore (Eds.), *Handbook of complementary methods in education research* (pp. 375-385). Routledge.

Creswell, J. W. (2013). Qualitative inquiry & research design: Choosing among five approaches. Sage Publications.

Denzin, N. K., & Lincoln, Y. S. (Eds.). (2018). The Sage handbook of qualitative research. Sage Publications.

Erickson, F. (1986). *Qualitative methods in research on teaching.* In M. Wittrock (Ed.), *Handbook of research on teaching* (3rd ed., pp. 119-161). Macmillan.

Giorgi, A. (2009). *The descriptive phenomenological method in psychology: A modified Husserlian approach.* Duquesne University Press.

Glaser, B. G., & Strauss, A. L. (1967). *The discovery of grounded theory: Strategies for qualitative research.* Aldine Transaction.

Grossman, P. L., Wilson, S. M., & Shulman, L. S. (1989). Teachers' Understanding of Teaching Reconsidered. *Teachers College Record, 91*(3), 384–405.

Hammersley, M., & Atkinson, P. (2007). *Ethnography: Principles in practice* (3rd ed.). Routledge.

Lareau, A. (2003). *Unequal childhoods: Class, race, and family life.* University of California Press.

Merriam, S. B. (2009). *Qualitative research: A guide to design and implementation.* John Wiley & Sons.

Merriam, S. B., & Tisdell, E. J. (2015). Qualitative research: A guide to design and implementation. John Wiley & Sons.

Mills, J., Bonner, A., & Francis, K. (2006). The development of constructivist grounded theory. *International Journal of Qualitative Methods, 5*(1), 25-35.

Moustakas, C. (1994). *Phenomenological research methods.* Sage Publications.

Patton, M. Q. (2014). Qualitative research & evaluation methods: Integrating theory and practice. Sage Publications.

Riessman, C. K. (2008). Narrative methods for the human sciences. Sage Publications.

Smith, J. A., & Osborn, M. (2007). Understanding the lived experience of being a novice English language teacher: The development of a phenomenological model. *Teaching and Teacher Education, 23*(7), 1027-1043. https://doi.org/10.1016/j.tate.2006.07.009

Spindler, G., & Spindler, L. (Eds.). (1987). *Interpreting ethnographic data: An ethnographic perspective.* Sage Publications

Stake, R. E. (1995). *The art of case study research.* Sage Publications.

Strauss, A., & Corbin, J. (1998). *Basics of qualitative research: Techniques and procedures for developing grounded theory.* Sage Publications.

van Manen, M. (2016). *Phenomenology of practice: Meaning-giving methods in phenomenological research and writing.* Routledge.

Wolcott, H. F. (2008). *Ethnography: A way of seeing.* AltaMira Press.

Yin, R. K. (2018). Case study research and applications: Design and methods. Sage Publications.

Chapter 12. Mixed Methods Research

This chapter will address the following learning objectives:
<ul><li>Identify the key characteristics of mixed-methods research in educational contexts.</li><li>Describe the mixed-methods research designs commonly employed in educational research, including sequential exploratory design, concurrent triangulation design, and concurrent embedded design.</li><li>Explain the process and rationale behind sequential exploratory design.</li><li>Analyze the advantages and disadvantages of sequential exploratory design in educational research, considering factors such as comprehensiveness, methodological synergy, and resource intensity.</li><li>Explain the principles and procedures of concurrent triangulation design, including simultaneous data collection and separate analysis of qualitative and quantitative data.</li><li>Evaluate the strengths and limitations of concurrent triangulation design in educational research, considering factors such as triangulation of findings and complexity of analysis.</li><li>Compare and contrast the advantages and disadvantages of concurrent embedded design in educational research, considering factors such as methodological robustness and difficulty in data integration.</li><li>Analyze the use of embedded design to explore a specific educational intervention or phenomenon.</li><li>Synthesize the key principles and considerations of mixed-methods research in educational contexts to inform evidence-based practices and contribute to advancements in the field.</li></ul>

Mixed methods research in education is a dynamic approach that combines qualitative and quantitative methodologies to investigate educational phenomena (Johnson & Onwuegbuzie, 2004). It acknowledges the complexity of educational issues and aims to provide a comprehensive understanding by integrating both numerical data and rich contextual insights (Creswell & Plano Clark, 2018). This methodological framework allows researchers to explore diverse aspects of education, such as teaching methods, student learning outcomes, policy effectiveness, and educational interventions, in a holistic manner.

In mixed methods research, researchers typically collect and analyze both quantitative data, such as surveys, standardized test scores, or demographic information, and qualitative data, including interviews, observations, or open-ended responses (Creswell & Creswell, 2017). By triangulating these different types of data, researchers can validate findings, gain deeper insights into the research questions, and generate more robust conclusions.

This approach is particularly valuable in education because it enables researchers to explore complex educational phenomena from multiple perspectives, taking into account both the statistical significance and the nuanced meanings embedded within educational experiences (Teddlie & Tashakkori, 2009). Mixed methods research in education not only enhances the rigor and validity of educational research but also fosters a more comprehensive understanding of the multifaceted nature of teaching, learning, and educational systems.

Mixed Methods Research Designs

In educational research, several mixed-methods designs are commonly employed to explore complex educational phenomena. The most common are sequential exploratory designs, concurrent triangulation designs, and concurrent embedded designs. These mixed-methods research designs offer flexibility and robustness in exploring educational phenomena from multiple perspectives, combining the strengths of both qualitative and quantitative approaches.

Sequential Exploratory Design

In this design, researchers initially collect and analyze qualitative data to explore a phenomenon. In this design, one method is dominant and is supplemented or enriched by the other method. This design is useful when the phenomenon is not well understood or when there is a need to explore diverse perspectives before conducting quantitative research (Creswell & Plano Clark, 2018).

In the sequential exploratory design, researchers begin by conducting qualitative research to explore a phenomenon thoroughly. This qualitative phase involves collecting and analyzing data through methods such as interviews, observations, or focus groups to gain a rich understanding of the research topic. After analyzing the qualitative data, researchers use the insights gained to inform the development of quantitative research instruments or surveys. The quantitative phase then follows, allowing researchers to collect numerical data from a larger sample size to test or generalize the findings obtained from the qualitative phase. Finally, the researchers integrate the results from both phases to provide a comprehensive understanding of the research question.

This design is particularly useful when the phenomenon under investigation is not well understood or when there is a need to explore diverse perspectives before conducting quantitative research. It allows researchers to build on qualitative findings to develop quantitative measures that capture essential aspects of the phenomenon.

Example of Sequential Exploratory Mixed Methods Study in Educational Research
Title: "Understanding the Impact of Peer Tutoring Programs on Student Learning Outcomes in Mathematics Education"
Qualitative Phase: In the qualitative phase of the study, researchers conduct in-depth interviews with mathematics teachers and students to explore their perceptions and experiences with peer tutoring programs. The interviews aim to uncover the effectiveness of peer tutoring in improving student learning outcomes, as well as to identify the factors that contribute to successful peer tutoring interventions. Themes that may emerge from the qualitative data include student engagement, peer relationships, teacher support, and perceived benefits and challenges of peer tutoring.
Quantitative Phase: Based on the insights gained from the qualitative phase, researchers design a

Example of Sequential Exploratory Mixed Methods Study in Educational Research
quantitative survey to assess the impact of peer tutoring programs on student learning outcomes in mathematics. The survey is administered to a larger sample of students who have participated in peer tutoring programs and those who have not. Quantitative data are collected on variables such as academic performance (e.g., test scores, grades), self-efficacy, and attitudes toward mathematics. Statistical analyses, such as regression analysis or ANOVA, are conducted to examine the relationships between participation in peer tutoring and student outcomes while controlling for relevant variables. **Integration:** Finally, the qualitative and quantitative findings are integrated to provide a comprehensive understanding of the research question. Researchers compare the qualitative themes with the quantitative results to identify patterns, contradictions, or areas of convergence. For example, qualitative data may reveal that students value peer support and collaboration in peer tutoring programs, while quantitative data may show a significant improvement in academic performance among students who participated in peer tutoring compared to those who did not. The integrated findings shed light on the mechanisms through which peer tutoring influences student learning outcomes and provide insights for improving the design and implementation of peer tutoring programs in mathematics education. This example demonstrates how a sequential exploratory mixed methods study can be conducted to investigate the impact of peer tutoring programs on student learning outcomes in mathematics education, combining qualitative insights with quantitative data to provide a comprehensive understanding of the research question.

Sequential exploratory designs offer valuable insights and a nuanced understanding of educational phenomena, making them a popular choice in educational research, particularly when studying complex or multifaceted issues. When conducting sequential exploratory studies, researchers should consider both the advantages and disadvantages of this method.

Advantages:

Comprehensive Understanding. Sequential exploratory designs allow researchers to gain a comprehensive understanding of complex phenomena by initially exploring them qualitatively and then confirming or expanding on the findings through quantitative methods.

Richness of Data. The qualitative phase of this design provides rich, detailed data that can offer insights into participants' experiences, perspectives, and contexts.

Enhanced Instrument Development. Qualitative findings from the initial phase can inform the development of quantitative instruments, ensuring that the quantitative measures capture relevant aspects of the phenomenon under study.

Methodological Triangulation. By using both qualitative and quantitative methods, researchers can achieve methodological triangulation, enhancing the validity and reliability of the study's findings.

Flexibility. Sequential exploratory designs offer flexibility, allowing researchers to adjust their approach based on the insights gained from the qualitative phase.

Disadvantages:

Time-Consuming. Conducting two separate phases of data collection and analysis can be time-consuming and may require a longer timeframe compared to single-method studies.

Resource Intensive. Sequential exploratory designs may require more resources in terms of staffing, funding, and participant recruitment, particularly if researchers need to collect data from multiple sources or settings.

Complexity of Analysis. Analyzing data from two different phases using different methods can be complex and challenging, requiring researchers to integrate findings from qualitative and quantitative analyses effectively.

Potential for Bias. Researchers may introduce bias during the integration of qualitative and quantitative data if they selectively prioritize certain findings over others or if their interpretation is influenced by preconceived notions.

Risk of Discrepancies. There is a risk of discrepancies between qualitative and quantitative findings, which may require additional exploration and explanation to reconcile conflicting results.

Concurrent Triangulation Design

Concurrent triangulation research designs in education involve collecting both qualitative and quantitative data simultaneously, analyzing them separately, and then comparing the findings to identify convergence, divergence, or complementarity. (Creswell & Plano Clark, 2018). In concurrent triangulation designs, researchers collect quantitative and qualitative data concurrently and analyze them independently. This simultaneous data collection allows researchers to examine the research question from multiple angles and to compare the findings from different methods. Quantitative data may include surveys, standardized tests, or other numerical measures, while qualitative data may consist of interviews, observations, or document analysis. After collecting the data, researchers conduct separate analyses for each dataset, focusing on identifying patterns, themes, or trends within each set. Finally, researchers integrate the findings, comparing the results to gain a more comprehensive understanding of the research question.

Example of Concurrent Triangulation in Educational Research

Research Question: How does the implementation of a flipped classroom approach impact student engagement and learning outcomes in a high school science class?

Study Design: A concurrent triangulation design is employed to investigate the research question. Data collection occurs simultaneously using both quantitative and qualitative methods.

Quantitative Data Collection and Analysis:

- Quantitative data are collected through pre- and post-intervention surveys administered to students enrolled in the science class.

- The surveys include Likert-scale items to measure student perceptions of engagement, satisfaction, and learning outcomes.

- Student grades on quizzes, tests, and assignments are also collected as objective measures of learning outcomes.

- Quantitative data are analyzed using descriptive statistics, such as means and standard

---

Example of Concurrent Triangulation in Educational Research

---

deviations, to identify trends and patterns in student responses and performance.

Qualitative Data Collection and Analysis:

- Qualitative data are collected through classroom observations and semi-structured interviews with the teacher and select students.

- Classroom observations focus on student participation, interactions, and engagement during flipped classroom activities.

- Interviews with the teacher and students explore their experiences with the flipped classroom approach, including perceived benefits, challenges, and suggestions for improvement.

- Qualitative data are analyzed using thematic analysis to identify recurring themes and patterns in the interview transcripts and observational notes.

Integration of Findings:

- The quantitative and qualitative findings are compared and contrasted to provide a comprehensive understanding of the impact of the flipped classroom approach on student engagement and learning outcomes.

- Convergence, divergence, and complementarity between the two sets of data are examined to triangulate evidence and draw robust conclusions.

By employing a concurrent triangulation design, this study aims to offer insights into the effectiveness of the flipped classroom approach in enhancing student engagement and improving learning outcomes in high school science education.

This design is advantageous because it allows researchers to validate findings by triangulating evidence from multiple sources. It also enables researchers to explore the same phenomenon using different methods, providing a more holistic perspective. However, it can be challenging to manage and analyze two sets of data simultaneously, and researchers must carefully consider how to integrate the findings effectively. Below are some advantages and disadvantages of concurrent triangulation designs:

Advantages:

Comprehensive Understanding. Concurrent triangulation designs allow researchers to gain a comprehensive understanding of the research question by integrating both quantitative and qualitative data. This approach provides a more holistic perspective on the phenomenon under study (Creswell & Plano Clark, 2018).

Methodological Triangulation. By using multiple data sources and methods, researchers can achieve methodological triangulation, enhancing the validity and reliability of the study's findings. Triangulation helps to overcome the limitations of using a single method and strengthens the overall research design (Teddlie & Tashakkori, 2009).

Confirmation of Findings. Concurrent triangulation designs enable researchers to corroborate findings across different data sets. Consistency in findings across quantitative and qualitative data sources increases confidence in the results and conclusions drawn from the study (Johnson & Onwuegbuzie, 2004).

Enhanced Interpretation. The integration of quantitative and qualitative data allows for a more nuanced interpretation of the research findings. Qualitative data can provide insights into the contextual factors influencing quantitative results, leading to a deeper understanding of the research topic (Teddlie & Tashakkori, 2009).

Greater Insight into Complex Phenomena. Concurrent triangulation designs are particularly well-suited for exploring complex educational phenomena that cannot be fully understood using either quantitative or qualitative methods alone. The combination of approaches offers a more complete picture of multifaceted issues in education (Creswell & Plano Clark, 2018).

Disadvantages:

Resource Intensive. Concurrent triangulation designs can be resource-intensive in terms of time, funding, and expertise required for data collection, analysis, and integration. Managing multiple data sets and conducting analyses in parallel may increase the workload for researchers (Creswell & Plano Clark, 2018).

Complex Analysis. Analyzing both quantitative and qualitative data concurrently can be challenging, requiring researchers to possess diverse analytical skills and expertise. Integrating findings from different methods may involve complex statistical procedures and qualitative interpretation techniques (Teddlie & Tashakkori, 2009).

Potential for Discrepancies. There is a risk of discrepancies between quantitative and qualitative findings, which may arise due to methodological differences, sampling biases, or interpretation biases. Resolving inconsistencies and reconciling conflicting results may require additional exploration and explanation (Johnson & Onwuegbuzie, 2004).

Difficulty in Data Integration. Integrating quantitative and qualitative data sets while preserving their integrity and richness can be challenging. Researchers must carefully consider how to combine the findings to ensure that the integrated results provide a coherent and meaningful interpretation of the research question (Creswell & Plano Clark, 2018).

Limited Generalizability. Concurrent triangulation designs prioritize depth over breadth, focusing on understanding specific contexts and phenomena in-depth. As a result, the findings may have limited generalizability to broader populations or settings, particularly if the sample size is small or the study is context specific (Teddlie & Tashakkori, 2009).

Concurrent Embedded Design

In this design, one method is dominant and is supplemented or enriched by the other method. Quantitative data collection and analysis usually occur first, with qualitative data collection and analysis embedded within the quantitative process. The qualitative data provide additional insights or explanations to enhance the understanding of the quantitative findings (Creswell & Plano Clark, 2018).

In concurrent embedded designs, researchers primarily use one method (quantitative or qualitative) and embed the other method within it. For example, researchers may collect quantitative survey data from a large sample of students and then select a subset of participants for in-depth qualitative interviews to provide additional insights into the quantitative findings. Alternatively, researchers may use qualitative data to enrich the interpretation of quantitative results.

Example of Concurrent Embedded Design in Educational Research

Research Question: Does the use of a specific teaching intervention improve students' mathematics achievement in elementary school?

Concurrent Embedded Design:

1. **Quantitative Component:**

   - Researchers administer a pre-test to a large sample of elementary school students to assess their mathematics achievement levels.

   - The students are then divided into two groups: one group receives the teaching intervention, while the other serves as the control group and receives standard instruction.

   - After the intervention period, researchers administer a post-test to both groups to measure any changes in mathematics achievement.

2. **Qualitative Component (Embedded within Quantitative Design):**

   - From the group that received the teaching intervention, researchers purposefully select a subset of students, teachers, and parents for in-depth qualitative interviews.

   - Interviews are conducted to gather rich insights into participants' experiences with the teaching intervention, including perceived benefits, challenges, and suggestions for improvement.

   - Qualitative data from interviews are analyzed thematically to identify common patterns, themes, and perspectives related to the effectiveness of the teaching intervention.

Integration:

- Quantitative data from pre-tests and post-tests are analyzed using statistical methods to compare the mathematics achievement levels between the intervention and control groups.

- Qualitative findings from interviews are integrated with quantitative results to provide deeper insights into the mechanisms underlying the observed changes in mathematics achievement.

- The qualitative data help contextualize and explain the quantitative findings, shedding light on factors such as instructional practices, student engagement, and parental involvement that may influence the effectiveness of the teaching intervention.

By embedding qualitative data collection and analysis within the quantitative design, this concurrent embedded research design provides a comprehensive understanding of the impact of the teaching intervention on students' mathematics achievement in elementary school.

This design allows researchers to capitalize on the strengths of both quantitative and qualitative methods while prioritizing one approach over the other. By embedding qualitative data collection and analysis within the quantitative process, researchers can provide deeper insights, contextual understanding, or explanatory power to complement the numerical data. Nevertheless, researchers must consider both the advantages and limitations of this method:

Introduction to Educational Research

Advantages:

Comprehensive Understanding. Embedded mixed methods designs allow researchers to gain a comprehensive understanding of the research question by integrating both quantitative and qualitative data within a single study. This approach enables researchers to explore the same phenomenon from multiple perspectives, enriching the depth and breadth of the investigation (Creswell & Plano Clark, 2018).

Methodological Synergy. By combining quantitative and qualitative methods within a single research design, embedded mixed methods designs leverage the strengths of both approaches. Quantitative methods provide statistical rigor and generalizability, while qualitative methods offer rich contextual insights and understanding of participants' perspectives (Teddlie & Tashakkori, 2009).

Triangulation of Findings. Embedded mixed methods designs facilitate methodological triangulation, allowing researchers to validate and corroborate findings across different data sources and methods. Triangulation enhances the credibility, validity, and reliability of the study's findings by minimizing the limitations of using a single method (Johnson & Onwuegbuzie, 2004).

Enhanced Interpretation. Integrating quantitative and qualitative data within a single study enables researchers to provide deeper insights and richer interpretations of the research findings. Qualitative data can help contextualize quantitative results, elucidate underlying mechanisms, and generate hypotheses for further investigation (Creswell & Plano Clark, 2018).

Efficiency and Cost-Effectiveness. Embedded mixed methods designs offer efficiency and cost-effectiveness by allowing researchers to collect and analyze multiple types of data within a single research study. This approach minimizes the need for separate studies and maximizes the utility of available resources (Teddlie & Tashakkori, 2009).

Disadvantages:

Complexity of Analysis: Analyzing both quantitative and qualitative data within a single study can be complex and challenging, requiring researchers to possess diverse analytical skills and expertise. Integrating findings from different methods may involve intricate statistical procedures and qualitative interpretation techniques (Creswell & Plano Clark, 2018).

Potential for Bias. There is a risk of bias in embedded mixed methods designs, particularly if researchers selectively prioritize certain findings over others or if their interpretation is influenced by preconceived notions. Researchers must remain vigilant to minimize bias and ensure the integrity of the study's findings (Johnson & Onwuegbuzie, 2004).

Resource Intensive. Embedded mixed methods designs can be resource-intensive in terms of time, funding, and expertise required for data collection, analysis, and integration. Managing multiple data sets and conducting analyses across different methods may increase the workload for researchers (Creswell & Plano Clark, 2018).

Difficulty in Data Integration. Integrating quantitative and qualitative data while preserving their integrity and richness can be challenging. Researchers must carefully consider how to combine the findings to ensure that the integrated results provide a coherent and meaningful interpretation of the research question (Teddlie & Tashakkori, 2009).

Limited Generalizability. Embedded mixed methods designs prioritize depth over breadth, focusing on understanding specific contexts and phenomena in-depth. As a result, the findings may have limited generalizability to broader populations or settings, particularly if the sample size is small or the study is context-specific (Creswell & Plano Clark, 2018).

In conclusion, mixed-methods research designs offer valuable approaches for investigating complex educational phenomena by integrating both quantitative and qualitative methods. These designs provide researchers with the flexibility to explore research questions from multiple perspectives, enhancing the depth and breadth of understanding. By combining the strengths of quantitative rigor and qualitative richness, mixed methods designs facilitate methodological synergy, triangulation of findings, and enhanced interpretation. While mixed-methods research designs present challenges such as complexity of analysis, potential bias, and resource intensity, their advantages in providing comprehensive insights, methodological robustness, and efficiency make them increasingly popular in educational research. Overall, mixcd-methods research designs contribute significantly to advancing knowledge and informing evidence-based practices in education.

Summary

The chapter provides an overview of mixed-methods research in educational contexts, highlighting its significance, methodologies, and common designs. Mixed-methods research, characterized by its integration of qualitative and quantitative methodologies, is depicted as a dynamic approach that aims to comprehensively investigate educational phenomena. The chapter describes various mixed-methods research designs commonly employed in educational research, including sequential exploratory design, concurrent triangulation design, and concurrent embedded design.

Sequential exploratory design, where qualitative data collection and analysis precede quantitative methods, is detailed along with an illustrative example of its application in studying the impact of peer tutoring programs on mathematics learning outcomes. Concurrent triangulation design, involving simultaneous data collection and separate analysis of qualitative and quantitative data, is described alongside its advantages, disadvantages, and an example exploring the effectiveness of a flipped classroom approach in science education. Concurrent embedded design, where one method dominates while the other is embedded to enrich understanding, is elucidated, along with a detailed example investigating the effects of a teaching intervention on mathematics achievement in elementary school.

Advantages and disadvantages of each mixed-methods design are outlined, emphasizing factors such as comprehensiveness, methodological synergy, triangulation of findings, complexity of analysis, potential bias, resource intensity, difficulty in data integration, and limited generalizability. Despite challenges, mixed-methods research is depicted as essential for advancing knowledge and informing evidence-based practices in education due to its ability to offer comprehensive insights, methodological robustness, and efficiency. Overall, the chapter serves as a guide to understanding mixed-methods research in educational contexts, providing researchers with insights into its methods, designs, advantages, and limitations.

Suggestions for Students

Key Questions

1. What is mixed-methods research, and why is it considered valuable in educational research?
2. Can you differentiate between sequential exploratory, concurrent triangulation, and concurrent embedded designs in mixed-methods research? Provide examples of each.

3. What are the advantages and disadvantages of using mixed-methods research designs in educational research? How might these designs enhance or limit our understanding of educational phenomena?

4. Describe the process of integrating qualitative and quantitative data in a mixed-methods study. Why is this integration important, and what benefits does it offer?

5. Can you identify common challenges researchers may encounter when conducting mixed-methods research in education? How might researchers address these challenges to ensure the rigor and validity of their studies?

6. How might the findings of a mixed-methods research study contribute to evidence-based practices in education? Give examples of how mixed-methods research has been used to inform educational policies or interventions.

7. Suppose you are planning a mixed-methods research study to investigate the impact of technology integration on student learning outcomes in a middle school science class. What research design would you choose, and why? Outline the steps you would take to conduct this study.

8. Discuss the ethical considerations that researchers should consider when conducting mixed-methods research in educational settings. How can researchers ensure the ethical conduct of their studies and protect the rights of participants?

9. Reflect on your own learning from this chapter. What key insights have you gained about mixed-methods research in education, and how might you apply this knowledge in your future research endeavors or professional practice?

10. In what ways might the integration of qualitative and quantitative data in mixed-methods research contribute to a deeper understanding of educational phenomena compared to using either method alone? Provide examples to support your argument.

Suggestions for Instructors

Suggested Learning Activities

The following learning activities aim to engage students in active learning experiences that deepen their understanding of mixed-methods research in educational contexts and equip them with skills for designing and analyzing research in the field.

Reading Assignment: Assign students to read the chapter on mixed-methods research in education. Encourage them to highlight key concepts, methods, and examples provided.

Suggestions for Instructors

Group Discussion: Divide students into small groups and facilitate a discussion on the advantages and disadvantages of sequential exploratory, concurrent triangulation, and concurrent embedded designs. Encourage students to share their perspectives and insights based on the chapter's content.

Case Study Analysis: Provide students with examples of mixed-methods research studies in educational contexts. Ask them to analyze the research designs used, data collection methods employed, and how qualitative and quantitative data were integrated to address the research questions.

Research Proposal Development: Task students with developing a research proposal for a mixed-methods study in an educational setting. Provide guidelines for selecting a research question, choosing appropriate research designs, outlining data collection methods, and discussing potential advantages and challenges.

Data Integration Exercise: Present students with sets of qualitative and quantitative data from a hypothetical mixed-methods study. In groups, instruct them to integrate the data and draw conclusions based on the combined analysis. Encourage critical thinking about how qualitative insights can enhance the interpretation of quantitative findings.

References

Creswell, J. W. (2014). A concise introduction to mixed methods research. Sage publications.

Creswell, J. W., & Creswell, J. D. (2017). Research design: Qualitative, quantitative, and mixed methods approaches. Sage publications.

Creswell, J. W., & Plano Clark, V. L. (2018). Designing and conducting mixed methods research. Sage publications.

Johnson, R. B., & Onwuegbuzie, A. J. (2004). Mixed methods research: A research paradigm whose time has come. Educational researcher, 33(7), 14-26.

Teddlie, C., & Tashakkori, A. (2009). Foundations of mixed methods research: Integrating quantitative and qualitative approaches in the social and behavioral sciences. Sage.

Chapter 13. Action Research

This chapter will address the following learning objectives:
• Define action research and explain its significance in educational research.   • Describe the cyclical process of action research, including its key steps and stages.   • Differentiate between various types of action research, such as collaborative action research, participatory action research (PAR), practitioner research, teacher-led action research, and action learning.   • Analyze examples of action research in education, identifying how they address specific educational challenge and informs instructional practices.   • Compare and contrast action research with formal research, highlighting similarities and differences in purpose, methodology, audience, and outcomes.   • Evaluate the advantages and disadvantages of action research in educational settings, considering factors such as relevance, empowerment, flexibility, professional development, validity, data analysis, resistance to change, and ethical considerations.   • Apply principles of action research to design and conduct a research project aimed at addressing a real-world problem or challenge within an educational context.   • Reflect on the role of collaboration, reflection, and continuous improvement in action research and its implications for promoting positive change in educational practice.

Action research is a participatory approach to educational research that focuses on addressing real-world problems or challenges within educational settings through a collaborative process of inquiry, reflection, and action. Unlike traditional research approaches, which often involve researchers studying subjects from a detached perspective, action research actively involves educators, administrators, and other stakeholders in the research process, empowering them to take ownership of and make meaningful changes in their practice.

Action research in education involves a cyclical process of planning, acting, observing, and reflecting, with the goal of improving teaching and learning practices and addressing specific issues or concerns within educational contexts. It emphasizes collaboration, critical reflection, and the integration of theory and practice.

In action research, educators identify an area of interest or concern, formulate research questions, and design interventions or strategies aimed at addressing the identified issue. They then implement these interventions in their classrooms or schools, collecting data to monitor their effectiveness and make informed decisions about future actions. Throughout the process, educators engage in ongoing reflection, drawing on both qualitative and quantitative data to critically examine their practice and its impact on student learning outcomes.

Action research is characterized by its participatory nature, with educators actively involved in all stages of the research process. This collaborative approach fosters a sense of ownership and empowerment among practitioners, as they work together to identify challenges, implement solutions, and assess the impact of their actions on teaching and learning.

Steps in Action Research

Action research typically involves a cyclical process of planning, acting, observing, and reflecting, with the goal of addressing practical problems or challenges within a specific context. Below are the main steps involved in action research:

1. Identification of the Problem or Area of Interest:

- Identify a specific problem, challenge, or area of interest within the educational context that you wish to investigate or address. This could be related to student learning outcomes, teaching practices, classroom management, or other aspects of education.

2. Planning:

- Develop a research question or questions that clearly define the focus of the inquiry.

- Determine the scope and objectives of the research project.

- Consider the appropriate research methods, data collection techniques, and sources of data that will help you address the research question(s).

- Create a research plan outlining the timeline, procedures, and resources needed to conduct the research.

3. Implementation:

- Implement the planned interventions, strategies, or changes in practice within the educational setting.

- Collect data systematically using a variety of methods, such as observations, interviews, surveys, or document analysis, to monitor the effects of the interventions and gather evidence related to the research question(s).

4. Observation and Data Collection:

- Observe and document the implementation of the interventions and their effects on the identified problem or area of interest.

- Collect data on relevant variables, behaviors, or outcomes using the chosen data collection methods.

- Ensure that data collection is ongoing and systematic, capturing both quantitative and qualitative information.

5. Reflection:

- Reflect on the data collected and analyze it to identify patterns, trends, and insights related to the research question(s).

- Consider the successes, challenges, and unexpected outcomes of the interventions or changes in practice.

- Engage in critical reflection on your own assumptions, biases, and perspectives, as well as the broader context in which the research is taking place.

6. Action:

- Based on the analysis of the data and reflection on the findings, take informed action to address the identified problem or improve practice.

- Make adjustments to the interventions, strategies, or changes in practice as needed, informed by the evidence collected during the research process.

7. Evaluation:

- Evaluate the effectiveness of the actions taken in response to the research findings.

- Assess the impact of the interventions or changes in practice on the identified problem or area of interest.

- Consider the implications of the research findings for future practice, policy, or research.

8. Sharing and Dissemination:

- Share the research findings, insights, and recommendations with relevant stakeholders, such as colleagues, administrators, policymakers, or the broader educational community.

- Disseminate the research outcomes through presentations, reports, publications, or other channels to contribute to the collective knowledge base in education.

In conclusion, action research is a dynamic and iterative process that empowers educators to address practical problems or challenges within their educational contexts. The steps involved in action research, including problem identification, planning, implementation, observation, reflection, action, evaluation, and sharing, form a cyclical and iterative framework for inquiry and improvement. By systematically engaging in these steps, educators can collaboratively explore, understand, and address issues in their practice, leading to continuous improvement, enhanced student learning outcomes, and the advancement of education.

Tyes of Action Research

Action research encompasses various approaches and methodologies that educators can employ to investigate and address issues within their educational settings. Below are descriptions of some common types of action research:

Collaborative Action Research. In collaborative action research, educators work together in teams or communities of practice to identify shared concerns, develop interventions, and collaboratively reflect on their practice. This approach emphasizes collective inquiry and collaboration among educators, fostering a sense of shared responsibility for improving teaching and learning.

Participatory Action Research (PAR). Participatory action research involves collaboration between researchers and participants, often including students, parents, and community members, in all stages of the research process. PAR emphasizes the importance of empowering marginalized groups and promoting social justice through research that addresses issues of equity, diversity, and inclusion within educational contexts.

Practitioner Research. Practitioner research refers to action research conducted by practicing educators within their own classrooms or schools. Educators use practitioner research to investigate specific teaching and learning challenges, develop innovative practices, and improve student outcomes. This approach emphasizes the integration of research and practice, with educators serving as both researchers and agents of change within their educational settings.

Teacher-led Action Research. Teacher-led action research involves individual teachers or teaching teams conducting research to improve their practice and enhance student learning. Educators identify areas of interest or concern, develop research questions, and implement interventions or instructional strategies informed by their research findings. This approach emphasizes the professional development of teachers and the importance of reflective practice in promoting continuous improvement.

Action Learning. Action learning combines elements of action research with principles of organizational learning and leadership development. In action learning, individuals or teams engage in a structured process of inquiry, action, and reflection to address complex problems or challenges within educational organizations. This approach emphasizes the development of leadership skills, critical thinking, and collaborative problem-solving abilities.

Example of Action Research in Education

Improving Reading Comprehension through Peer Tutoring
The following example demonstrates how action research can be used to address practical challenges in education, engage stakeholders in collaborative problem-solving, and inform instructional practices to support student success.

Background: A fifth-grade teacher notices that several students in her class are struggling with reading comprehension skills. Despite various instructional strategies employed, some students continue to struggle with understanding and analyzing texts. Concerned about their progress, the teacher decides to engage in action research to address this issue.

Action Research Question: How can peer tutoring improve reading comprehension among struggling readers in a fifth-grade classroom?

Action Plan:
1. **Identifying Participants:** The teacher selects four struggling readers from her class to participate in the intervention.
2. **Training Peer Tutors:** The teacher provides training to four high-achieving students who will serve as peer tutors. The training includes strategies for effective tutoring, such as asking questions, summarizing, and providing feedback.
3. **Intervention Implementation:** The peer tutoring sessions are conducted twice a week for 60 minutes each session. During these sessions, peer tutors assist struggling readers with reading comprehension strategies while reading assigned texts.

Example of Action Research in Education

4. **Data Collection:** The teacher collects data on reading comprehension using pre-tests, post-tests, and ongoing observations of student progress during tutoring sessions.
5. **Reflection and Adjustment:** Throughout the intervention, the teacher reflects on the effectiveness of peer tutoring and makes adjustments as needed. This may include modifying tutoring strategies, providing additional support, or changing groupings.

Results and Reflection:
- After several weeks of peer tutoring sessions, the teacher observes improvements in the reading comprehension skills of struggling readers. They demonstrate increased ability to identify main ideas, make inferences, and summarize texts.
- Both struggling readers and peer tutors report positive experiences with the intervention, citing increased confidence and motivation to engage with texts.
- The teacher reflects on the success of the intervention and considers incorporating peer tutoring into her ongoing teaching practices to support struggling readers in future classes.

Conclusion: Through action research, the teacher successfully implemented a peer tutoring intervention to improve reading comprehension skills among struggling readers in her fifth-grade classroom. The collaborative and reflective nature of action research allowed her to address a specific educational challenge, implement a targeted intervention, and assess its impact on student learning outcomes.

Action Research versus Formal Research

Action research and formal research share similarities in their commitment to systematic inquiry and the generation of knowledge. However, they also exhibit distinct differences in terms of purpose, methodology, and outcomes.

Similarities:

Systematic Inquiry. Both action research and formal research involve systematic inquiry aimed at exploring, understanding, and addressing specific phenomena or problems within a given context. They rely on rigorous methods of data collection, analysis, and interpretation to generate empirical evidence and insights.

Evidence-Based Practice. Both types of research aim to inform evidence-based practice by providing empirical support for decision-making in education and other fields. They seek to identify effective strategies, interventions, or policies that can improve outcomes and inform practice.

Ethical Considerations. Both action research and formal research adhere to ethical guidelines and principles to ensure the protection of participants' rights and well-being. They prioritize informed consent, confidentiality, and the responsible conduct of research throughout the research process.

Differences:

Purpose. The primary purpose of formal research is to contribute to the general body of knowledge within a particular field by testing hypotheses, establishing theories, or exploring phenomena. In contrast, the primary purpose of action research is to address practical problems or challenges within specific contexts and to inform improvements in practice.

Methodology. Formal research typically follows a predetermined research design, such as experimental, correlational, or descriptive methods, and often involves large-scale data collection from diverse populations. In contrast, action research is characterized by its flexible and iterative nature, with researchers engaging in cycles of planning, acting, observing, and reflecting to address specific issues within their own practice or context.

Audience. The audience for formal research is often fellow researchers, academics, policymakers, or other stakeholders interested in advancing knowledge within a particular field. In contrast, the audience for action research is typically practitioners, educators, administrators, and other stakeholders directly involved in the context being studied, with a focus on informing practice and promoting improvement.

Outcomes. The outcomes of formal research often include publications in peer-reviewed journals, presentations at conferences, or contributions to academic discourse. In contrast, the outcomes of action research are typically focused on practical changes or improvements within educational settings, such as the implementation of new strategies, interventions, or policies informed by research findings.

Advantages and Disadvantages of Action Research

Action research is vitally important in education as it empowers educators to collaboratively address real-world challenges within their classrooms and schools. By engaging in a cyclical process of inquiry, reflection, and action, educators can develop practical solutions, enhance teaching practices, and improve student learning outcomes. Action research promotes a culture of continuous improvement and innovation, fostering professional growth, and ultimately contributing to the ongoing advancement of education. Nevertheless, researchers must consider all advantages and disadvantages of using this method:

Advantages:

Relevance and Practicality. Action research is focused on addressing real-world problems and challenges within educational settings. This makes the research process highly relevant to the needs and concerns of practitioners, leading to the development of practical solutions that can be implemented to improve teaching and learning outcomes.

Empowerment and Ownership. Action research actively involves educators, administrators, and other stakeholders in the research process, empowering them to take ownership of and make meaningful changes in their practice. This collaborative approach fosters a sense of agency and efficacy among practitioners, leading to increased engagement and commitment to the improvement of educational practices.

Flexibility and Adaptability. Action research is characterized by its flexible and adaptive nature, allowing researchers to tailor interventions and strategies to the specific needs and contexts of their classrooms or schools. This flexibility enables educators to experiment with different approaches, make adjustments based on ongoing feedback, and refine their practices over time.

Professional Development. Engaging in action research provides valuable opportunities for professional development and growth. Through the process of inquiry, reflection, and action, educators deepen their understanding of teaching and learning processes, enhance their problem-solving skills, and develop a reflective stance towards their practice. This continuous learning contributes to ongoing improvement and innovation in education.

Promotion of Reflective Practice. Action research encourages educators to engage in critical reflection on their practice, drawing on both qualitative and quantitative data to evaluate the effectiveness of their interventions and make informed decisions about future actions. This reflective stance fosters a culture of continuous improvement and self-evaluation among practitioners, leading to enhanced teaching and learning outcomes.

Disadvantages:

Time and Resource Intensive. Action research can be time-consuming and resource-intensive, requiring educators to allocate significant time and effort to planning, implementing, and evaluating interventions. This may pose challenges for busy teachers who already have demanding workloads and limited resources.

Validity and Generalizability. The findings of action research studies may be subject to limitations in terms of validity and generalizability. Because action research typically focuses on specific contexts and small sample sizes, the findings may not be easily generalizable to broader populations or settings. Additionally, the validity of findings may be affected by factors such as researcher bias or subjectivity.

Complexity of Data Analysis. Analyzing data in action research can be complex, particularly when using qualitative methods such as thematic analysis or grounded theory. Educators may require training and support in data analysis techniques to effectively interpret and make meaning of the data collected during the research process.

Resistance to Change. Implementing changes based on the findings of action research may encounter resistance from stakeholders who are comfortable with existing practices or skeptical about the need for change. Overcoming resistance to change requires effective communication, collaboration, and buy-in from all stakeholders involved in the research process.

Ethical Considerations. Action research raises ethical considerations related to informed consent, confidentiality, and the potential for harm to participants. Educators must ensure that research activities adhere to ethical guidelines and safeguard the rights and well-being of all individuals involved in the research process.

Despite these challenges, action research remains a valuable approach for improving educational practices, promoting professional growth, and enhancing student learning outcomes. By leveraging the strengths of action research and addressing its limitations, educators can effectively address real-world challenges and contribute to continuous improvement in education.

Summary

The chapter on action research in educational settings provides a comprehensive overview of this participatory approach to research. It begins by defining action research as a collaborative process aimed at addressing real-world problems or challenges within educational contexts through inquiry, reflection, and action. The chapter outlines the cyclical process of action research, including steps such as problem identification, planning, implementation, observation, reflection, action, evaluation, and sharing. Furthermore, the chapter discusses various types of action research, including collaborative action research, participatory action research (PAR), practitioner research, teacher-led action research, and action learning. Each type emphasizes different aspects of collaboration, participation, and leadership in the research process. Additionally, the chapter explores an example of action research in education, illustrating how a fifth-grade teacher uses peer tutoring to improve reading comprehension among struggling readers. This example demonstrates the practical application of action research to address specific educational challenges and inform instructional practices. Moreover, the chapter compares action research with formal research, highlighting similarities and differences in purpose, methodology, audience, and outcomes. While both approaches aim to generate knowledge and inform practice, action research prioritizes practical solutions and collaboration with stakeholders. Finally, the chapter discusses the advantages and disadvantages of action research in educational settings. It acknowledges the benefits of relevance, empowerment, flexibility, professional development, and reflective practice, while also addressing challenges related to time, validity, data analysis, resistance to change, and ethical considerations. In summary, the chapter provides a comprehensive overview of action research in educational research, emphasizing its importance as a collaborative and empowering approach to addressing real-world challenges and driving continuous improvement in education.

Suggestions for Students

Key Questions

1. What is action research, and why is it important in educational research?

2. Describe the cyclical process of action research. What are the main steps involved, and how do they contribute to addressing educational challenges?

3. Can you differentiate between different types of action research, such as collaborative action research, participatory action research (PAR), practitioner research, teacher-led action research, and action learning? Provide examples of each.

4. Analyze an example of action research in education provided in the chapter. How does this example demonstrate the application of action research principles to address a specific educational challenge?

5. Compare and contrast action research with formal research. What are the main similarities and differences between these approaches in terms of purpose, methodology, audience, and outcomes?

6. Evaluate the advantages and disadvantages of action research in educational settings. What are some of the benefits and challenges associated with implementing action research in educational contexts?

7. Reflect on the role of collaboration, reflection, and continuous improvement in action research. How do these principles contribute to promoting positive change in educational practice?

8. Apply principles of action research to design a research project aimed at addressing a real-world problem or challenge within an educational context. What steps would you take to plan, implement, and evaluate your action research project?

Suggestions for Instructors

Suggested Learning Activities

Case Study Analysis: Provide students with case studies of action research projects conducted in educational settings. Divide students into small groups and ask them to analyze the case studies, identifying the key steps of the action research process, the types of action research employed, and the outcomes of the projects. Facilitate a class discussion where groups share their analyses and insights, comparing the different approaches and outcomes of the action research projects.

Action Research Simulation: Divide students into small groups and assign each group a specific educational challenge or problem to address through action research. Guide students through the action research process, including problem identification, planning, implementation, data collection, reflection, and action. Have each group present their action research plan, including their research question, proposed interventions, data collection methods, and expected outcomes. Facilitate a debriefing session where students reflect on their experiences, discuss the challenges encountered, and identify lessons learned from the simulation.

Peer Review and Feedback: Ask students to conduct peer reviews of action research proposals or reports created by their classmates. Provide students with rubrics or guidelines for evaluating the quality and effectiveness of action research projects, focusing on criteria such as clarity of research questions, appropriateness of methodologies, thoroughness of data analysis, and implications for practice. Pair students up and have them exchange feedback on each other's work, offering constructive criticism and suggestions for improvement. Encourage students to revise their action research projects based on the feedback received and submit final versions for evaluation.

Field Observation and Reflection: Arrange for students to observe action research projects in real educational settings, such as classrooms, schools, or community organizations. Provide students with observation guides or reflection prompts to help them document their observations and reflections on the action research process, including how the research is conducted, the challenges encountered, and the impact on teaching and learning. Facilitate a discussion where students share their observations and reflections, highlighting key insights and lessons learned from their field experiences.

Action Research Proposal Development: Assign students to develop action research proposals focused on addressing specific educational challenges or problems of interest to them. Guide students through the process of formulating research questions, designing research methodologies, selecting data collection methods, and planning interventions. Have students present their action research proposals to the class, explaining their rationale, objectives, methods, and expected outcomes. Facilitate a peer review session where students provide feedback on each other's proposals, offering suggestions for refinement and improvement.

References

Creswell, J. W. (2014). Research design: Qualitative, quantitative, and mixed methods approaches. Sage Publications.

Fraenkel, J. R., Wallen, N. E., & Hyun, H. H. (2014). How to design and evaluate research in education. McGraw-Hill Education.

Kemmis, S., & McTaggart, R. (2005). Participatory action research: Communicative action and the public sphere. In N. K. Denzin & Y. S. Lincoln (Eds.), The Sage handbook of qualitative research (3rd ed., pp. 559-603). Sage Publications.

McNiff, J., & Whitehead, J. (2006). All you need to know about action research. Sage Publications.

Mills, G. E. (2014). Action research: A guide for the teacher researcher (5th ed.). Pearson.

Sagor, R. (2017). The action research guidebook: A four-step process for educators and school teams (4th ed.). Corwin.

Stringer, E. T. (2007). Action research (3rd ed.). Sage Publications.

Zeichner, K., Payne, K. A., & Brayko, K. (2015). Democratizing knowledge in the transition from preparation to teaching: Can we realize Dewey's vision? Teachers College Record, 117(10), 1-45.

Chapter 14. Writing Research Proposals

This chapter will address the following learning objectives:
• Explain the purpose of research proposals in educational research.
• Identify the key components of a research proposal, including the introduction, literature review, methodology, and ethical considerations.
• Explain why research proposals are important in educational research, including their role in clarifying research objectives, guiding the research process, and securing funding.
• Analyze the process of writing a research proposal, including steps such as formulating research questions, selecting appropriate methodologies, and addressing ethical considerations.
• Describe the various contexts and situations in which research proposals are required in educational research, such as grant applications, academic research projects, ethical reviews, collaborative research projects, and conference presentations.
• Evaluate the advantages and disadvantages of research proposals in educational research.
• Reflect on the overall role and significance of research proposals in advancing knowledge and promoting evidence-based practices in education.

What Are Research Proposals?

A research proposal in educational research is a formal document that outlines a planned study, including its objectives, methodology, significance, and feasibility. It serves as a roadmap for conducting the research and provides a clear rationale for why the study is important and how it will be carried out. Research proposals are typically submitted to funding agencies, academic institutions, or research committees for review and approval before the research is conducted. Here are some definitions of research proposals from authoritative sources:

According to Fraenkel, J. R., Wallen, N. E., & Hyun, H. H. (2019), a research proposal is "a written plan that describes in detail how a research study will be conducted. It includes the research question, a rationale for the study, a description of the research design and methodology, a discussion of the ethical considerations involved, and a timeline for completion."

Leedy, P. D., & Ormrod, J. E. (2014) define a research proposal as "a written plan or outline that specifies the research question(s), describes the research design and methodology to be used, outlines the procedures for data collection and analysis, and provides a rationale for the study."

Gall, M. D., Gall, J. P., & Borg, W. R. (2007) describe a research proposal as "a detailed plan for a research study that specifies the research question, provides a rationale for the study, outlines the research design and methodology, describes the procedures for data collection and analysis, and discusses the significance and implications of the study."

These definitions highlight the key components of a research proposal, including the research question, rationale, design, methodology, data collection procedures, and significance. Research proposals play a critical role in educational research by providing a structured framework for planning and conducting research studies in the field of education.

Why Are Research Proposals Important?

Research proposals play a crucial role in educational research by providing a blueprint for conducting a study and outlining the key elements of the research project. Below are several reasons why research proposals are important in educational research:

Clarifying Research Objectives. A well-written research proposal clearly articulates the objectives, aims, and purpose of the study. It helps researchers to define the scope of the research, identify the research questions or hypotheses, and specify the intended outcomes.

Guiding the Research Process. Research proposals provide a roadmap for conducting the study, outlining the research design, methodology, data collection procedures, and analysis techniques. They serve as a guide for researchers to follow throughout the research process, ensuring that the study is conducted in a systematic and organized manner.

Facilitating Peer Review. Research proposals are typically subjected to peer review by experts in the field before the research is conducted. Peer review helps to evaluate the quality, feasibility, and ethical considerations of the proposed study. Feedback from peer reviewers can help researchers refine their research plans and address any methodological or conceptual issues before beginning the study.

Ensuring Ethical Conduct. Research proposals outline the ethical considerations and procedures that will be followed during the research, including informed consent, confidentiality, and participant rights. By addressing ethical concerns upfront, research proposals help to ensure that the study is conducted in an ethical and responsible manner.

Securing Funding. Many research projects require funding to cover expenses such as materials, equipment, participant compensation, and personnel. Research proposals provide a justification for why the research is important, how it will be conducted, and how the funds will be allocated. A well-written research proposal increases the likelihood of securing funding from grant agencies, foundations, or other sources.

Promoting Transparency and Reproducibility. Research proposals promote transparency by clearly documenting the research plan, including the research design, methodology, and data analysis procedures. This transparency allows other researchers to evaluate the study's methods and findings and facilitates the replication of the study by other researchers.

Contributing to Scholarly Dialogue. Research proposals contribute to the ongoing scholarly dialogue in the field of education by proposing new research ideas, theories, or methodologies. Even if the proposed study is not ultimately conducted, the research proposal can still stimulate discussion, generate new ideas, and inspire future research directions.

Overall, research proposals are essential documents in educational research as they provide a framework for planning, conducting, and evaluating research studies. By clearly outlining the research objectives, methodology, and significance, research proposals help researchers to communicate their research plans effectively to reviewers, funders, and stakeholders in the field of education.

What are the Components of Research Proposals?

Writing a research proposal in educational research involves outlining a clear plan for conducting a study that addresses a specific research question or problem within the field of education. Below is a step-by-step guide on how to write a research proposal in educational research:

1. **Title Page:**

    • Include a descriptive title that succinctly summarizes the research project.

    • Provide your name, institutional affiliation, department, and contact information.

    • Include the date of submission.

2. **Abstract:**

    • Write a concise summary of the proposed research, including the research question, objectives, methodology, and anticipated outcomes.

    • Highlight the significance of the research and its potential implications for theory, practice, or policy in education.

    • Keep the abstract brief, typically no more than 250 words.

3. **Introduction:**

    • Provide background information on the topic of study, including relevant literature, theories, and research findings.

    • Clearly state the research problem or question that the study aims to address.

    • Justify the importance of the research by explaining its relevance to the field of education and identifying gaps or limitations in existing knowledge.

    • Clearly articulate the purpose and objectives of the study.

4. **Theoretical Framework:**

    • Develop a theoretical framework that provides a conceptual lens for understanding the research problem and guiding the analysis.

    • Identify relevant theories, models, or conceptual frameworks that inform the study's approach and methodology.

    • Explain how the theoretical framework aligns with the research question and objectives.

5. **Literature Review:**

    • Conduct a comprehensive review of relevant literature on the topic, including empirical studies, theoretical frameworks, and conceptual models.

- Synthesize and critically analyze the existing research to identify key themes, trends, and debates in the field.

- Identify theoretical perspectives or conceptual frameworks that will guide the study.

- Discuss how previous research informs the research question and methodology of the proposed study.

6. **Methodology:**

    - Describe the research design, including whether the study will be qualitative, quantitative, or mixed methods.

    - Outline the sampling strategy, including the target population, sampling method, and sample size.

    - Detail the data collection methods, such as surveys, interviews, observations, or document analysis.

    - Discuss how data will be analyzed, including specific techniques or procedures for data coding, thematic analysis, or statistical analysis.

    - Address ethical considerations, including informed consent, confidentiality, and the protection of participants' rights.

7. **Timeline:**

    - Provide a detailed timeline for conducting the research, including key milestones, data collection periods, and analysis phases.

    - Specify the duration of each phase of the research project and the anticipated completion date.

8. **Budget:**

    - Estimate the costs associated with conducting the research, including expenses for materials, equipment, participant compensation, travel, and personnel.

    - Justify the budget by explaining how each expense contributes to the successful completion of the research project.

9. **References:**

    - Provide a list of references cited in the proposal, formatted according to the appropriate citation style (e.g., APA, MLA, Chicago).

    - Ensure that all sources are properly cited and referenced throughout the proposal.

10. **Appendices:**

- Include any additional materials or documents that support the proposal, such as informed consent forms, survey instruments, interview protocols, or data analysis plans.

Writing a research proposal in educational research requires careful planning, organization, and attention to detail. By following these steps and guidelines, researchers can develop a comprehensive and well-structured proposal that effectively communicates the rationale, objectives, methodology, and significance of their study to reviewers and stakeholders in the field of education.

Example of a Research Proposal Plan in Educational Research

The following example is a plan for a research proposal in education and demonstrates how to structure and organize a proposal for investigating a specific research problem related to teaching and learning. It provides a detailed overview of the proposed study, including its objectives, methodology, theoretical framework, ethical considerations, significance, and practical implications.

Title: Enhancing Student Engagement Through Flipped Learning: A Mixed-Methods Study

1. **Introduction:** The introduction will provide background information on the topic of flipped learning and its potential impact on student engagement in educational settings. It will highlight the importance of student engagement for academic success and outline the rationale for conducting the proposed study.

2. **Research Problem:** The research problem will be identified as the need to enhance student engagement in the classroom, particularly in the context of traditional lecture-based instruction. The proposal will discuss how flipped learning has emerged as a promising instructional approach to address this problem by shifting the focus from teacher-led instruction to student-centered learning activities.

3. **Objectives:** The objectives of the study will be to:

   - Investigate the impact of flipped learning on student engagement levels in a high school mathematics classroom.

   - Explore student perceptions and experiences of flipped learning in relation to their engagement and motivation.

   - Identify effective strategies and best practices for implementing flipped learning to enhance student engagement.

4. **Theoretical Framework:** The theoretical framework will draw on theories of student engagement, self-regulated learning, and constructivist pedagogy to provide a conceptual basis for the study. It will discuss how flipped learning aligns with these theoretical perspectives and has the potential to promote active learning and deeper understanding among students.

5. **Method**:

   - **Research Design:** The study will employ a mixed-methods approach, combining quantitative surveys with qualitative interviews and classroom observations.

   - **Participants:** The participants will include high school students enrolled in a mathematics course where flipped learning is being implemented, as well as their teacher.

   - **Data Collection:** Data will be collected through pre- and post-surveys to measure changes in student engagement levels, semi-structured interviews to explore student perceptions and experiences, and classroom observations to document instructional

Example of a Research Proposal Plan in Educational Research

practices.

- **Data Analysis:** Quantitative data will be analyzed using descriptive statistics and inferential tests, while qualitative data will be analyzed thematically to identify key themes and patterns.

6. **Ethical Considerations:** The proposal will address ethical considerations related to informed consent, confidentiality, and participant rights. It will outline procedures for obtaining consent from participants and ensuring their anonymity and privacy throughout the study.

7. **Significance:** The proposal will discuss the significance of the study for educational practice and research. It will highlight the potential benefits of flipped learning for promoting student engagement, academic achievement, and lifelong learning skills.

8. **Timeline and Budget:** The proposal will include a timeline outlining the various stages of the research project, from recruitment and data collection to analysis and dissemination of findings. It will also provide a budget estimate for expenses such as materials, participant incentives, and data analysis software.

9. **References:** The proposal will include a list of references cited in the document, formatted according to the appropriate citation style (e.g., APA, MLA).

When Are Research Proposals Necessary?

Research proposals are required in educational research in various contexts and situations. Below are some common scenarios in which research proposals are typically needed:

Grant Applications. Researchers often submit research proposals as part of grant applications to funding agencies, foundations, or government organizations. These proposals outline the planned research project, its objectives, methodology, and anticipated outcomes, along with a budget and timeline. Funding agencies use research proposals to evaluate the quality, significance, and feasibility of proposed research projects and allocate funding accordingly.

Academic Research Projects. In academic settings, graduate students, faculty members, and researchers may be required to submit research proposals as part of their coursework, thesis or dissertation projects, or independent research initiatives. Research proposals provide a structured framework for planning and conducting research studies, guiding students and researchers through the process of formulating research questions, designing studies, and collecting and analyzing data.

Ethical Review. Research proposals are often required to undergo ethical review by institutional review boards (IRBs) or ethics committees before research involving human participants can be conducted. Ethical review ensures that research studies adhere to ethical guidelines and protect the rights and well-being of participants. Research proposals submitted for ethical review typically include detailed information on informed consent procedures, data collection methods, and procedures for ensuring participant confidentiality and privacy.

Collaborative Research Projects. When researchers collaborate on interdisciplinary or multi-institutional research projects, they may be required to develop research proposals to outline their respective roles, responsibilities, and contributions to the project. Research proposals facilitate collaboration and communication among research team members, ensuring that everyone is aligned with the project's objectives and methodology.

Conference Presentations. Researchers may submit research proposals to academic conferences as abstracts or proposals for presentations, workshops, or poster sessions. Conference proposals provide an opportunity for researchers to share their research findings, methods, and insights with colleagues, receive feedback from peers, and contribute to the scholarly dialogue in the field of education.

Overall, research proposals are required in educational research to plan, organize, and communicate research projects effectively, whether for securing funding, obtaining ethical approval, conducting academic research, collaborating with other researchers, or presenting research findings at conferences. They serve as a formal document that outlines the rationale, objectives, methodology, and significance of the proposed research study, guiding researchers through the process of designing and conducting high-quality research in the field of education.

Challenges in Writing Research Proposals

Writing research proposals in education can present several challenges due to the complexity of educational research and the diverse range of topics and methodologies involved. Below are some common challenges in writing research proposals in education, along with references for further reading:

Identifying a Research Gap. One of the initial challenges in writing a research proposal is identifying a gap in the existing literature that warrants further investigation. Researchers must conduct a thorough review of the literature to identify gaps, inconsistencies, or unanswered questions in the field of study (Boote & Beile, 2005).

Formulating Research Questions. Formulating clear and focused research questions that address the identified research gap can be challenging. Research questions should be specific, feasible, and relevant to the research objectives, requiring researchers to carefully define the scope and purpose of their study (Gall et al., 2007).

Selecting a Suitable Methodology. Choosing an appropriate research methodology and study design is essential but can be challenging, particularly for novice researchers. Researchers must consider factors such as the research questions, objectives, population, and available resources when selecting a methodology (Creswell, 2014).

Addressing Ethical Considerations. Ensuring that research proposals address ethical considerations related to participant rights, informed consent, and confidentiality can be challenging. Researchers must develop clear procedures for obtaining informed consent, protecting participant privacy, and ensuring the ethical conduct of research studies (Hensley, 2013).

Developing a Realistic Timeline and Budget. Creating a realistic timeline and budget for the proposed research project can be challenging, as researchers must balance the scope of the study with available resources and time constraints. Researchers must carefully plan and allocate resources to ensure the successful completion of the research project (Fraenkel et al., 2019).

Writing Clearly and Concisely. Communicating complex research ideas and methodologies in a clear and concise manner can be challenging, particularly for researchers with limited writing experience. Researchers must effectively communicate their research objectives, methodology, and significance in a way that is accessible to reviewers and stakeholders (Kelley et al., 2003).

Addressing Reviewer Feedback. After submitting a research proposal for review, researchers may receive feedback and suggestions for revision from peer reviewers or funding agencies. Addressing reviewer feedback and revising the proposal accordingly can be challenging, requiring researchers to critically evaluate and revise their proposed research plans (Davis, 2011).

Navigating Institutional Requirements. Researchers must navigate institutional requirements and guidelines when preparing research proposals, such as formatting guidelines, submission deadlines, and institutional review board (IRB) requirements. Adhering to institutional requirements while maintaining the integrity of the research proposal can be challenging (Fowler, 2014).

Overall, writing research proposals in education requires careful planning, attention to detail, and a thorough understanding of the research process. By addressing these common challenges and seeking guidance from relevant literature and resources, researchers can develop high-quality research proposals that contribute to the advancement of knowledge in the field of education. While research proposals play a crucial role in educational research by providing a framework for planning, organizing, and conducting research projects, they also have limitations and challenges that researchers must consider. By understanding the advantages and disadvantages of research proposals, researchers can develop more effective research proposals and navigate the research process more successfully.

Benefits and Downsides of Writing Research Proposals

Research proposals in education offer several benefits, including providing a structured framework for planning and conducting research studies, clarifying research objectives and methodologies, securing funding opportunities, and addressing ethical considerations. However, they also have downsides, such as the time and effort required for development, the potential for rigid structures to limit creativity, and the subjective nature of the review process. Despite these limitations, research proposals play a crucial role in guiding and facilitating high-quality educational research. Below is a summary of the benefits and drawbacks of writing research proposals with references for further reading:

Benefits:

Clarity and Focus. Research proposals help researchers to clarify their research objectives, methodology, and intended outcomes before embarking on a study. By clearly defining the scope and purpose of the research, proposals ensure that researchers stay focused on addressing relevant research questions and objectives (Bitchener & Basturkmen, 2006).

Planning and Organization. Research proposals provide a structured framework for planning and organizing research projects. They outline the research design, methodology, data collection procedures, and analysis techniques, helping researchers to systematically plan and conduct their studies (Fraenkel et al., 2019).

Peer Review and Feedback. Research proposals undergo peer review by experts in the field, such as funding agencies, academic institutions, or ethics committees. Peer review provides valuable feedback and suggestions for improving the quality, feasibility, and ethical considerations of proposed research projects (Kelley, Clark, Brown, & Sitzia, 2003).

Ethical Considerations. Research proposals address ethical considerations related to informed consent, participant confidentiality, and data protection. By outlining procedures for ethical conduct, proposals ensure that research studies adhere to ethical guidelines and protect the rights and well-being of participants (Hensley, 2013).

Funding Opportunities. Research proposals are essential for securing funding from grant agencies, foundations, or government organizations. They provide a rationale for why the research is important, how it will be conducted, and how the funds will be allocated, increasing the likelihood of securing funding for research projects (Fowler, 2014).

Downsides:

Time and Effort. Developing a research proposal requires significant time, effort, and resources. Researchers must thoroughly review the literature, formulate research questions, design the study, and prepare the proposal, which can be time-consuming and challenging, particularly for novice researchers (Leedy & Ormrod, 2014).

Rigid Structure. Research proposals often follow a rigid structure, with specific sections and formatting requirements. This structure may limit researchers' creativity and flexibility in designing and conducting research studies, leading to a standardized approach that may not be suitable for all research projects (Silverman, 2016).

Subjectivity in Review Process. The peer review process for research proposals can be subjective, with reviewers' opinions and biases influencing the evaluation of proposed research projects. This subjectivity may result in inconsistencies in the review process and biases against certain types of research or researchers (Davis, 2011).

Rejection and Resubmission. Research proposals may be rejected by funding agencies or ethics committees, requiring researchers to revise and resubmit their proposals for further review. The rejection and resubmission process can be time-consuming and demoralizing for researchers, delaying the start of research projects and limiting funding opportunities (Fain, 2015).

Limited Generalizability. Research proposals often focus on specific research questions, contexts, or populations, which may limit the generalizability of research findings. Researchers must carefully consider the applicability of their findings to broader populations or settings and acknowledge any limitations in generalizability in their proposals (Denzin & Lincoln, 2011).

Overall, while research proposals play a crucial role in educational research by providing a framework for planning, organizing, and conducting research projects, they also have limitations and challenges that researchers must consider. By understanding the advantages and disadvantages of research proposals, researchers can develop more effective research proposals and navigate the research process more successfully.

In conclusion, research proposals play a pivotal role in educational research by providing a roadmap for planning, organizing, and conducting rigorous studies. They serve as a tool for clarifying research objectives, methodologies, and ethical considerations, while also facilitating the securing of funding opportunities and guiding researchers through the peer review process. Although research proposals have limitations, such as the time and effort required for development and the potential for rigid structures to constrain creativity, their importance in guiding high-quality educational research cannot be overstated. Ultimately, research proposals contribute to the advancement of knowledge in education by ensuring the systematic and ethical conduct of research studies, thereby promoting evidence-based practices and the improvement of educational outcomes.

Summary

The chapter explores the significance, components, necessity, challenges, and benefits of research proposals in educational research. It begins by defining research proposals as formal documents outlining planned studies, including objectives, methodology, significance, and feasibility. These proposals serve as roadmaps for research, clarifying why the study is essential and how it will be conducted. Next, it highlights the importance of research proposals in educational research, emphasizing their role in clarifying objectives, guiding the research process, facilitating peer review, ensuring ethical conduct, securing funding, promoting transparency, and contributing to scholarly dialogue. The chapter outlines the components of research proposals, including title page, abstract, introduction, theoretical framework, literature review, methodology, timeline, budget, references, and appendices. It provides a step-by-step guide for writing a research proposal, incorporating examples and authoritative references. It discusses when research proposals are necessary, such as grant applications, academic research projects, ethical review, collaborative research, and conference presentations. Moreover, it addresses the challenges in writing research proposals, such as identifying research gaps, formulating research questions, selecting methodologies, addressing ethical considerations, and navigating institutional requirements. Furthermore, the chapter explores the benefits and limitations of research proposals, highlighting their role in providing clarity, planning, peer review, ethical conduct, and funding opportunities, while acknowledging challenges like time constraints, rigid structures, subjective review processes, rejection, and limited generalizability. In conclusion, the chapter emphasizes the pivotal role of research proposals in educational research, serving as essential tools for planning, conducting, and evaluating rigorous studies. It underscores the importance of understanding and addressing challenges while leveraging the benefits of research proposals to advance knowledge and promote evidence-based practices in education.

Suggestions for Students

Key Questions

9. What is the purpose of a research proposal in educational research?
10. What are the key components of a research proposal, and why are they important?
11. How does a research proposal contribute to the planning and organization of a research study?
12. Why is it essential to address ethical considerations in a research proposal?
13. In what contexts or situations are research proposals typically required in educational research?
14. Can you explain the process of writing a research proposal, including the steps involved?
15. What are some advantages and disadvantages of research proposals in educational research?
16. How do peer review processes contribute to the quality of research proposals?
17. How do research proposals help researchers secure funding for their projects?
18. What is the significance of research proposals in advancing knowledge and promoting evidence-based practices in education?

Suggestions for Instructors

Suggested Learning Activities

Case Study Analysis: Provide students with examples of research proposals from different fields of education. Ask them to analyze these proposals, identifying key components such as the research question, methodology, theoretical framework, and ethical considerations. Encourage students to discuss the strengths and weaknesses of each proposal and propose improvements.

Proposal Writing Workshop: Organize a workshop where students work in small groups to develop their own research proposals. Provide them with a research topic or allow them to choose their own. Guide students through the process of formulating research questions, selecting methodologies, and outlining the significance of their proposed studies. Encourage peer review and feedback to refine their proposals.

Peer Review Simulation: Divide students into pairs or small groups and assign each group a research proposal to review. Provide guidelines for evaluating proposals based on criteria such as clarity, feasibility, and ethical considerations. After reviewing the proposals, have students provide constructive feedback to the authors and discuss their observations as a class.

Ethical Dilemma Discussion: Present students with hypothetical scenarios involving ethical dilemmas in educational research (e.g., issues related to informed consent, confidentiality, or participant rights). Facilitate a class discussion where students analyze the ethical implications of each scenario and propose solutions based on ethical guidelines and principles.

Grant Writing Exercise: Assign students the task of writing a grant proposal for a research project in education. Provide them with guidelines and criteria for grant applications, including information on budgeting, timeline development, and funder expectations. Encourage students to integrate concepts learned from the chapter into their grant proposals.

Research Proposal Presentation: Have students present their research proposals to the class or a panel of faculty members and peers. Encourage them to effectively communicate their research objectives, methodologies, and significance within a limited time frame. Provide constructive feedback on presentation skills, clarity of content, and overall coherence of the proposals.

Guest Speaker Series: Invite experienced researchers or professionals in educational research to share their insights and experiences in writing research proposals. Allow students to ask questions and engage in discussions about real-world challenges and best practices in proposal development and submission.

References

Bitchener, J., & Basturkmen, H. (2006). Perceptions of the difficulties of postgraduate L2 thesis students writing the discussion section. Journal of English for Academic Purposes, 5(1), 4-18.

Boote, D. N., & Beile, P. (2005). Scholars before researchers: On the centrality of the dissertation literature review in research preparation. Educational Researcher, 34(6), 3-15.

Cohen, L., Manion, L., & Morrison, K. (2017). Research methods in education (8th ed.). Routledge.

Creswell, J. W. (2014). Research design: Qualitative, quantitative, and mixed methods approaches (4th ed.). Sage Publications.

Davis, G. (2011). A quality approach to peer review. ASME Journal of Mechanical Design, 133(4), 041004.

Denzin, N. K., & Lincoln, Y. S. (2011). The SAGE handbook of qualitative research (4th ed.). Sage Publications.

Fowler, A. (2014). How to write a successful research funding application: A guide for social scientists. Sage Publications.

Fraenkel, J. R., Wallen, N. E., & Hyun, H. H. (2019). How to design and evaluate research in education (11th ed.). McGraw-Hill Education.

Gall, M. D., Gall, J. P., & Borg, W. R. (2007). Educational research: An introduction (8th ed.). Pearson.

Hensley, L. C. (2013). Considerations for ethical guidelines in educational research. IAFOR Journal of Education, 1(1), 1-15.

Kelley, K., Clark, B., Brown, V., & Sitzia, J. (2003). Good practice in the conduct and reporting of survey research. International Journal for Quality in Health Care, 15(3), 261 266.

Leedy, P. D., & Ormrod, J. E. (2014).

Merriam, S. B., & Tisdell, E. J. (2015). Qualitative research: A guide to design and implementation (4th ed.). Jossey-Bass.

Punch, K. F. (2013). Introduction to social research: Quantitative and qualitative approaches (3rd ed.). Sage Publications.

Robson, C. (2011). Real world research: A resource for users of social research methods in applied settings (3rd ed.). Wiley.

Silverman, D. (2016). Qualitative research (4th ed.). Sage Publications.

Made in the USA
Columbia, SC
10 June 2024

36864000R00137